D0592418

Praise for *Close the Gap & Get Your Share*

"In a world where financial misinformation is all too common, *Close the Gap & Get Your Share* provides a trusted source of investing advice. Here you will find a path forward to financial stability and practical guidance toward closing the wealth gap."
—Burton G. Malkiel, Author of *A Random Walk Down Wall Street*, 50th Anniversary Edition, 2023, and Professor of Economics at Princeton University

"Cacho, Conkling, and Herrera have written a great book to help unsophisticated investors design their investment strategies and feel comfortable with their decision throughout the ups and downs of the market. Although written with migrant families in mind, the book is a fabulous resource for any household in need of guidance in navigating the complex universe of financial products to achieve higher returns on your savings."
—Alejandro Werner, Founding Director, Georgetown Americas Institute, and former Director, International Monetary Fund

"If you're looking to learn about the different investment options available today, I highly recommend *Close the Gap & Get Your Share*. This comprehensive guide provides an accessible and easy to understand overview of the investment landscape. Whether you're a seasoned investor or just getting started, *Close the Gap & Get Your Share* is a must-read that will help you make informed investment decisions in today's world."
—Pedro De Garay, CEO, GBM Grupo Bursatil Mexicano

"As novices about investing and financial planning, *Close the Gap & Get Your Share* gave us the confidence and knowledge we needed to take control of our financial future. It's a must-read for anyone who wants to build financial wealth and security, regardless of background or financial situation. We highly recommend this book to anyone looking to start investing to build a bright financial future."
—Hanna Perez and Ashley Perez of the American Latin pop duo *Ha*Ash*.

Close the Gap &
Get Your Share

Close the Gap & Get Your Share

How Immigrants and Their Families Can Build and Protect Generational Wealth in the US

Julio Cacho, PhD, and Cole Conkling, JD, with Juan Carlos Herrera

Matt Holt Books
An Imprint of BenBella Books, Inc.
Dallas, TX

This book is designed to provide informational financial guidance. Neither the author nor the publisher is engaged in rendering legal, accounting, or other professional services by publishing this book. If any such assistance is required, the services of a qualified financial professional should be sought. The author and publisher will not be responsible for any liability, loss, or risk incurred as a result of the use and application of any information contained in this book.

Close the Gap & Get Your Share copyright © 2023 by Julio Cacho, Cole Conkling, and Juan Carlos Herrera

All rights reserved. No part of this book may be used or reproduced in any manner whatsoever without written permission of the publisher, except in the case of brief quotations embodied in critical articles or reviews.

Matt Holt is an imprint of BenBella Books, Inc.
10440 N. Central Expressway
Suite 800
Dallas, TX 75231
benbellabooks.com
Send feedback to feedback@benbellabooks.com

BenBella and *Matt Holt* are federally registered trademarks.

Printed in the United States of America
10 9 8 7 6 5 4 3 2 1

Library of Congress Control Number: 2022061560
ISBN 9781637743942 (hardcover)
ISBN 9781637743959 (electronic)

Editing by Camille Cline
Copyediting by Michael Fedison
Proofreading by Kellie Doherty and W. Brock Foreman
Indexing by WordCo Indexing Services, Inc.
Text design and composition by PerfecType, Nashville, TN
Cover design by Brigid Pearson
Printed by Lake Book Manufacturing

Special discounts for bulk sales are available. Please contact bulkorders@benbellabooks.com.

To my wife, Claudia; my children, Julito, Pau, and Rex; and my parents.
—Julio Cacho

*To Rachel, for standing beside me and supporting me on this journey.
To Elle and Lily, for giving me so much joy. To my parents, for
always believing in me and giving me every opportunity.*
—Cole Conkling

To Hanna and Mathilda with all my love.
—Juan Carlos Herrera

◄ CONTENTS ►

CONTENTS

◀ PART III ▶
BEHAVIOR, AND HOW TO CONTROL IT

◀ FOREWORD ▶

Think of this book as the ultimate toolbox in your journey to financial literacy. The term might sound scholastic, but its contents will inspire, inform, and empower migrants with a vision to help close the wealth gap by providing culturally relevant experiences and practical ways to help them reimagine financial wellness. I'm confident that the work by the authors will become a trusted source of information for those looking to overcome current financial challenges and better prepare for a more prosperous future. As a first-generation immigrant, I know what it's like to live a life of constant change and adaptation. Most migrants have no access to banking and other mainstream financial services when they arrive in the U.S., and even after establishing themselves, their financial needs evolve over time, depending on the vulnerability they experienced, their human and social capital, and their plans. That generates important obstacles on their way to self-reliance and economic independence. Because without a bank account and access to basic financial services, migrants lack a trusted place to save and receive money and have far fewer options to make payments or access loans. In short, they can't fully participate in our country's economy or build a stable life for themselves and their families.

Through my work as a Mexican American journalist serving Latinos in the U.S., I've seen firsthand how, despite being one of the largest demographic groups with substantial purchasing power, Latinos still face significant financial challenges with money management and long-term financial security. Learning to save, predatory lending practices, and poor or insufficient credit history are just some of the barriers that prevent those in the community from reaching financial stability. And when each of these compounds, Latino families are unable to invest their money and create generational wealth. This book offers a path forward to overcome those obstacles as well as policy constraints and access barriers to financial inclusion whether they are cultural or systemic. As you'll learn here, one of the most serious financial hurdles for un-banked communities is their inability to build wealth through the proper investing tools. Opening a bank account and building a healthy credit history may be the first steps toward financial security, but that's just one piece of the puzzle to creating long-term financial stability. It can be tricky, even intimidating, to move into the public markets due to a lack of access and information surrounding this decision, but getting that education is key to gaining the confidence needed to take the kind of financial steps that will help immigrants build a better future for themselves and their families.

This book provides a space to learn about money without feeling judged or pressured. Many Latinos grew up looking at money as a taboo, and the best way to tackle that stigma is by becoming financially literate. By having candid conversations about short- and long-term goals, parents can teach their children the actual value of money as well as healthy financial habits. But the contents of this book go beyond a specific community and can help all migrants break down barriers and feelings of anxiety that finance or investing isn't for them, or that it's too hard to understand. By leading with education and reinforcing the theme of saving and personal investing, the book is designed to help close the wealth gap, and that's a goal that should be welcomed as a crucial contribution not just to minority communities, but to our collective economic well-being.

Enrique Acevedo
Journalist, CBS News and El Tiempo Latino
November 2022

◄ INTRODUCTION ►

From January 1992 to September 2022, Standard & Poor's 500 index, known as the S&P 500, which tracks the stocks of the largest five hundred public companies in the United States, rose a staggering 1,485 percent. If you had invested $10,000 in January 1992, it would have been worth more than $158,000 by September 2022. If you had done what many Americans do, and continually added to your initial investment each year, say $10,000, by September 2022 you would have had over $1,800,000.

Over that same period, if you had instead chosen to forego investing in the U.S. economy by keeping your $10,000 in cash, that $10,000 would, of course, only be worth $10,000 today. If you had chosen to leave it in a bank savings account earning an average interest rate of around 2 percent, it would be worth a little over $18,000 today. And while adding $10,000 a year would have seen your savings account increase to over $400,000, that's a far cry from the over $1,800,000 you could have earned investing in the S&P 500.

As you can see, the decision of whether to invest your hard-earned money is one that comes with life-changing consequences. While saving money and keeping it in cash might feel safe, over time it will leave you worse off. If you are an immigrant to the United States, not investing might have indeed been a good move in your home country. Maybe your home country's economy was not ripe for investment, even to this day. Or perhaps there was simply too much corruption to entrust your cash with someone else, even—or especially—the government. But, in America, much of its citizens' wealth is formed through investment in its economy. By failing to properly invest, immigrants new and old have fallen behind and will continue to do so, ever increasing the wealth disparity gap. To help close that gap, immigrants to the United States need to become comfortable with investing so that they can get their share of the American Dream. The returns from the American economic machine are there for anyone and are ready for the picking—if you know where to look. That is what we want to share with you with this book.

If you come away with anything, we hope it is a shift, however slight, in how you view money and investing. We hope you'll see it's not too complicated. Not too hard. Not too difficult to understand and master for your purposes. Know that most of the investment industry makes investing seem complicated to make a handsome profit off your hard-earned savings. Financial jargon, like all industry jargon (for example, law and medicine), exists as a type of moat to keep outsiders out and insiders in. Middlemen, many hordes of them, are there to siphon off fees and expenses, rarely providing any value. Sometimes, entire companies' only mandate is to exploit your behavioral weaknesses and biases. They know human psychology better than any learned psychologist, many of which are under their employ. They'll get you to do things. Lots of things. They'll get you to do them regularly. Because doing things, such as buying . . . selling . . . trading . . . going to cash . . . buying the dip . . . changing your "allocation" . . . changing your "exposure" . . . doing things, you see, makes them money. Mind you, this is not all nefarious. Some simply don't know. Some truly believe in what they're selling. They are always selling.

If you're an immigrant to the United States, you face an even steeper challenge. Immigrants have a median income of around $53,000 compared to $58,000 for American-born households. And, as of 2016, over 19 percent of immigrants lived in poverty compared to the overall U.S. average of around 12 percent. Indeed, one reason may be that many immigrants cannot or do not rely on the social safety nets that are available to many U.S. citizens, compounding the problem.[1]

Faced with all this, immigrants must wade through the cash-sucking minefield of the investment industry like everyone else. To do this, you must discard much of your money-related worldviews and biases you may have from your home country that will not serve you well in the United States. You will first need to change your outlook on money and investing. You will then need to understand the basics of finance and investing. You don't have to be an expert, but you should know enough to be dangerous. You'll also need to become familiar with some of the major investment theories and debates that exist—primarily because, again, the industry will try and make things complicated for you so that they make money *off* you, not *for* you. We see many investors fall prey to the industry simply because they lack a lot of this basic, fundamental knowledge.

Once you understand the basics of investing, you will then need to understand yourself. You will have to know, and we mean really know, that you are a flawed, biased human being. That you come preprogrammed with emotions, which will often do you a grave disservice when investing money. We will explore these biases, not to place judgment, but to make you a better investor. Because you can save and invest to your heart's content and screw it all up with one bad decision.

You do not have to be a victim to the investment industry machine. Not you. Not if you follow the peer-reviewed, academic research. Not if you follow the objective data that's been available for more than fifty years to anyone who cares to look. Not if you have a solid financial plan that you believe in and stick with through thick and thin. Not if you control your emotions, including, among others, fear and greed.

We know the strategies to make decent, respectable investment returns over the long term. Everyone who has studied the facts of investing knows them too. All business school students have learned these strategies; most have forgotten them or have chosen to ignore them in the "real world" outside the classroom. Warren Buffett knows them. So does Ray Dalio, and countless other titans of investing. You can know them too.

This book will be a journey; or should be, at least. For the reader, many of whom may be recent immigrants to the United States, the journey is literal: you physically traveled through space and time to the United States to provide a better life for you and your family. Indeed, all Americans were, at some point in time, immigrants. Every person, save Native Americans, currently here now had an ancestor that was, first and foremost, an immigrant to America. It's why we're called "a nation of immigrants." Julio is a recent immigrant to America, having come here originally for his doctoral studies at Princeton University. Juan Carlos was born and raised in the United States, but his parents grew up in Mexico, immigrating here prior to his birth. And while Cole's family has been here many generations, someone down the line was also an immigrant. Every one of us has a unique story to tell.

A journey can also, of course, be figurative: say, for our purposes, the educational journey to learn more about proper investing and how to get your "fair share of the pie." For the authors, the quest for investment knowledge and truth is long-standing, but the journey continues in earnest to spread our findings far and wide to people just like you. We hope to share with you how immigrants, new and old, can best invest their hard-earned money to create a better financial future. We will share with you what works best, and which of your held beliefs from your home country may not. Indeed, much of what we will cover may be information that is new to you, since many investment opportunities that Americans regularly take for granted may not have even existed for you before—you don't know what you don't know.

We assume that you, the reader investor, already has or will have money to invest. This book is not about budgeting—there are many out there that are—and we assume you already have a budget or can get help in creating and sustaining one so you can save and invest as much money as possible. Indeed, the single biggest factor that will decide whether you meet your long-term financial goals is the amount of money you regularly save and put to good investment use. No other action by you will matter so much as that. Every dollar you can save today is a dollar you can invest and watch grow over time—or perhaps bequeath to later generations, or give away. Remember: today's savings are tomorrow's spendings. If you want to enjoy a comfortable life, retire, or build generational wealth, there's no getting around the need for having a robust savings system working for you in the here and now.

Our goal with this book is to take you on a journey where, at the end, your financial and investment worldview will be forever changed. This book will challenge your beliefs about money and investing, some of which might be well established and deep-seated—a "part of you," if you will. This is understandable; however, we ask you to have an open mind. As you'll see, the investment data presented in this book are based on rigorous academic research; they are not our opinions. Nevertheless, investing is a practical thing involving flesh-and-blood human beings. You are not a spreadsheet! Your feelings about money and investing (i.e., your behavior) are probably the most important variables of all. We aren't preachers. We aren't going to ask you to believe anything on faith. We'll show you the way toward successful investing, but you'll have to be the one to take it, stay on the path, and eventually get to your destination, wherever that may be.

We will look at how most U.S. immigrants, and people generally, view money and investing and how some of those beliefs are flawed and counterproductive—or are at least incomplete. To do so, we will present peer-reviewed, academic research showing the best way to accumulate wealth over time. We'll provide pros and cons of various approaches and which ones give investors the highest probability of success. We'll explore the different beliefs (e.g., beliefs about luck versus success) and biases (e.g., overconfidence) that can bring even the savviest of investors down for the count, knocked off the trail, too bruised and battered to continue.

This book will be primarily educational and fact based. Our guidance is either supported by research or by our own experiences advising clients in the real world. As independent registered investment advisors by day, we have nothing to sell to the reader—no product or scheme—except for our recommendations provided herein. When our commentary drifts away from academic findings and becomes based more upon our working experience, we will let you know. Our approach and suggestions are meant to be open and constructive—not a black box. As you'll discover, proper investing is usually boring and requires patience, above all. It's not about trying to get rich quick by picking stocks, obsessively awaiting earning reports, or binge-watching CNBC. If you want entertainment, we suggest looking elsewhere. Boring is usually good for your money and financial future; find an exciting hobby outside the markets if you need a regular adrenaline fix.

Getting you to the end will require some financial education and understanding of what a market is and why investors are unlikely to outperform one. We'll talk about different types of assets and what returns can be expected from those assets. You'll learn about proper diversification and risk and return. We'll show you various investment theories, along with real-world applications of those theories. Importantly, at the end of this journey you should be more equipped to understand investment risk, especially your own unique risk tolerance. Understanding risk—what it is, how it can be managed, and the types of risk one should and should not take—is paramount.

We hope this book will give you the knowledge and tools to successfully complete whatever investment journey you're on—whether you're just starting out, charging through the middle, or approaching the end. So, take this journey with us and become a dangerous investor. One who is ready to take financial control of your life to better yourself and your family. One who is prepared to fight off all the bad actors trying to knock you off your path. One who is confident that you will meet your goals, and maybe more. One who is ready to examine your long-held beliefs and biases to arm yourself for the good times and bad. And one who is ready to finally become financially secure and free.

◄ PART I ►

Change Your View,
Change Your Future

◄ 1 ►

What You Might Not Know About Investing

If you're reading this book, you likely want to learn something about investing that you didn't know before. And if you're an immigrant to the United States, you likely want to learn something about investing here in the U.S. that you didn't know before. So let's get this out of the way up front: not knowing is *okay*. Indeed, not knowing is part and parcel of any investment journey. That's because nobody knows the future. And we mean *nobody*: Not us. Not the talking heads on TV. Not the academic experts. And not the billionaire hedge fund managers, either. Fortunately, great investing doesn't require knowing the future. It does, however, require humility. It also requires making decisions based on probability in a world of uncertainty. It requires patience, as well as discipline. It also requires knowing yourself—what kinds of biases you may have, as well as knowing how you'll respond in times of market excess and despair. This book will help you make investment decisions in a world of uncertainty where nobody knows the future. It will also help you patiently stick with those decisions through the good times and the bad.

As you already know, however, investing involves money. And money is personal. To you. To us. To everyone. We all have different views about money: How we use it. What we use it for (and what we don't). How we feel about making it. And how we feel about losing it—whether temporarily, say due to a drop in the market, or permanently, say because a company that you invested in failed. Where we grew up will affect our views about money. And so will our families. And so will the period in which we grew up. For example, most people who lived through the Great Depression swore off stocks for the rest of their lives. And why wouldn't they? Stocks lost about 90 percent of their value during that time.

If you're an immigrant to the U.S., perhaps you faced obstacles in your home country that don't exist here. Therefore, you'll have a different perspective about money and investing too. Or maybe you have viewpoints and feelings about investing that do not apply here, are incomplete, are outdated, or are simply inaccurate. We have worked with immigrants in our investment advisory practice and have observed some common characteristics and beliefs that many share. For example, when most immigrants think about where to invest their money, three options usually come to mind: (1) raw, undeveloped land; (2) real estate, meaning developed land, like a personal residence, rental house, apartment complex, or a commercial property, like a shopping center; or (3) starting one's own small business or investing in a friend's or family member's small business. These options are not "wrong," because you may have very good reasons for choosing them. Maybe people don't invest in the stock, bond, and commodities markets in your home country because many do not have access. Or maybe those markets are just not that developed compared to the United States. In that case, we probably would share the same beliefs if we grew up there too! After all, investing in land has historically been the primary way that people created wealth.

One goal with this book is to show you that investing, especially in the U.S., is much more than land, real estate, and small business. There are more options available to you—many more. Some of them might be foreign to you. Other investments might be known to you, but you've never considered them because you thought they were too risky. The stock market easily comes to mind as an example. We've seen many immigrants shun stocks, believing them more akin to gambling at a casino than a safe investment.

To be clear, we are not saying that investing in land, real estate, and small businesses are bad investments—far from it! They can often be lucrative, especially if you pick the right one at the right time. But what we *are* saying is that many think these investments are safer than they really are—in other words, they are not aware of the risks. Moreover, you could be taking too much risk without earning enough return; what if you could have gotten *more* return with *less* risk somewhere else? For example, many immigrants believe that starting a small business is a safe way to build wealth, but the data show that more than half of new businesses fail within the first six years, with close to two-thirds failing within ten years.[1]

Investing in the right things will also help ensure that you get a piece of the economic pie above and beyond what you can earn with your labor alone. While your day job might earn you a decent living, it is unlikely to create generational wealth—there are, after all, limited hours in the day. Saving some of your labor earnings for investment, however, will help you get a leg up—to "close the gap"—between your labor income and wealth accumulation goals. Indeed, a great investment will make money for you while you sleep, without your having to lift a finger.

Good investing, at its core, is about taking calculated risks that give you the highest probability of making more money than you started with—in other words, a "return" or a "reward." Your investment return is primarily dependent on how much risk you are willing to bear. Consequently, you'll often hear that "risk and return are linked" or that "risk and return are two sides of the same coin; you cannot have one without the other." Indeed, the cardinal rule of investing is that if you want a high return, you'll have to take on some risk; and if you want low risk, you'll have to settle for a low return.

But not all risks are the same. In fact, many risks are not worth taking, since they are not expected to provide you with *any* reward whatsoever—in other words, you should expect to lose some, or all, of your money. And that's okay too—if you know it. It's akin to gambling where you're aware that the odds are against you, but you do it anyway for the thrill of it, or because there's a small chance you could strike it big.

What we will show you in this book is that you do not need to gamble to make a decent return that can change your life forever. Proper investing is not gambling. Far from it. It doesn't have to be scary. And it doesn't have to be complicated either. But it does require patience, discipline, and some basic knowledge. So, let's next explore a very crucial concept: private versus public investments and why great investing requires patience above all else.

PRIVATE VS. PUBLIC INVESTMENTS— WHY PATIENCE PAYS

The investment arena is, at its most basic, divided between private and public markets. Public investments are listed on public market exchanges, like the New York Stock Exchange, where the prices of the listed assets, like stocks and bonds, are reported every second of every trading day. As denoted by the word "public," anyone can participate in them. Public markets are heavily regulated, which means that companies must provide detailed financial statements and reports on the health of their businesses. Investors large and small can then analyze those reports to decide whether to invest in a certain company or not. Public markets are also highly liquid, which means that investors can almost immediately turn their public investments into cash with the click of a button.

On the other hand, private markets exist outside of the public purview and do not report prices daily. They are not readily open to the public. You might not even know about certain private markets, and you will certainly not know all the participants and investments that occur within them. Private markets include things like private equity (investing in private company stock), venture capital (investing in startup company stock), private real estate deals, and private debt deals. Even a loan between two friends would be a private investment. Because private markets exist outside of the public's purview, the prices of private investments are largely unknown day to day. There certainly is no "ticker" on TV revealing what the daily market prices are.

While the difference between private and public markets may sound obvious to you, many investors frequently trip up when comparing the two. One reason is that many tend to believe that private markets are safer because they cannot see the price of their investments moving daily as they do with public markets. It is this public market "volatility," or constant price movement, that is very hard to handle in real time and which causes a lot of bad investor behavior that we regularly witness in our day jobs as investment advisors.

Turn back to what many immigrants first think of when investing: raw land and developed real estate. Imagine you buy a farm perfectly suited for growing crops on land you feel confident will grow in value over time. Some years the crop yields are great; some years . . . not so much. Or suppose you buy a rental house in an up-and-coming part of town. Some years the property leases out for a high rent; other years . . . not so much. But again, you feel confident that, over time, the value of your rental property will increase.

In both examples, you receive cash flow every year and have no plans of selling because you believe in the long-term prospects of the investment. You are, therefore, unmoved by the short-term news of the day; nor are you concerned with what you could get if you sold the investment today— because, again, you're not selling for many years. Over time, both the farm and the rental house appreciate substantially in value. When you sell, many years later, you receive a nice profit, all while earning cash flows each year. Here, you were a patient investor and it paid off.

Now imagine you buy a publicly traded index fund that invests in the stocks of every publicly traded company in the world. The fund holds over nine thousand stocks in firms like Apple, Google, Tesla, Toyota, Sony,

Nestle, J.P. Morgan, and Tencent. Imagine you also invest in all the bonds in the world—more than nineteen thousand bonds, issued by governments and companies—along with all the world's commodities, things like oil, gold, wheat, and silver. Over time, the stocks, bonds, and commodities also appreciate substantially in value.

This time, however, you don't go into the investment planning to hold for many years. Instead, you buy and sell based upon what the market is doing, along with how you feel about what the market *might* do in the future. Every day, you check the price on your phone, either seeing red or green, each color sending you into despair or euphoria. You follow the market news incessantly, paying close attention to what every supposed expert has to say about this or that. Sometimes you sell a position and earn a tidy profit; other times you sell at a loss. In the end, however, you end up performing worse than you did on your private farm and rental house investments— not because the public market investments did worse, but because of your behavior. In fact, if you had just bought and held the public investments, you would have done much better than the farm and rental house.

So, why the difference? Why do we tend to be patient investors with private investments and impatient investors with public investments? After all, the risks are much higher with private investments because there is less liquidity, less transparency, and much less diversification. By "liquidity" we mean the ease in which an investment is readily turned into cash. So, for example, your personal residence is illiquid because it takes time to turn it into cash. Apple stock, on the other hand, is highly liquid; you can sell it and turn it into cash at the push of a button.

Highly liquid investments mean there is always someone offering to buy your investment. By the way, this is a wonderful benefit because you can quickly turn your investment into cash when you need it. The problem with liquidity, however, is that the price of your investments will move *constantly* depending on how the markets are processing new information. These price movements tempt investors to constantly buy and sell in hopes of quick profits, or to avoid temporary losses. They also cause investors to swing between greed and fear whenever the market moves up or down. The price of a private investment, on the other hand, is unknown because there's no active market of buyers constantly knocking on your door each day making an offer to buy your farm or rental property. Ignorance is often bliss with private markets.

In the private markets, investors tend to focus more on cash flows from the investment while paying little to no attention to the actual value of the asset itself. This is one of the main reasons investors believe their private investments are less volatile and "safer" than public investments. But this is an illusion; the actual value of a private investment is largely unknown. Its true value is only known when a bona fide offer to buy is received, which, in most cases, does not happen until a sale is completed. Let's break this crucial point down further.

If you own a home and want to sell it today, the actual cash value to you is zero. Yes, zero! That's because you presumably don't have a current offer to buy it and, therefore, it cannot readily be converted to cash. Your house is, thus, an illiquid asset. Even with a ready cash buyer, it will take some time for the transaction to close and for you to receive the money in hand. You might object, however, that you know your home's true value because you have an appraisal. Or maybe your neighbors recently sold their house, which is comparable to yours. Appraisals and comparables, however, are not the same as bona fide offers to buy; nor are they the same as a closed transaction with cash in hand. What if the market changes from when the appraisal was done? What if a latent defect is discovered during the inspection process that drastically lowers your home's value? What if interest rates shoot up, making your buyer pool smaller and less able to finance the purchase? You might *think* your home is worth a certain amount, but if you're in urgent need of the money today and nobody is there to make an offer and close today, then the price is zero until the deal is done.

Private business owners often make this mistake as well when they compare the value of their public investment portfolios with the paper valuations of their private, illiquid company or other private investments. They mistakenly believe their public investments have gone to hell in a handbasket while their private investments have held strong. What they do not consider is that since their private investments exist within the same economic machine as their public ones, both have likely lost value in tandem.

The laws of risk and return apply to all investments, not just liquid, public investments. And the correlations between asset classes in the private and public markets are very high. If the economy is strong, both public and private assets will do well; if the economy is weak, both will suffer. You may not realize how much your private investments are suffering because you cannot readily see the market price, but you'll find out if you try to sell.

Investors need to approach investing in public markets the same way they do private markets. They should view liquidity in public markets as a benefit instead of letting price swings sway them emotionally. Investors are better off ignoring all the news and noise regarding the public markets just as they do when evaluating how their private investments are doing.

We realize public markets can seem overly complicated, with numbers constantly whizzing by on TV screens all day and prices moving like a roller coaster. Many get overwhelmed and go to private markets or deals that they can "touch and see," "know," or "understand." This, however, may result in earning less on a private investment than one could with a similar, or superior, public investment. Moreover, some investors take on more risk for the same return they could have gotten in the public markets. Others might hire a professional advisor to help them with their public investments, without really understanding what's going on—"I'll let him deal with it," they might say. Unfortunately, this blind, ignorant trust usually ends when markets crash, resulting in a phone call to the advisor to "get out and get out now." Indeed, one of the main reasons investors sell during temporary drawdowns is they don't understand their investments and fear they will never come back.

Let's go back to the private investment farm example again. Imagine you're not ready to sell, but someone offers to buy it for 15 percent less than you think it's worth. Would you sell? If you don't need the money and remain confident the farm will appreciate over time, then probably not. You know and understand the farm and that it should appreciate over time. You'll likely think to yourself, "That buyer is wrong—he doesn't know what he's talking about; he doesn't understand this market or my farm. What a lunatic. Goodbye, good sir!"

Public markets should be viewed the same. Most people get into trouble because they don't really know what's in their public investment portfolios and view price swings like a casino, randomly fluctuating with no rhyme or reason. But just because you can buy and sell at any time doesn't mean you should. As an investor, you must understand and believe in the assets you're holding, while keeping in mind that the daily gyrations in price are akin to the hypothetical buyer offering to buy your farm or rental property for 15 percent less than what you paid for it. In both examples, you have the choice to ignore the offer or not.

For a concrete example with real numbers, let's look at average U.S. home values since the year 2000:

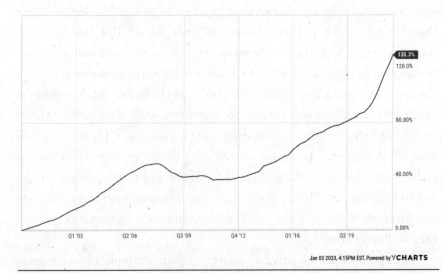

Jan 03 2023, 4:15PM EST. Powered by YCHARTS

Figure 1. Aggregate House Price Index Percent Change. Data illustrated by Ycharts.com

It looks like a smooth curve going up with little volatility, right? That's because, again, homes are illiquid assets. Here, the measurement used to calculate the housing market's value is the average home price *sales* throughout the United States, not the actual, daily prices of every home on the market. This is important. Consider what the value of your home would be the day after a devastating fire. It would drop by a lot, wouldn't it? That drop, however, doesn't show up on the chart above because you're not selling it. Next consider what the value of your home would be after you got the insurance money and rebuilt the home. Maybe you even improved upon it and the value now increases above and beyond what it was pre-fire. That, too, does not appear on the chart if you're not selling. Private markets, therefore, hide and smooth out the daily price swings that the public markets so readily advertise every single trading day.

Let's next consider what would have happened if you had invested in the S&P 500 over the same period as the housing market example:

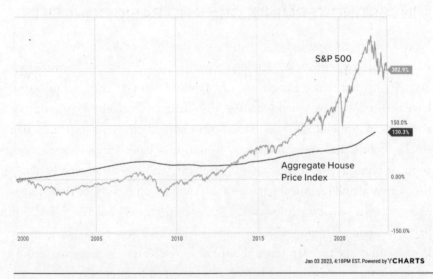

Figure 2. Aggregate House Price Index vs. S&P 500 Total Return Level Percent Change. Data illustrated by Ycharts.com

As you can see in Figure 2, the S&P 500 is more volatile, especially if you zoom in to shorter time periods, meaning the price moves more dramatically from day to day, compared to the housing market. But, if you can ignore the volatility, your investment would have grown more than three times compared with housing. However, while it's easy to illustrate this in hindsight, it's understandably difficult to live through the ups and downs of daily liquidity in real time.

If you treat your public investments like your private investments, you'll realize that the daily price movements of public assets are simply the cost for immediate liquidity—they're a feature, not a bug. If you don't like the price, then don't sell, just as you wouldn't sell your farm or house. Warren Buffett famously said that "the stock market is a device for transferring money from the impatient to the patient." Investing, as opposed to speculating or gambling, takes time above all else, so it pays to be patient.

INVESTING TERMINOLOGY AND BASIC CONCEPTS

Now let's try to simplify the often-complicated world of investing. Like many industries, investing comes prepackaged with lots of terminology and jargon that many people are not familiar with. If this includes you, have no fear. We have provided an index of investing terminology and basic concepts in Appendix I. There, you'll find basic definitions for things like stocks, bonds, and commodities, as well as quick overviews of some concepts, such as active versus passive investing, and the difference between fundamental and technical security analysis. Note that many of these terms and concepts will be explored in more detail throughout the book, but having a basic grasp now will, we hope, make this a more pleasant journey. If you would like to learn more about these terms and concepts, we recommend turning to Appendix I before moving on to chapter two.

◄ 2 ►

Save, Invest, and Limit Speculation

We want to start this journey by stressing the importance of *investing* your money, as opposed to simply saving it. While saving money is certainly a prerequisite to investing it, saving money alone without putting it to good investment use will likely not be enough to reach your financial goals. So, having a savings plan in place is where you should start your journey. After that comes investing.

WHY INVEST AT ALL?

Maybe you are from a part of the world where saving does not equal investing. Maybe you grew up in a household that kept all their money in physical cash or precious metals. This could have been completely understandable, especially if you heard stories of people investing and losing their life's savings. Perhaps preservation of savings was the only thing that mattered; risking those savings on a complicated investment was just not worth it.

You should understand, however, that simply saving money in cash is not the right approach if you want to build wealth over time. That's because of inflation, which, contrary to popular belief, is not always a negative. In fact, inflation is a crucial part of any country's capitalist-based economy.

So, what is it? Inflation is defined as the percentage increase in the price of goods and services. It's complicated and not entirely understood, even by economists. The gist is that inflation erodes the value of the currency—dollars, pesos, euros, whatever—and, therefore, one's purchasing power. When you hear that inflation is up 5 percent this year, it means that a predefined basket of consumer goods and services, on average, is up 5 percent from the last reported period (i.e., month, quarter, year). So, if a bunch of bananas normally costs $3 but, because of inflation, now costs $5, it greatly affects your purchasing power. The same amount of money now cannot buy the same amount of goods and services as it used to. Inflation is why you'll hear older people lament about how "such and such" used to cost "such and such" when they were kids.

Above and beyond wanting to make a decent return on your money, keeping up your purchasing power over time is the primary reason you should try to be fully invested with your savings. If you do not invest, but instead hold your savings in cash, it means you are *guaranteed* to lose 2 to 3 percent of your money every year. While that $1,000 in cash may still say "$1,000" one, five, and ten years from now, it will not be *worth* the same because of inflation. In other words, that $1,000 will not be able to buy as many goods and services as it did before. And because what you can buy with your money is the only thing that matters, inflation matters. A lot. As you can see in Figures 3 and 4, 2 to 3 percent inflation every year can reduce the value of your cash savings tremendously over time.

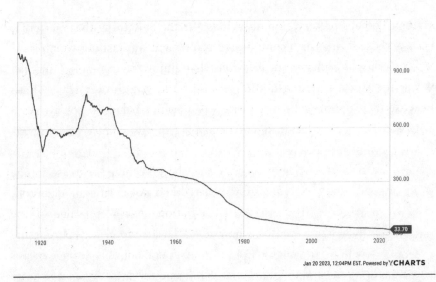

Figure 3. U.S. Consumer Price Index: Purchasing Power of the Consumer Dollar. Illustrated by Ycharts.com

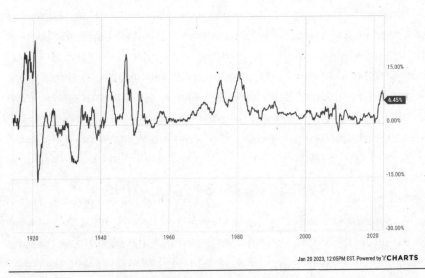

Figure 4. U.S. Inflation Rate. Data illustrated by Ycharts.com

Central banks across the world—such as the Federal Reserve in the United States, the Mexican Central Bank, and the European Central Bank—have a mandate to create inflation at about 2 to 3 percent annually. What that means is that inflation *will* happen. This mandate is directed by the congressional branches of these governments because they want their citizens to either (1) spend money by purchasing goods or services or (2) invest the money. Since one person's spending is another person's income, spending your money to buy goods or services in the economy contributes to economic growth. And if you do not need to spend all your money in the present, investing that money with others that can put it to better productive use likewise grows the economy. What does *not* grow the economy is people hoarding cash, whether physically or in a bank account; therefore, governments want a modest amount of inflation of around 2 to 3 percent to encourage either spending or investing.

Inflation higher than 2 to 3 percent is not good for economic growth because it erodes people's purchasing power too quickly and results in myriad damage to businesses and families, especially those of modest means with no assets. Inflation lower than 2 to 3 percent is also undesirable because it does not incentivize people to spend or invest their money. Indeed, deflation, which is a *decrease* in the price of goods and services, is catastrophic for modern economies. That's because if your money is worth more tomorrow than it is today, people are incentivized to hoard cash above all else, which greatly damages economic growth and prosperity.

INVESTING VS. SPECULATING

Let's now explore what investing is, and what it is not. Specifically, we want to delineate the difference between investing and speculating, because many a fortune has been lost by those blurring the line between the two.

From the beginning of markets, investors and speculators have always coexisted to some degree or another. Markets need speculators to help provide price discovery and liquidity (i.e., cash) to function properly.

There's nothing inherently wrong with speculation, but it's important to know if you're doing it or not. What gets people into trouble is when they think they're investing but really speculating. So, let's try to ferret out the differences.

Back in 1930, Philip Carret, in *The Art of Speculation*, wrote that motive is the primary distinguisher between investing and speculating. "The man who bought United States Steel at 60 in 1915 in anticipation of selling at a profit is a speculator . . . On the other hand, the gentleman who bought American Telephone at 95 to enjoy the dividend return of better than 8 percent is an investor."[1] Carret felt that investors were more concerned with the long-term economics of a business, while speculators were primarily concerned with how to make a quick buck from price changes. "Speculation may be defined as the purchase or sale of securities or commodities in expectation of profiting by fluctuations in their prices," said Carret.

Benjamin Graham is one of the most famous investors of all time, is widely known as the father of value investing, and was the major influencer and mentor of Warren Buffett. Graham also tried to define investing in his popular book *The Intelligent Investor*. There, he famously proffered that "[a]n investment operation is one which, upon thorough analysis, promises safety of principal and satisfactory return. Operations not meeting these requirements are speculative."[2] This definition, we believe, can be particularly helpful to ponder.

An investment implies that the investor reasonably believes his money is safe long term and will not go to zero. For example, as we'll get into later, we believe investing in a low-cost, diversified index fund of stocks that are "market-capitalization" weighted is a great move for most individuals. Such an investment will no doubt fluctuate but should never go to zero.* On the other hand, buying a single stock because you believe its price will quickly

---

* If the S&P 500 goes to zero, the world (or at least the United States) would probably no longer have functioning markets or would be "over" to some degree or another—apocalyptic times would truly be upon us.

appreciate in the hopes of selling it in a day, week, or month looks more like speculation. That's because individual stocks can, and very often do, go to zero—or lose most of their value. Thus, under Graham's definition, most individual stock picking isn't really an investment because "safety of principal" is lacking. Moreover, since most stocks fail to beat the market index, investing in just one does not usually provide a satisfactory return when compared to the alternatives.

More recent commentators believe it's better to look at speculation versus investment on a time continuum, with speculation lying to the left and investment to the right.[3] On the left, we have short-term traders, making moves that occur within seconds, minutes, hours, or days. We can place "day traders" in this group. Moving toward the middle and on to the right, we have decisions that last weeks, months, years, and decades. The farther to the right, under this theory, the more the activity looks like "investing."

Jack Bogle, the late founder of Vanguard, which now manages over $7 trillion in assets, likewise believed that investing meant long-term ownership of a company or asset, while speculation meant short-term trading. What's more, he warned against speculation, providing evidence that investors outperform speculators over the long term:

> In the eight virtually consecutive decades from 1926 through 1997, the nominal dividend yield has averaged 4.5 percent, and earnings growth has averaged 4.2 percent. The sum of these two components is a fundamental stock return of 8.7 percent, slightly less than the 10.5 percent nominal return actually provided by stocks over the same rolling periods. We can chalk up the remaining 1.8 percent to speculation . . . In short, the fundamentals of investment— dividends and earnings growth—are the *right* things to remember about things past. In the very long run, the role of speculation has proven to be a neutral factor in the shaping of returns. Speculation cannot feed on itself forever. Periods in which speculation has enhanced returns have been followed by periods in which

speculation has diminished returns. No matter how compelling—or even predominant—the impact of speculation on returns is in the short run, expecting it to repeat itself leads our expectations down the wrong road. Speculation is the *wrong* thing to remember when we peer into the future to consider things yet to come.[4]

Investors tend to be unconcerned about temporary price movements, whether up or down, because they feel confident in the economics of the businesses they own, whether it be their debt or equity. They understand that markets are cyclical and people fickle, but that long-term economic trends tend to increase cash flows, profits, and asset values. Speculators feed on and relish market volatility as opportunities to get rich quick, believing they can time the market. Investors "keep calm and carry on" through the downturns, happily receiving their dividends while patiently waiting for long-term growth. Brave investors may even *look forward* to bad times as opportunities. Warren Buffett certainly fits this mold, having famously said one should "be fearful when others are greedy. Be greedy when others are fearful."[5]

Burton Malkiel, author of the seminal investment book *A Random Walk Down Wall Street*, sums it up nicely:

> I view investing as a method of purchasing assets to gain profit in the form of reasonably predictable income (dividends, interest, or rentals) and/or appreciation over the long term. It is the definition of the time period for the investment return and the predictability of the returns that often distinguish an investment from specula-tion. A speculator buys stocks hoping for a short-term gain over the next days or weeks. An investor buys stocks likely to produce a dependable future stream of cash returns and capital gains when measured over years and decades.[6]

A speculator's primary goal is to outperform the market, or the "index." So, a speculator buys a single stock because they believe that stock will earn more than the stock market's return as a whole. Indeed, if the speculator did not believe this, they would simply buy the entire stock market through a low-cost index fund.

The main problem with speculating, however, is that, in the end, it's a zero-sum game. We'll get into the details of what that means in chapter nine, but for now, you should understand that the market return is simply the average return of all the investors in that market. Consequently, for every speculator that outperforms the market, there must be a speculator that underperforms the market.* Add in transaction costs, taxes, and fees, and the average speculator will certainly underperform the market. It is simple math because, by definition, the index's return *is the market return*, less any transaction costs, taxes, and fees. The indexer is guaranteed not to underperform the market because the indexer *is the market*.

The rub, however, is that the indexer is also guaranteed not to outperform the market either. Nevertheless, the chance to outperform and get rich quick, however improbable, is the siren call so many speculators fall victim to on their investment journeys, often to ruinous results.

Numerous studies show most speculators do not perform well, *at all*. For example, one study found that 97 percent of Brazilian futures traders lost money over a time span of three hundred days. Another found that, between 1995 and 2006, only 5 percent of day traders in Taiwan were profitable. In the United States, a study by the SEC found that more than 70 percent of currency traders lost money every quarter, and typically lost 100 percent of their money within twelve months.[7] Indeed, myriad academic studies spanning the last twenty years show day traders and other active traders do not make money except over very short and fleeting time

---

* A common misconception is that the zero-sum game means that one side of the trade will always lose money. This is not true. Under certain conditions, like a rising market, both speculators on a trade can make money. One can still underperform a benchmark and make money (e.g., the market return was 10 percent and the speculator's return was 5 percent).

periods.[8] One study concluded that "it is virtually impossible for individuals to day trade for a living."[9]

You will, however, no doubt be bombarded by stories of speculative success. You'll see and hear traders making millions of dollars on a single trade. You'll have serious fear of missing out, or FOMO. You'll want to do it too. But you should stop and think about your reasons for wanting to do so. The trade that reaped millions for the braggart on your Twitter feed is gone now—poof! You can't go buy that stock and expect the same result. Moreover, you only saw the one trader that succeeded, not the thousands that failed. We refer to this as "survivorship bias," which is only seeing the winners, and not the many, many losers. It's like seeing the Mega Millions lottery winner on TV and thinking, "If I only were to buy a lottery ticket, I could be a mega-millionaire too!" You instinctively know that's not how it works—and that it's not how it works with investing either. We're not saying it can't *ever* work—it obviously has—but wild success is usually due more to luck than anything else. And luck, by its very nature, cannot be reliably repeated.

FIRM-FOUNDATION THEORY VS. CASTLES-IN-THE-AIR THEORY

Burton Malkiel also raises another point we should consider here, since it flavors investors' views of the world in innumerable ways. He begins by noting that "[a]ll investment returns—whether from common stocks or exceptional diamonds—are dependent, to varying degrees, on future events. That's what makes the fascination of investing: it's a gamble whose success depends on an ability to predict the future."[10] He posits that serious investors use one of two theories to value assets: (1) the firm-foundation theory or (2) the castles-in-the-air theory, also called the "greater fool theory."

The firm-foundation theory states that all assets have what's called "intrinsic value," which smart investors can determine by studying the asset's present condition and future prospects. Upon this careful consideration, investors can decide whether an asset is a good buy, when the price of the asset falls, or is a smart sell, when the price of the asset rises. "Investing then becomes a dull but straightforward matter of comparing something's actual price with its firm foundation of value," writes Malkiel.[11]

For common stocks, one can determine the present, firm foundation value by analyzing the stream of earnings that company should generate in the future and discounting the value of those future earnings to today's prices to give fair value. It goes without saying that a company's stream of future earnings is not set in stone. Instead, it's highly unpredictable and difficult for even the best Wall Street analysts to get right. But many, oh so many, try. This, by the way, is why the prices of assets like stocks change so much from day to day—investors all over the globe are continually examining and reevaluating businesses' prospects based on the steady flow of new information.

The castles-in-the-air, or greater fool, theory posits that investors should be less concerned with an asset's future income stream. Instead, investors should focus on "analyzing how the crowd of investors is likely to behave in the future and how during periods of optimism they tend to build their hopes into castles in the air. The successful investor tries to beat the gun by estimating what investment situations are most susceptible to public castle-building and then buying before the crowd."[12] This can be compared to a beauty contest with ten judges, you being one, where you're asked *not* to pick the most beautiful contestant in the show *to you*, but to pick which contestant the *rest of the judges* will think is the most beautiful. In this kind of contest, you must be adept at understanding what the crowd thinks is beautiful, whether you agree or not. So, for example, you may think a company has poor long-term prospects, but have knowledge that everyone else will pile into its stock for one reason or another. In that case, you'd try to buy first.

This theory was popularized by the famous economist John Maynard Keynes who stated that fundamental, firm foundation analysis is of little use if everyone else is building castles in the sky. "It is not sensible to pay

25 for an investment of which you believe the prospective yield to justify a value of 30, if you also believe that the market will value it at 20 three months hence."[13] In this world, it doesn't really matter whether an investment is "good" in the sense that it has the chance for superior future cash flows. All that matters is that there's another person, a "greater fool," out there who is ready and willing to buy your asset for a higher price than you bought it for. A master castle-in-the-air investor has a keen understanding of how many greater fools are left out in the field. When none are left, he better sell quickly as there are no fools left to buy.

We see the castle-in-the-air phenomenon play out commonly in assets that have little to no fundamental value—meaning that they do not have cash flows—not now, not ever. One example is gold. Gold has some intrinsic value as jewelry and in technological applications, but its intrinsic value is well below its historical and current market value. That is because gold has had a castle-in-the-air value to humans for millennia. We have collectively thought of gold as a store of value. We believe gold has worth above its material, intrinsic uses because other people do too. If everyone stopped believing that everyone believed gold had such value, its price would plummet down to its much lower value as jewelry and for use in certain technology.

When you start thinking this way, you will quickly see how circular things can become and how many assets only have value because people believe so. Collectibles, art, and cryptocurrency are all like gold in this respect—they have no cash flows. Their value depends on what other people think their value is. Gold has been around a long time and has held its value remarkably well, but other fads like Beanie Babies and many cryptocurrencies have not.

HAVE A LONG-TERM PERSPECTIVE AND RIDE THE COATTAILS OF THE MARKET

Now that you have a basic grasp of the long-standing debate between the firm foundationalists and the castles-in-the-airers, we'd suggest it is usually best to take a step back for some perspective. In our view, both theories are probably right, to some degree, at various times in the market and in individual asset prices. Just look at the recent GameStop saga where an almost bankrupt company exploded in growth as a result of a meme. If you bet on that trade as a firm foundationalist, you probably lost your shirt. But were you wrong? No, not necessarily. Under the firm-foundation theory, the stock's value was, and still is as of this writing, lacking a firm foundation-based price! Its future income and growth prospects are not ideal. But if you were a castle-in-the-airer, and somehow knew that the meme crowd would bid the price of the stock up, you could have made a fortune. But were you right? Yes, on the market psychic, but wrong on the prospects of the business.

What we'll see, again and again, is that being right doesn't always make for a good investment. And sometimes, being wrong can make you a windfall. Nobody ever said investing was fair. You can win for the wrong reasons and lose for the right ones.

It's our belief that markets, in the short term, can do crazy, unpredictable things when all the castle-in-the-airers gain traction and there are lots of greater fools out there in the market. On the other hand, the firm foundationalists will often do things like stay out of the market during huge bull runs because "the fundamentals are out of whack; we're staying in cash until things settle down." Maybe so—fundamentals do indeed get "out of whack," regularly—but being right about the fundamentals on the sidelines can cost you a lot of money too.

Our suggestion to most investors is to simply ride the coattails of the two camps and let them duke it out. Do you really care if the market is going up because of fundamentals or greater fools? We sure don't. While the evidence shows that markets tend to go up or down based on fundamentals over the long term, there are certainly periods, sometimes very long, where markets are building huge castles in the air. And no matter which theory is at play, you should always try to be in the market to reap its long-term benefits no matter which camp wins out in the end. We will look at how to best ride the coattails of the global markets later in the book when we discuss our Three Buckets Approach for financial planning.

IF YOU SPECULATE, DO SO SPARINGLY

There's nothing inherently wrong with speculating. And recall that there's a spectrum between investing and speculation. Indeed, since investing necessarily involves predicting an uncertain future, all investors must speculate in that way. Some may even enjoy speculating for the thrill of it. For example, many like researching companies and picking a few stocks. For them, it's a source of entertainment and it doesn't really matter whether they win or lose. It's akin to going to a casino on vacation, fully aware of the odds, but taking part anyway for the fun of it. However, if you do like to speculate with the markets, we suggest knowing the odds of underperformance, which are about 97 percent.[14] We will get into what underperformance means exactly in chapter nine but it's simply not what you want your money to be doing.

Whether you want to speculate because you believe a certain company will take off, or you want to day trade for pure entertainment—no matter the reason—keep it to a minimum. We typically advise that clients speculate with no more than 5 percent of their overall investment portfolio. Then set your number beforehand and stick to it—like how responsible, casual gamblers set a maximum amount of money they're willing to lose on their Vegas vacation. Do that, and you can feed the itch to have some fun and play the lottery, while also keeping your financial future on track.

However, if you are the type that doesn't feel the need to speculate, we recommend avoiding it altogether. That's because every dollar you will likely waste speculating could have been put into investments that have had, and are expected to continue to have, some fantastic returns over time. By fantastic, no, we do not mean that you're going to get rich overnight. And no, we don't mean you'll be able to quit your day job anytime soon. But, if you do it right, you will position yourself to receive the formidable returns the markets are giving away to anyone who has the patience and discipline. So, let's look next at the returns the markets have produced over the years to give you an idea of what you might expect.

GET YOUR SHARE OF LONG-TERM INVESTMENT RETURNS

We will now look at what those long-term returns have been in the U.S. for stocks and bonds. As you can see in Figure 5, if you had invested $10,000 in the S&P 500 at the end of 1989, by November 2022 it would be worth almost $215,000.

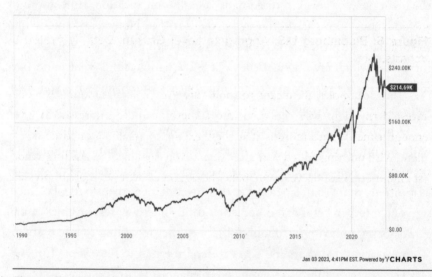

Figure 5. S&P 500 Total Return Level Growth. Data illustrated by Ycharts .com

Figure 6 likewise shows the growth of $10,000 in the total U.S. bond market. Ten thousand dollars invested in May 1996 would be worth almost $30,000 by November 2022.

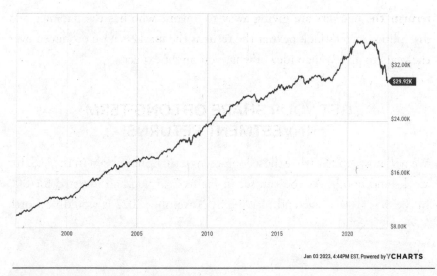

Figure 6. Bloomberg U.S. Aggregate Level Growth. Data illustrated by Ycharts.com

These examples are meant to show that even a small amount of money invested the right way can turn into something quite impressive if given enough time. What's more is that these examples assume a onetime investment, with nothing added year after year as you earn income. Adding a modest amount of $5,000 a year will make the figures above even more impressive.

◀ 3 ▶

Follow the Facts,
Avoid the Myths

While investing invariably involves numbers and data, most investors are anything but data driven when it comes to making investment decisions. If investors were data driven, we'd see the bulk of them piling into low-cost, passive index funds and exchange traded funds (ETFs), instead of higher-cost, active funds. We see the opposite, even though the trend has gotten somewhat better lately. We'd also see most investors shunning investments that are too speculative and have low, or even zero, long-term expected returns. Instead, we see investors buying up cryptocurrencies, some of which are literally jokes, with reckless abandon. If investors were data driven, we'd see properly diversified portfolios based on global market capitalizations. Instead, we see that most investors have outsized U.S. equity exposure, limited to no international exposure, and, frequently, zero exposure to entire asset classes altogether (e.g., bonds and commodities). If investors were data driven, we'd see most of them buying up assets on the cheap when they're down, such as during a crash or recession. Instead, we see many investors selling out of fear at the worst possible times.

The data are out there, ripe for the picking. Will you be like most investors and give into fear, greed, and get-rich-quick schemes? Or will you follow the data to give you and your family the best chance for long-term financial success? Proper, evidence-based investing is simple, but it's far from easy.

Most of the investment industry acts in opposition to the objective data because to do otherwise would forgo massive profits. What's more, even if the paid investment professionals know the evidence—or interestingly, even if their own clients do, too—nobody really thinks it applies to *them*. "This time is different." "The market's too hot; I'll wait to buy the dip." "This stock is massively undervalued." "This stock is too expensive." On and on.

In our investment advisory practice, we tell clients that if they stick with our investment plan for the long term, there is a very high probability of things working out in their favor, but that their behavior is the one place where they can really mess things up. We like to use an example that many of them are familiar with: dieting.

If you want to lose weight, it's relatively simple: burn more calories than you consume. All else equal, if you follow this formula, you'll lose weight. Yet, as we all very well know, doing this day in and day out is anything but easy. Life, and more especially our behavior, gets in the way. This behavioral problem is, of course, well known and regularly exploited by the dieting industry, which is keen to provide all sorts of products and services promising an easy fix. So, you get the endless fads. The gurus. The charlatans there to serve you up an easy way out. Do this diet craze. Take this pill. Buy my kale-watermelon-chia seed detox shake system for only twenty-seven easy payments of $19.99! Who needs discipline when you can lose those pounds before that weekend pool party? All charge cards accepted.

We are our own worst enemy. We know what we should do, yet we do not do it. But don't beat yourself up about it—it's a distinctly human trait we all share. Indeed, the apostle Paul, writing in Romans, recognized long ago: "I do not understand what I do. For what I want to do I do not do, but what I hate I do."[1] This well-known trait has led to myriad dieting books, trends, and gimmicks that we just can't seem to get enough of. The concept is easy. It's the behavior that's the problem. And boy, do companies love to profit from our bad behavior.

So, too, with investing. Based on rigorous academic research, we know what works over the long term. Yet there are thousands of books, blogs, and "strategies" on investing—most of them offering a new get-rich-quick scheme. But oh, we would be so lucky if it were just books being hawked! No, the more disturbing reality is that it's an entire industry, set up like a sea monster with hundreds of ever-growing, uncontrollable tentacles designed to cash in on our innately poor behavior and biases at the expense of our financial well-being. It's asset managers creating whatever funds they think can be sold to meet a current fad; it's cable news shows and magazines constantly bombarding viewers with tales of greed, followed by fear; it's unscrupulous brokers and advisors earning commissions on products they sell you, no matter if they're appropriate or not; and, yes, it's all the "experts" making forecasts that never pan out. For the most part, the entire investment industry is designed to get you to buy and sell, and to do it *regularly*. Because it's not about earning you sufficient long-term returns, but rather raking in as much profit as possible today.

There is a better way, which is why we wrote this book. It doesn't happen overnight. It doesn't have the sexiest narrative. But it works. However, it takes planning, discipline, and time—*when* you start makes a big difference. As we know, the longer you wait to get your physical health in order, the harder it is to right the ship. You get older, slowly put on weight, and before you know it, you're in a deep hole. Same with investing: if you delay too long doing what we know works, you'll have a lower chance of achieving your financial goals. Don't delay—the clock is ticking.

Proper investing—investing based on data—is not new. Anyone who's ever taken a college or graduate-level investment course will find the concepts in this book familiar; sadly, few apply them. As noted previously, the concepts we'll be exploring in this book have been around since at least the early 1950s. Back then, however, implementing these strategies was almost impossible; it was certainly cost-prohibitive for all but the wealthiest of investors. Today, there's no excuse: the technology and affordable funds available to virtually every investor are abundant and blessedly cheap. You only need to make the right choices, and then stick with them through thick and thin.

While most people believe they make financial decisions based on their best interests, several hidden and unnecessary risks shape their choices. In a 2011 study, economists Ulrike Malmendier and Stefan Nagel found that Americans largely make financial decisions based on their prior experiences, including familial upbringing and cultural customs, not objective data and what's in their best interests.[2] Relying on personal experience can be especially dangerous for immigrants and their descendants, who come to a new country with the baggage of foreign financial beliefs. They may be accustomed to different tax systems, or, if their country of origin had universal pensions, they may not be familiar with the concept of having to save for retirement all by themselves. Their home countries may not have had a stock exchange, or a volatile currency may have informed their investment philosophy. For example, Venezuelan immigrants would no doubt have been exposed to rampant, savings-killing inflation in their home country.

Ridding yourself of certain biases stemming from your own experience is extremely difficult without a concerted and prolonged effort. It would be completely understandable, for example, for Venezuelan immigrants to be irrationally afraid of inflation for the rest of their lives and make subpar financial moves as a result in America. Certain financial beliefs may have served them well in the past, but they do not always hold up now.

Humans learn by making mistakes and applying their newfound knowledge to future situations, so it makes sense that people make decisions based on their experiences. However, when it comes to investing, learned behavior does not always lead to the best choices. Making decisions based on the objective data and thinking in terms of probability will serve most investors better.

Our goal is to help you understand the truth about investing so you can make better investment decisions. Even savvy investors make unconscious and harmful mistakes, either because they do not have the relevant information or because their previous experience persuades them to ignore the facts. Usually, investors think "this time is different," or "the facts don't apply to me." For example, just because someone's father's business remained lucrative for thirty years does not mean that the same business model will work for thirty more. Indeed, in the late 1970s, the average life span of an S&P 500 company (i.e., the largest and most successful companies in the United States) was thirty-five years. Today, it's around twenty years, and only growing shorter.[3] Nevertheless, many investors trust their personal experience rather than statistical probability.

DON'T TRUST THE DEVIL YOU KNOW

The idiom "better the devil you know than the devil you don't" suggests that it's preferable to deal with someone or something you're familiar with, even if it's not perfect. Maybe your current job isn't perfect but switching to another company might be even worse—better to stay put! Or maybe you're stuck in a bad relationship, but someone else might make you even more miserable—or you simply don't want to be alone. Better to grit your teeth!

With money, people frequently choose the devils they know, when they'd be much better off considering other options. We see this frequently, and in various ways. For example, many real estate professionals like to invest all their personal savings into real estate—it is, after all, what they know best. They fail to recognize, however, that by doing so their labor income now mimics their personal investments. If real estate does poorly, they may be out of a job and a retirement portfolio! We've likewise had to talk people in the car industry out of putting a big chunk of money into a single car company stock.

Sticking to what you know can often, no doubt, be good life advice—like honing one skill on which to build a successful career. So, it's understandable and unsurprising that, in general, people feel more comfortable investing in real, physical assets they can touch and see (e.g., real estate; equipment; precious metals, like gold and silver; one's personal business) over non-real assets that they cannot (e.g., stocks and bonds). With immigrants this preference is usually even more pronounced.

Sociologists Jody Agius Vallejo and Lisa A. Keister have shown that "the accumulation of tangible assets, such as home and business ownership, often hold particular significance for immigrants, suggesting that wealth accumulation closely approximates immigrants' own conceptions of mobility and sense of belonging in the host country."[4] And because many immigrants are familiar with real assets, they cling to the idea that it's safer to invest in things they can see. This can be especially true for immigrants coming from seriously corrupt home countries, where contract law and the judicial system cannot always be trusted. In America, however, this mindset will usually limit your long-term financial success.

Americans become accustomed to financial assets—non-physical assets whose value comes from a contractual claim, like bank deposits, stocks, and bonds—from a young age. Many children have college savings plans (e.g., a "529 Plan"—after Section 529 of the U.S. Tax Code*) set up in their names from the day they're born. Or a parent or grandparent might open a custodial brokerage account on behalf of a child to deposit birthday money or other gifts. Some may even help children buy securities in the account to encourage lifelong savings and investment habits. Young employees are

---

* A 529 Plan allows parents (or anyone else) to contribute money into an investment account set up for a child's future education, including room and board, and other educational-related expenses. Money is typically invested in investment funds that will be liquidated upon that child entering their college years. If the money is used for education, none of the capital gains or income earned on the investments in the account are ever taxed.

encouraged to open a 401(k) retirement savings account the moment they're hired at their first job. Indeed, many employers are now automatically opening 401(k) accounts for new employees, requiring those employees to "opt out" if they don't want to participate. And even most non-investing Americans have at least some exposure to the stock market—it is in the news *all the time.*

In contrast, when people in Latin America, for example, buy something, they typically want to see it, touch it, feel it. They're often skeptical of investing in financial assets like mutual funds. This may be because they feel they'll end up getting fleeced, or because they think there are too many middlemen lined up to take their hard-earned money. Some may equate investing to gambling, because popular TV shows and movies sometimes portray it as such. In truth, however, investing in intangible assets is usually less risky than the investments they're used to. Immigrants have historically invested in real estate because it has usually been the easiest way for them to invest in something. Indeed, there were no ETFs and very few index funds until around twenty years ago, so this is not surprising. It was not as easy to build and invest in a well-diversified portfolio for the average investor.

Financial assets—like well-diversified index funds, mutual funds, and ETFs—are usually a safer bet. When investors buy a single piece of real estate, like a rental property, they're wholly responsible for its maintenance and bear major risk if it gets destroyed, say by flood or fire. They're also exposed to other risks unique to that property—like a bad neighbor, overbearing homeowners association, or the neighborhood or city falling out of favor with buyers. In contrast, when you buy a financial asset, like a Real Estate Investment Trust (REIT)—a type of investment fund that owns a lot of different real estate assets—you don't have to worry about your one and only property getting destroyed, since you have exposure to hundreds (or even thousands) of others.

Entrepreneurship and investing in small businesses are also quite risky. Small businesses have a 50 percent failure rate within the first five years. That's a much riskier track record than a well-diversified portfolio of public company stock, which might rise and fall, but should never wipe out an investor's entire savings. Nevertheless, many people, especially immigrants, start new businesses every year, with the assumption that the failure rate data do not apply to *them*. To mitigate their financial risks more effectively, immigrants need to understand the opportunity costs that come with these types of investments.

Real assets become even more of a liability when people become attached to them. We refer to this as the "IKEA Effect." Once you've poured several hours of blood, sweat, and tears into building that super complicated desk you bought from IKEA, you're much less likely to return it to the store, or to sell it. Indeed, because you put your labor into that desk, it's likely worth more to you than anyone else. IKEA is aware of this effect, and it's one of the reasons they purposefully make their customers build their own furniture. Likewise, when someone labors to grow their small business or to buy and renovate a property, they don't always recognize when it's time to let go. That's why, if you ever find yourself in a bidding war when buying a home, writing a personal letter to the sellers about how great their house is, especially any updates they personally made, can sometimes win the day, even if you're not the highest bidder.

People who trust the devil they know usually miss valuable opportunities to sell their assets at the highest price, properly diversify, or grow their wealth even more. Don't be one of them.

MISSING THE BIG PICTURE

When investors approach their finances based primarily on their personal experiences, they tend to miss the big picture. For example, investors frequently overlook the hidden costs, risks, and fees attached to certain assets. You may think of real estate as a secure investment, but when you're saddled with a $20,000 roof replacement you didn't anticipate, you quickly realize your investment wasn't so secure. Financial assets like retirement and investment accounts also include many hidden fees. These costs may seem small on a month-to-month basis, causing investors to overlook them, but compounded over time they can add up to significant amounts. Investors also frequently make financial decisions with little thought, rather than considering the long-term impacts of their choices.

This tendency is even more dangerous when combined with volatile emotions. Even the most rational investors give in to their emotions, often justifying their behavior after the fact. We commonly see this when markets fluctuate. A dip in the stock market generates fear, and investors respond by withdrawing their money with the justification that they're protecting against further decline. Big-picture investors control their fear and recognize that the natural patterns of market fluctuations follow a random up-and-down cycle. Plus, the stock market is only one asset class, and if investors have diversified properly, their other investments may be experiencing gains. That's why having some historical perspective on markets and asset class performance can help investors. Being able to see the forest for the trees and ignoring all the short-term noise is a skill any successful investor must have.

Additionally, people don't know how to gauge whether the price of an asset or investment already reflects the relevant factors that could cause the price to rise or fall. Ambitious investors believe they'll discover a hidden gem, without considering that other smart investors are also seeking diamonds in the rough. Imagine you just read an article about a company that created a revolutionary new technology. You immediately decide to invest in the company, assuming its stock will rise. What you aren't seeing are all the other savvy investors reading the same article, behaving the same way, and expecting the same results. The stock price you're seeing may already reflect investors' newfound interest. Moreover, there's no guarantee the actual technology will succeed or that the price will rise further.

Even *knowing* the future with a hypothetical crystal ball won't always translate into knowing how *markets* will react to that future. For example, let's say at the end of 2019 you knew for certain that COVID-19 would cause a global pandemic, shutting down most of the world economy in

2020. What would you have predicted the markets to do that year? Would you have predicted that the S&P 500 would have a total return of over 18 percent? Be honest.

Investors also commonly look at only a small portion of the financial world and mistakenly assume that it's representative of the whole. That's why people are so readily misled by survivorship bias—a tendency to make conclusions solely based on successes without taking the total number of failures into account. Have you ever caught yourself saying, "I wish I had bought stock in Apple. I knew it was going to go up."? We beat ourselves up that we didn't follow our alleged past hunches to realize huge gains. Meanwhile, we forget about the fifty other companies we thought about investing in, and we conveniently ignore that if we had followed through on all of them, we would have lost money. Apple only stands out because it was successful.

These are a few of the many ways investors assume they're looking at the full picture when they're only seeing part of it. To reliably grow your wealth, you must train yourself to reject your emotional reactions and take a broader perspective before you invest.

THERE IS NO "RIGHT" TIME TO INVEST

We frequently hear from our clients, "I'll wait to invest after the election," or "Let's wait until the quarterly report," or "Let's just wait a few months to see how things shake out." They believe they can time the market to make greater returns. Wrong. There is no "right time" to invest. The "right time" has less to do with when you invest and more to do with your risk tolerance and how long you let your investments grow. As the old saying goes, it's not timing the market, but time *in* the market that counts.

For example, if you invested $10,000 in an S&P 500 index fund in January 2003 and never touched it until January 2022, you would have made just over a 9 percent compounded return, per year. Your $10,000 would have become over $54,000.

You may think you could have gotten better returns from strategic buying and selling. If you flawlessly missed the worst market days during that twenty-year period and hit the best days, you'd be right. Your $10,000 would become $252,117.29. There's certainly an allure to market timing; if you can get it all right, you stand to make a killing. But the problem is just that: getting it all exactly right. That's like winning the lottery; the probability is very low. It's likelier that you'd miss some good days and hit some bad ones.

THE ALLURE of Market Timing: **Missing the Worst Days**
20 Years (1/1/2000–12/31/2019)

$10,000 invested in S&P 500 Index	Annualized Return	Value of $10K at end of period
All trading days	6.02%	$32,192.93
Less the 5 biggest losing days	8.30%	$49,300.06
Less the 10 biggest losing days	10.01%	$67,338.55
Less the 20 biggest losing days	12.81%	$111,428.95
Less the 40 biggest losing days	17.51%	$252,117.29

THE PROBLEM with Market Timing: **Missing the Best Days**
20 Years (1/1/2000–12/31/2019)

$10,000 invested in S&P 500 Index	Annualized Return	Value of $10K at end of period
All trading days	6.02%	$32,192.93
Less the 5 biggest gaining days	3.87%	$21,359.95
Less the 10 biggest gaining days	2.42%	$16,122.15
Less the 20 biggest gaining days	.07%	$10,145.77
Less the 40 biggest gaining days	**-3.79%**	$4,615.42

Figure 7. Timing the Market Is Hard. 2000–2019: Missing the Worst Days vs. Missing the Best Days

So, let's assume you didn't time everything correctly and you missed the five best days in that twenty-year period. Five days may not seem like much, especially over the course of twenty years, but compared to leaving your investment untouched, those five days would cost you more than $10,000. Your rate of return would drop to 3.87 percent ($21,359.95).

When you look at financial data, the evidence is clear: you cannot time the market; and if you try, you'll usually end up performing worse than if you left your money alone. Missing out on the best days of the market penalizes you more than missing out on the worst.

Another way people try to "time" the market is by succumbing to FOMO. They hear about an investment that keeps increasing in value, and instead of doing their usual due diligence, they give in to the pressure of the "limited-time" offer. When people think about the possibility of missing out on an opportunity, they experience anticipatory regret, which drives them to make an investment without considering the implications.[5] So, next time you're scrambling to invest your money in the "new hot thing" before it's "too late," slow down and make sure you're doing your due diligence and not just succumbing to FOMO.

While time no doubt affects every investment, the constant deluge of red and green stock tickers causes investors to overemphasize short-term movements, always stressing whether now is the best possible time to buy and sell. That pressure is an illusion. Tickers play on your emotions. When you can see the price of an asset going up and down every day, your emotions go up and down with it. Investors who monitor their stocks all the time not only experience more stress, but they also make emotional decisions that undermine their financial success.

Think of it this way: If you own a home, the value of your home always fluctuates, but you don't think about those changes daily. The value of your home isn't listed on a ticker next to the front door. You might estimate your home's value, based on what you paid for it, or what a neighbor's home recently sold for, but you don't truly know its worth until someone makes you a bona fide offer. An asset's value depends entirely on what someone will pay for it.

Imagine how your attitude would change if someone knocked on your door every day to make a bid on your home. One day, you hear, "I'll give you $500,000." The next, "I'll give you $475,000." The next, "$515,000." You would see how every paint color, appliance purchase, and landscaping decision sent the price up or down by a few dollars. You would also see how things completely out of your control—like the local or national economic outlook, interest rates, and a thousand other things—would affect the daily price. In the end, having that level of knowledge about your home's value would become nerve-wracking, and the constant price movements would likely generate anxiety. You would also probably evaluate your investment on your home differently, thinking it might not be as safe and stable as you thought.

That's exactly why people think of the stock and bond markets differently than they think of real assets, when really, their values fluctuate in the exact same way. The markets make an offer on those kinds of financial assets every minute of the day, so it feels like you're getting constant knocks on your portfolio's door. The best thing you can do is to think of those knocks like a nosy neighbor and ignore them. Don't answer the door until you're ready to sell, and you'll have a lot more peace of mind.

OVERCONFIDENCE AND OPTIMISM CAN LEAD YOU ASTRAY

Sometimes, investors are fully aware of the facts. They know small businesses are risky and their money would be safer elsewhere, but they go ahead and start one anyway. It's not because they're crazy or self-sabotaging; usually, it's because they've fallen victim to the overconfidence effect or optimism bias. Starting a business is great for the overall economy, no doubt, and we need people to take on that risk. Unfortunately, the risk is usually taken by people who don't have the means to take it, like a lot of immigrants who arrive here with very few assets and zero safety net.

The overconfidence effect is exactly what it sounds like: a bias in which a person's confidence in their own judgment is much higher than the objective data would suggest. We can see it at work in surveys consistently reporting that three-quarters of American drivers claim to be better than average. Statistically, that just can't be true.

A related bias, the optimism bias, causes people to believe they are less likely to experience unfortunate events. For example, even though 606,520 people in America died from cancer in 2020, no one believed they would be among them.

These may seem like benign delusions, but in his bestselling book, *Thinking, Fast and Slow*, Daniel Kahneman called the optimism bias "the most significant of the cognitive biases."[6] It exaggerates our ability to forecast the future, which leads to overconfidence and poor decision making. Overconfidence and the optimism bias are especially pernicious when it comes to financial decisions.

Over the long run, approximately 95 percent of fund managers who try to beat the market fail. That includes professional investors as well as hedge fund and private equity firm managers who have staked their reputation on success.[7] Statistically, they have a mere 5 percent chance of success, yet they assume they'll be among those lucky few. Their gut-level impressions and overconfidence persuade them to ignore the risk. When individuals make financial decisions based on how they feel, rather than on facts, they're setting themselves up for failure.

In his book, *The Four Pillars of Investing*, William J. Bernstein reports on a poll done by the *Wall Street Journal* asking readers how they think their personal investment portfolios will perform over the next year compared to the market index. The poll revealed the average investor believed they would beat the market by a whopping 2 percent! And while some might, it obviously cannot be true mathematically, since the market *is the average*.[8] Bernstein goes on to explain how overconfidence is so pernicious in investing because "[t]he more complex the task, the more inappropriately overconfident we are," because one's efforts cannot be easily "calibrated." What that means is that "[t]he longer the feedback loop, or the time-delay, between our actions and the results, the greater the overconfidence."[9] He then describes how "meteorologists, bridge players, and emergency room physicians are generally well-calibrated because of the brief time span separating their actions and their results. Investors are not." He points to two main overconfidence errors most investors make:

> The first is the "compartmentalization" of success and failure. We tend to remember those activities, or areas of our portfolios, in which we succeeded and forget about those areas where we didn't . . . The second is that it's far more agreeable to ascribe success to skill than to luck.[10]

Given the data, it would serve you well to recognize any overconfidence you may have and to attempt to control it. One way is to think long and hard before doing two things: (1) buying individual stocks (or other assets) and (2) timing the market. Both are very tempting because the short-term gains can be immense. Both, however, are likely to make you worse off, as we will show. But even if you do not know how much the cards are stacked against you, understanding what you're up against will help. Bernstein again makes this argument nicely, first on picking stocks and funds:

> Right now . . . [anyone] could screen a database of the more than 7,000 publicly traded U.S. companies according to hundreds of different characteristics, or even [their] own customized criteria. There are dozens of inexpensive, commercially available software programs capable of this, and they reside on the hard drives of hundreds of thousands of small and institutional investors, each and every one of whom is busily seeking market-beating techniques. Do you really think that you're smarter and faster than all of them?

On top of that, there are tens of thousands of professional investors using the kind of software, hardware, data, technical support, and underlying research that you and I can only dream of. When you buy and sell stock, you're most likely trading with *them*. You have as much chance of consistently beating these folks as you have of starting at wide receiver for the Broncos.[11]

You will find that by following the facts and controlling your emotions, your investment success is all but guaranteed. You will not get rich overnight, but done right, you'll succeed, which brings us to our next chapter: "Distinguishing Between Success and Luck."

◄ 4 ►

Distinguishing Between
Success and Luck

There's no shortage of financially successful people everywhere you look. Indeed, with the advent of social media, it often seems *everyone* is having a better go at it than us. Everywhere we look, we're presented with millionaires who've made it, billionaires who've reportedly pulled themselves up from their bootstraps, and immigrants who are living the American Dream. It's easy to be swayed by these inspiring tales of perseverance and triumph even though, statistically, we know the wealth gap in the U.S. continues to grow.

The United States has long attracted immigrants because of the conviction that America is the land of opportunity, but social science scholarship increasingly shows that the American Dream has become an elusive myth for most. In 2019, the median white family owned about $188,000 in family wealth, while the median Latino family owned only $24,000.[1]

These gaps mirror the extreme inequities many immigrants faced in their home countries.

Nevertheless, immigrants and their families can still attain upward economic mobility, particularly intergenerational economic mobility, if they are willing to confront traditional ideas about American opportunity. To efficiently maximize wealth, you must first overcome two pernicious myths: that (1) past success breeds future success, and (2) hard work is the only road to financial success.

SUCCESS DOESN'T ALWAYS BREED SUCCESS

Many investors believe past performance is indicative of future results. People assume that what was once a safe bet will continue to be a safe bet. But we saw just how risky that notion was when the COVID-19 pandemic hit. Pre-pandemic, Latino businesses were thriving, and Latino entrepreneurs were the fastest-growing cohort in "main street" businesses. But by October 2020, five million Latino families were at risk of bankruptcy in the U.S.; many never recovered.

Similarly, just because you've built and sold one successful business doesn't mean you can do it again. Initial successes lead investors to become overconfident, and they assume that because they've seized a so-called "opportunity," it will one day pay off. That rarely happens because, as we've already seen, overconfidence leads to bad decision making. Success doesn't always breed more success.

The mythology of success also applies to successful people. How many business owners have read profiles of Carlos Slim Helú, Mexico's richest man? How many finance enthusiasts have read biographies of Warren Buffett? There's a pervasive belief that successful people have actionable insight into leading a successful life. "This person succeeded this way," we tell ourselves, "so I can find success that way too." It's important to understand that extremely successful people of the Slim Helú/Buffett ilk may owe some, or even most, of their success to plain old luck.

SUCCESS AND LUCK

Just because you've been successful and just because you've
disrupted an environment, that doesn't mean you're a role
model or that you actually have anything to teach anybody.
There's an awful lot of luck and accident in the world,
and maybe you were just on the receiving end of that.
—MICHAEL LEWIS[2]

Imagine your next-door neighbor—we'll call him "Louie"—wins the lottery. Not just any lottery, mind you, but the Mega Millions. He's now a multi-millionaire beyond anyone's wildest dreams. Now imagine, you ask him, maybe as a joke, or out of a bit of spite, "Louie, how did you do it? How'd you win the lottery? Teach me your ways so I, too, can win the lottery and live happily ever after just like you." Louie, full of joy, and lots of pride, responds, "Well, fair neighbor, you're in luck. Listen here and you, too, can join me in multimillionaire land. First, you must drive your car to the gas station located on Main and 7th Street where I bought my ticket. You must do this on a Wednesday when the sun is shining and the temperature is a balmy seventy-five degrees, like it was for me. Now, don't just do it on any Wednesday all willy-nilly, no, you must do it on a Wednesday when good-ole' Carl the Cashier is working, because that's who I bought my winning ticket from. Anyways, when you speak with Carl the Cashier, be sure to get him to wish you 'good luck' like he did for me. Finally, you should buy exactly twenty dollars' worth of lottery tickets, but *do not* pay for them with a twenty-dollar bill. Like me, you should pay for them with a ten-dollar bill and *two* five-dollar ones. If you do all this exactly like I've laid out, I am positive you'll win the lottery, just like me!"

Do you think following Louie's lottery-winning instructions will also lead to you winning the lottery? Of course not! This is obvious and uncontroversial. It's a ridiculous premise that no one would try to implement on their own. The problem, however, is that many people try to emulate the success of others by following their playbook. They read biographies of Warren Buffett, Bill Gates, Elon Musk, and Steve Jobs and try to follow their path. But what many don't realize or fully appreciate is that any supremely successful person owes a huge chunk of their success to plain old luck. So, just as we wouldn't follow the advice of Lucky Lotto Louie, we should be careful following the advice of successful people. While most are surely smart, innovative, and hardworking, these skills are mere prerequisites to success. A little dose of luck is what turns the tide.

For example, your path to financial success will not be in following Bill Gates's path. While Mr. Gates is surely brilliant and worked hard, he was also lucky enough to be a middle schooler at one of the only schools in the entire United States at that time that offered unfettered access to a unique computer programming terminal. At that terminal, students were afforded the opportunity to submit their programs and receive immediate feedback on programming errors, which could then be corrected on the spot. The importance of this cannot be overstated. At that time, most terminals required programmers to submit their work and then wait at least a day for any error feedback. Gates, on the other hand, would submit his programs with immediate feedback. This allowed him, at a young age, to learn the intricacies of programming much faster and better than almost anyone else in the world. Gates himself has quipped that he'd be surprised if there were fifty kids on the entire planet that had this opportunity at the time. This, combined with other lucky events that happened to Gates when building Microsoft, goes a long way in explaining his phenomenal success.

You will likewise not find success by following the path of Warren Buffett. While Buffett is certainly one of the greatest investors of all time, his investment career began when he was around ten years old—much younger, likely, than any of you reading this book. This fact is recounted in Morgan Housel's *The Psychology of Money*, where he reports that, as of that writing, "Warren Buffett's net worth is $84.5 billion. Of that, $84.2 billion was accumulated after his 50th birthday. $81.5 billion came after he qualified for Social Security, in his mid-60s."[3] If Buffett had started investing in his thirties and retired in his sixties, like most of us, he would be unknown today. Housel points out that if Buffett had taken this typical path and earned his actual historical rate of return (22 percent), his net worth today would not be $84.5 billion, but $11.9 million! That's 99.9 percent less than what he is worth today. This goes to show that even if you got Buffett's ridiculous 22 percent returns for thirty years, you would be nowhere close to the actual Warren Buffett many revere and try to emulate today.[4]

Disentangling success from luck is notoriously difficult and not intuitive. How much does luck play a role in the life of a successful person? How much does it come into play in a winning investment strategy? The answers to these questions should change the way you look at success in life and in your investments. You might be surprised to learn that luck typically plays a pivotal role in most any highly successful person's trajectory.

As you may have noticed, the economic pie is not split evenly between an economy's participants—whether we're talking the global economy, or a single country like the United States. Competition for the best jobs and the most money is extremely fierce. There are millions of people trying to get their share. Hard work and talent alone are not enough to ensure you'll win the game. Why? Because there are many talented and hardworking people out there. Hard work and talent are necessary, but not sufficient. There are millions of talented and hardworking people who simply never become especially successful, financially speaking.

In his illuminating book *Success and Luck*, Cornell University economist Robert H. Frank lays out the argument that luck plays a huge role in the life of most successful people.[5] First and foremost, he finds that "roughly half of the variance in incomes across persons worldwide is explained by only two factors: country of residence and the income distribution within that country."[6] If you were born in a developed country like the United States, you won the birth lottery right off the bat. Warren Buffett credits this factor as a driver of his monumental success: "I've had it so good in this world, you know. The odds were 50 to 1 against my being born in the United States in 1930. I won the lottery the day I emerged from the womb by being in the United States instead of in some other country where my chances would have been way different." If you were also born in the U.S. to a well-off family, you, too, won the birth lottery. Studies show that the correlation between a child's income and their parents' is 50 percent—about the same as between a parent's and child's height.[7]

Professor Frank goes on to provide a helpful thought exercise. Imagine you have a merit-based contest that will be decided by objective performance, and there are lots of contestants. The contestants' performance will be comprised 98 percent by talent and effort, and 2 percent by pure luck. Given this, it's obvious that nobody could win this contest without being both talented and lucky. But what's surprising is that the winner of this hypothetical contest will likely be one of the luckiest of all the contestants. That's because, when you have a competition between many people, and even a little bit of luck is involved, almost everything must go right for the winner (i.e., he must be lucky). There will be many contestants at the top of the talent and effort metrics, but if those contestants aren't lucky, they won't win. In large groups, small differences—like luck—matter. A lot. Frank finds that "even when luck has only a minor influence on performance, the most talented and hardworking of all contestants will usually be outdone by a rival who is almost as talented and hardworking but also considerably luckier."[8]

It is also unwise to follow the financial advice of a wealthy person just because they are wealthy. Wealthy people don't necessarily possess better financial knowledge than the non-wealthy. Many were born into wealthy or middle-class families, or took advantage of seemingly merit-based opportunities, but that are, in reality, largely dependent on financial resources or "who you know." For example, students from low-income families cannot afford to accept non-paying internships, whereas students from wealthy families, who have readier access to a high-quality education, can afford to accept non-paying internships, and have access to resources like private tutoring or college preparation courses. We do not all start the race from the same starting blocks. Far from it.

Nor should you blindly trust the insights of self-made individuals who "struggled" to achieve their success. They took risks that paid off, but that doesn't mean their success is replicable. Moreover, we can never really know whether their path to success was due to hard work, skill, or luck. And even if we could figure out that mix, it would be likely impossible to replicate today in our unique circumstances.

We rarely hear cautionary tales about the mighty who have fallen, unless we're indulging in schadenfreude. Instead, we more commonly hear financial tales of legendary figures who overcame difficult socioeconomic circumstances to succeed. When investors take inspiration from these tales of success, they're engaging in a form of survivorship bias. They're not seeing the millions of other people who took the same risks and didn't make it. For one, they don't make good stories.

Latino entrepreneurs face a variety of unique obstacles, but we tend to only hear stories of the exceptional few who overcame those barriers. For example, in the U.S., Latino-owned businesses have up to a 60 percent lower chance of receiving a bank loan than white-owned ones. For every Jeff Bezos, there are thousands of Latino hopefuls who have struggled to even get their dream off the ground.

Success doesn't ride on the coattails of past successes. Every financial decision you make should be based on a clear-sighted view of your goals, the circumstances of the situation, and the characteristics of the investment—not whether it paid off in the past or whether someone wealthy swears by it.

HARD WORK DOESN'T ALWAYS GUARANTEE SUCCESS

Six out of ten Americans believe people can get ahead if they're willing to work hard. This belief goes hand in hand with the American Dream, and we take for granted that if we're smart and diligent, we will succeed.

Sadly, this is an illusion. As we saw above with luck and success, hard work and solid skills are not enough to secure success. Most people who start businesses work hard. They're passionate about what they do, and they're confident they have the skills to achieve their goals. Nevertheless, 70 percent of small businesses fail in the first ten years. Those failures don't happen because 70 percent of people get lazy or complacent. Maybe some do, but not 70 percent. They happen because, regardless of how hard they're willing to work, they are rarely the exception to the objective data we can all plainly see. Extreme financial success isn't something you can engineer, no matter how hard you try.

The myth that hard work will lead to wealth accumulation is especially pervasive in Latino communities. Many people commit to unflagging work, then use their earnings to invest in a business, with the intention of working even harder and starting another business. Their persistent cycle of hard work never ends, and they rarely stop to question whether there are more efficient and safer ways to save and diversify their money. This is true even among wealthy members of the Latino community. They think, "I have to put my money in real estate," instead of considering whether diversification may be better. As a Mexican immigrant, coauthor Julio knows precisely where these misguided patterns come from, as he felt many of them himself. Only after years of diligent academic study did he realize that hard work doesn't always correlate with outsized returns.

We don't deny that hard work matters; the blood, sweat, and tears that people put into their work is admirable. But it's imperative for investors to recognize that hard work alone isn't *sufficient*. While it may be a necessary condition to monetary success, it alone isn't usually enough. Just because a person works hard doesn't mean they will become financially successful. Success is contingent upon what you do with the fruits (i.e., income) of your labor, not upon the fact that you labored, however hard.

Moreover, as we've explored, luck plays a much bigger factor in wealth accumulation than people like to admit. In Mexico, many people say, "After the third generation, you lose all your money." It is a common pattern for someone to work hard, accumulate some wealth, and pass it on.

The second-generation heir thinks, "As long as I work hard, I will keep money," and they fail to account for the power of luck. They don't consthat perhaps their father was in the right business at the right time ohe had the right connections to make his dreams come true. Some ofactors may have been contingent on hard work, but not all. Thegeneration continues in their father's diligent footsteps, but thediversify or change their approach. After all, they see hard workkey to success. Suddenly, a new competitor moves in and steamarket share, and their highly successful business becomes oblittle they can pass on to the third generation is easily squandmatter of decades the family's wealth is back close to zero.

No matter how hard you work, luck is a real factor iwhy diversification is so important. You must hedge yourinvestment doesn't pan out. You must also learn thatreturns aren't based on hard work, but on the risks yoand your patience in awaiting to receive those returns.

◄ 5 ►

Be Humble: Diversify

We've touched on how our view of objective reality can become distorted to our detriment because of our innate biases. What we'll explore in more detail now is the biggest reality-killing culprit of all: overconfidence. You may be wondering why we're dealing with overconfidence now, since it's considered a behavioral bias, and chapter eighteen covers those. The answer is that overconfidence is so pervasive, so pernicious, so investment return–killing, that it deserves a chapter all its own—and early on, to boot. Moreover, recognizing and dealing with the overconfidence bias—whether it be in others or, more importantly, yourself—is crucial to any investor's long-term financial success. That's why we believe overconfidence deserves special recognition. We hope this discussion will begin to shift any deep-seated beliefs you might have.

Investors, by definition, have money available to invest that's not currently needed for day-to-day living. That usually means the investor has had some level of success in their career. While this should be applauded in and of itself, it comes with some tricky baggage. Because most investors have been successful one way or another, many run into the overconfidence trap. They believe that because they've made a lot of money in their day job, they're now capable of making even more money in the land of investing. How hard could it be? Whether you know it or not, this mindset usually makes one overconfident. And overconfidence kills.

You might also be wondering what overconfidence has to do with lack of diversification. Although not immediately obvious, we have noticed that many investors lack diversification *because* they are overconfident. They simply do not have the requisite humility that is required to be a successful long-term investor. Specifically, they are under-diversified because they are confident the asset they're over-concentrated in will outperform a properly diversified portfolio. Or maybe they're confident the future will look like the past. Or, maybe, they think they simply can predict the future. So, let's look at the overconfidence bias in detail first, and follow that up with how it can lead to a lack of diversification—and why that's such a bad thing.

OVERCONFIDENCE

Very few people believe they are average, and certainly not below average. Take a room full of people and ask them to raise their hands if they believe they're an above average driver compared to all the other drivers in the room. Well over half, usually about 70 percent, will raise their hands. Mathematically, this obviously cannot be true.

The chances a new business will survive within the first five years are about 35 percent.[1] When entrepreneurs were asked what the chances a "business like yours" (i.e., their industry) will survive those first five years, the response was 60 percent. And when asked what the likelihood of success would be for their personal business, the entrepreneurs said over 70 percent, with a third of those respondents saying they saw zero chance of failure.

We no doubt need entrepreneurs to start new businesses and drive innovation—our economy would not work without them. But, with investing, overconfidence can have some seriously negative consequences. More humility is what's needed.

LACK OF DIVERSIFICATION

Most investors are not well diversified. While many think they are, the data say differently. One common example can be found with the popular "60/40" portfolio, where 60 percent of the portfolio is weighted toward stocks and 40 percent toward bonds. One problem is that the portfolio is missing an entire asset class: commodities. Another is that, while stocks and bonds have historically tended to move in opposite directions—i.e., they are what we call "uncorrelated assets"—that's not always the case. For instance, at the time of this writing, in late 2022, the U.S. stock market is down around 16 percent for the year, while the U.S. bond market is down about 14 percent. Commodities, on the other hand, are up 19 percent year to date. If you owned the typical 60/40 portfolio thinking diversification would save you, you were out of luck.

The other problem with the 60/40 portfolio is that it delivers suboptimal returns per unit of risk. Consequently, most investors' portfolios are almost 100 percent correlated to global stock markets. Moreover, most investors own their homes, and maybe other real estate; and a lot of investors also own their own businesses. Both assets are equity investments that are almost 100 percent correlated to the global stock markets. This means that most investors are more exposed to equities than they realize; indeed, their investments are likely over 90 percent correlated to stocks. This may be fine during good times, but spells disaster when the bad times come, especially if they have not planned for such a disaster, are cash poor, and must sell their equity positions when they are down, missing out on the miracle of compound interest that only occurs after many decades.

Investors also tend to focus on allocating dollars rather than *risk*. So, because stocks carry much more risk than other asset classes, a portfolio that has 60 percent of its *money* invested in stocks has more like 80 percent or more of its *risk* allocated to stocks. This single issue dwarfs all others that investors face—by giving up diversification, investors are taking on too much risk and are leaving large amounts of return on the table.

We see this problem in other ways too. Many investors—especially in the U.S., but also in other countries—are over-concentrated in their own country's financial assets. This is what we call "home bias." Americans own too many U.S. stocks, Australians own too much of Australia's, Japanese too much of Japan's, and on and on. This lack of diversification can be beneficial if your country has a period of outperformance compared with other countries (e.g., the U.S.), but can be disastrous if you bought at the top and never recovered. This is what happened to Japanese investors in the 1980s. Japan was the hottest market in the world, with a market capitalization at one point much higher than the United States. Money flowed into Japan's stock market, especially from its own citizens. Unfortunately, those that bought at the top in the 1980s have still not seen those highs again to this day. So, when you look at whether you're diversified, consider whether you are too concentrated in your own country's investments, as so many are.

DIVERSIFICATION IS HARD TO HANDLE IN REAL TIME

The reason many investors are not properly diversified is because diversification is hard. That's because, by definition, being fully diversified means having exposure to all asset classes, all sectors, all regions, and all countries around the world. And guess what? These assets, sectors, regions, and countries perform differently over every period. Sometimes *very* differently. If you were fully diversified over the last decade, up until very recently, it was hard to own commodities. A well-diversified commodities portfolio didn't make any money for over a decade while stocks went on a barn-burning tear. Who wouldn't have been tempted to ditch those commodities and load up on stocks? It's human nature. But if you did hold onto your commodities, mid-2020 post-COVID showed up to finally reward you. Since COVID, commodities have been on a nice upward trend:

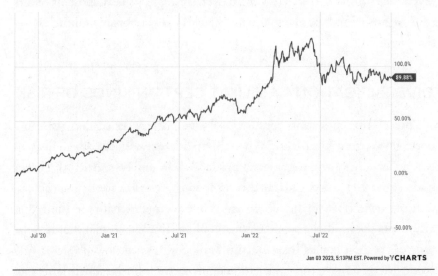

Figure 8. Bloomberg Commodity Index Total Return Level Percent Change. Data illustrated by Ycharts.com

Currently, bonds have been the asset class out of favor with most investors. They've gone through two straight years (2021 and 2022) of negative returns, which is highly unusual since bonds have a contractual right to repayment. Many people have shunned bonds because, again, they've been hard to own. While we don't know how much longer bonds will spend wandering in the proverbial desert, we'd wager that, one day, they'll come back with a vengeance just as commodities did.

To be fully diversified, you must get comfortable with owning things that others shun. You must get used to not being in the top 1 percent of investors for any given year. There will always be someone bragging about buying Tesla at the right time and striking it rich. Or the crypto billionaire that bought Bitcoin for $100. It happens and will continue to happen. You must resist the urge to concentrate your portfolio in the hot asset of the day. Because, one day, it will not be so hot and you'll be left holding the bag, lamenting why you sold your commodities after year 8 of paltry returns, when year 9 was the year of redemption. If you can remain well diversified through thick and thin, over time, you'll beat most investors who are trying to beat the market. As Jack Bogle famously quipped, "Stay the course."

DIVERSIFICATION CAN LIMIT CERTAIN KINDS OF RISK

We preach diversification because, over time, it reduces certain risks in a portfolio without sacrificing return. But while many know diversification is beneficial, few seem to understand exactly why and how. And even fewer understand the mathematical proof showing diversification reduces certain risks without sacrificing return. While the mathematics is somewhat arcane and beyond the scope of this book, a simple example should help. One of the best comes from Burton Malkiel's *A Random Walk Down Wall Street*. There, he asks the reader to imagine a tropical island with only two companies: (1) a resort hotel and (2) an umbrella business.[2] Being a tropical island, rainy weather greatly affects the fortunes of both businesses. When it's the sunny season, the resort does well, and the umbrella company does poorly. And when it's the rainy season, the umbrella company does great, while the resort's business is slow. Malkiel provides the following hypothetical table to show the investment returns of both businesses:[3]

	Umbrella Co.	Resort Co.
Rainy Season	50%	-25%
Sunny Season	-25%	50%

Next, assume that, on average, half the seasons are rainy, while half are sunny. If an investor purchased stock only in the umbrella company, then the investor's returns would be 50 percent half of the time, while the investor would lose 25 percent the other half of the time. Therefore, on average, the investor's return would be 12.5 percent. And if the investor had chosen instead to only invest in the resort company, the investor's returns would likewise be 12.5 percent. The risk, however, is if there are several sunny or rainy seasons in a row, because it's only half and half *on average*. If that likely scenario occurs, the investor will do worse than the 12.5 percent expected return if the wrong business was chosen.[4]

Now assume the investor had instead invested in *both* businesses—half in the resort and half in the umbrella company. During the sunny season, the investment would yield 12.5 percent. And during the rainy season, the investment would likewise yield 12.5 percent. By diversifying, the investor is *assured* of a 12.5 percent return. Malkiel explains further:

> Whatever happens to the weather, and thus to the island econ-
> omy, by diversifying investments over both of the firms, an inves-
> tor is sure of making a 12 ½ percent return each year. The trick
> that made the game work was that although both companies were
> risky (returns were variable from year to year), the companies were
> affected differently by the weather conditions. (In statistical terms,
> the two companies had a negative covariance.) As long as there
> is some lack of parallelism in the fortunes of the individual com-
> panies, diversification can reduce risk. In the present case, where
> there is a perfect negative relationship between the companies' for-
> tunes (one always does well when the other does poorly), diversifi-
> cation can totally eliminate risk.[5]

Now, this is not to say that diversification can "totally eliminate risk" in the real world—far from it. That's because many companies and industries do not have a perfectly negative covariance. To follow our example above, a recession may cause people to stop going on vacations *and* buying umbrel-las. But, as Malkiel points out, "because company fortunes don't always move completely in parallel, investment in a diversified portfolio of stocks is likely to be less risky than investment in one or two single securities."[6]

By understanding this simple example, we can now extrapolate further to see why diversification works in practice. It should now be obvious that owning more than one company is less risky than owning just one. The more companies you own, the more diversified you are and, therefore, the less risk you are taking on. The same goes for adding other asset classes, like bonds and commodities. By owning a well-diversified portfolio of stocks, bonds, and commodities from all over the world, investors can substantially reduce risk since these asset classes do not always move in tandem.

Unfortunately, again, things are not always so simple. In practice, if you were to build a well-diversified portfolio of stocks, bonds, and commodities, you'd end up with a portfolio that is low on what we call idiosyncratic risk (i.e., risk that only affects one company, for example), but still has exposure to systematic risk (i.e., risk that affects all companies equally, like a recession). We will explore those concepts more in chapters eleven, twelve, and thirteen. For now, know that a rational investor should want to eliminate as much idiosyncratic risk as possible through diversification, while maintaining a certain level of exposure to systematic risk based on the investor's risk tolerance and goals.

◄ 6 ►

Opportunity Costs, Scams, and Bad Deals

To be a good investor, sometimes, what you do *not* invest in can be even more important than the investments you *do* end up making. Unfortunately, the investment landscape is littered with scams, frauds, lies, bad deals, and deals that may not be terrible, but are just not right for *you*. Part II of this book will go into the details of how we think most of you should invest. This chapter is not about that—instead we will look at the things you should *avoid*. First, we will consider opportunity costs—which are the opportunities you forego anytime you invest in one thing over all the others. Next, we will try to set your mind right about what you should expect to see about investing in the popular culture and beyond, which is, frankly, a lot of misinformation, falsehoods, and outright lies. Finally, we will turn to all the things you should avoid, including obvious things like scams and frauds, but also most deals presented by friends and family. While avoiding these things is like our mandate of limiting speculation in chapter two, they are also different because, many times, investors in these situations fail to realize that they are speculating at all. The siren call of the "sure thing," "can't lose," "low risk, high return" pitch is just too tempting.

OPPORTUNITY COSTS

As investors, we only have finite dollars with which to invest. Every investment decision you make will be one choice, out of many, of where to put your hard-earned dollars to work. And there will be many choices. Too many, in fact. So many choices that you might become paralyzed and not invest at all; or, if you do invest, you might perpetually regret your choice. While making the right choice and largely sticking with it is the correct tack to take, as investors, we must always be aware of the choices we did *not* make. We call those roads not taken "opportunity costs." An opportunity cost is what you lose when you choose from two or more alternatives. It's a core concept for both investing and life in general. When you invest, opportunity costs can be defined as "the amount of money you might not earn by purchasing one asset instead of another."[1]

While we do not want you to second-guess every investment decision you make, you should be mindful of what opportunities you gave up when you do make one. This is where the concept of "benchmarks" comes in. A benchmark is "a standard or measure that can be used to analyze the allocation, risk, and return of a given portfolio."[2] A benchmark is simply a way for investors to measure their investment performance against an objective standard that is similar in risk characteristics.

For example, if you buy stock in a company listed on the S&P 500, say Microsoft, you should be comparing your investment performance against the S&P 500 index—that is your benchmark. Because purchasing an individual stock is riskier than purchasing the entire S&P 500 index, you should only be happy with your Microsoft investment if it beats the S&P 500 index over the life of the investment. So, if you hold your Microsoft stock for a year, and you get a return of 7 percent, was that a good investment? Without knowing what the benchmark did, it is impossible to say. If the S&P 500 returned 10 percent for the year, then your Microsoft investment does not look too good. You could have earned 10 percent investing in the S&P over Microsoft, while taking less risk. Your opportunity cost was too high for the Microsoft investment and, therefore, it was a bad investment. On the other hand, if the Microsoft investment netted you a return of 15 percent while the S&P only returned 5 percent, then we can objectively say that your choice to invest in Microsoft paid off handsomely, whether by luck or otherwise.

People regularly ignore opportunity costs. For example, we talk to many people who like investing in real estate by owning one or more rental properties. Some, for sure, enjoy owning rental properties for reasons that have nothing to do with superior investment performance, such as the reward of fixing up an old house to make it better than it was. But we also talk to many people who believe owning rental properties is a great investment. Maybe so, but these people rarely take the time to dig into the opportunity costs of those investments. They instead talk about the cash flows they are receiving from their tenants, the tax advantages, or the amount the property has increased in value. But owning a single rental property is not much different than owning a single stock. You are taking on a lot of idiosyncratic risk—or risk that is unique to that particular investment. So, for a rental property, that would include the risk of the local real estate market tanking, a fire or flood destroying the property, or the tenant losing their job and failing to pay rent for months on end.

If you wanted exposure to real estate as an investment, you could have done so in other ways. For real estate, you can invest in a broad, diversified real estate fund, often called a Real Estate Investment Trust (or REIT). There are myriad REITs, some of which exclusively hold single family rentals. So, just like in the stock example, if you own a rental property and earn 10 percent a year on it, just knowing that alone is not enough to determine whether your investment is a good deal. If a REIT of thousands of rental properties, spread out across the country, returned 15 percent over that time, you would have been much better off simply investing in that. And you would have taken less risk for more return. You also would not have had to deal with any of the issues that a typical landlord must deal with, like collecting rent, making repairs, paying taxes, or finding new tenants every year or two, among many others.

Incorporating opportunity costs into your investment worldview will have profound impacts that may not be immediately obvious. Instead of simply looking at your investment returns in a vacuum, you will start evaluating performance objectively against the data. Simply earning a "good return" will no longer be enough; instead, your performance will always depend on what your benchmark did. As we will show later, when you start comparing your performance, as well as the performance of professional, active fund managers that try to "beat the market," you will readily discover that the market is extremely hard to beat over the long run. You will learn, sooner or later, that taking the market return is usually a great deal. You will likewise begin to better understand the opportunities that you did not take, for better or worse.

INVESTING PARLANCE IN POPULAR CULTURE

It seems like everyone is an investor nowadays. Turn on the TV, and you will see celebrities hawking all sorts of ill-advised investment products, ranging from cryptocurrencies to reverse mortgages. It should go without saying that these people are not experts in what they are selling, nor do they have your best interests at heart. They likely believe in the product they are selling about as much as any other celebrity getting paid to endorse a product, whether it be a morning cereal or a car. Therefore, whenever you are enticed by an investing commercial, it is a good idea to take a deep breath and sleep on any tendency to buy that product. Really try and understand it and why you want to invest in it. Do you really know that much about it? Or do you just like Matt Damon's movies and are now transferring that affection to the crypto product he is pushing? Do your research. Talk to your friends and family—or, better yet, a fee-based financial advisor. Try and work out all the biases and influences that are pulling you toward wanting that shiny new investment in your portfolio. If you do all of this, we suspect you will decide on your own that the investment being heavily advertised to you is not such a good idea.

Whenever you are presented with an investment opportunity, you should immediately recall the "golden rule" of investing—that risk and return are inextricably linked. Therefore, if someone tells you they have a great investment with little to no risk, a red siren should go off in your head. Either the investment promoter knows what they are doing, but are lying to you about the risks, or they are ignorant of the risks. Either way, you should run from the "opportunity" like the plague. As we will show, simply earning the market return of around 10 percent that U.S. stocks have historically provided is anything but easy, and entails substantial risk—namely, volatility risk. Do you really think your friend has a real estate deal that promises 15 percent return within a year without *any* risk? If that were the case, don't you think every hedge fund on the planet would be chomping at the bit for that investment? Why are they asking you for money?

It is important to note here that the real estate deal promising a 15 percent return with no risk *might provide you with a 15 percent return*. That is beside the point. As we will show later, just because a risk never materialized does not mean that the risk did not exist. Maybe you just got lucky. Good on you. But that does not mean that things could not have gone the other way.

For example, think of planning a trip for your family to the beach next weekend and the weather forecast calls for a 50 percent chance of rain. You wonder whether to go or not but decide to take the risk anyway and begin packing up the car. You end up having your beach weekend with no rain. Great, you got lucky; the rain never came. But let's think about the risk. You might have been willing to take the 50 percent chance of rain because it was just an impromptu weekend getaway. If the rain did come, not ideal, but also no big deal. But what if you were instead planning an outdoor wedding for that weekend? Would you be willing to have the event outside with a 50 percent chance of rain? You likely will have invested a lot more money into the weekend for a wedding than an impromptu getaway. Maybe a 50 percent chance of rain is not something you're willing to risk for that.

The same goes for investments that are just too good to be true. You might get away with it once, twice, or more. But, eventually, the laws of risk and return will catch up to you and you do not want to find yourself stuck out in the rain with nothing to show for it.

AVOID SCAMS AND BAD DEALS

Some of the biggest opportunity cost killers are scams and bad deals. Nothing will set you back more on your investment journey than losing most, or all, of your money. And this happens. All the time. Immigrants are especially targeted by scammers, since they are often new to investing in the U.S. Often, in fact, immigrants are scammed by their fellow former countrymen who prey upon their shared culture and identity. This builds "trust" between the scammer and the immigrant investor, whereby the investor assumes the scammer has their best interests at heart. For example, one scammer case uncovered by the U.S. Securities and Exchange Commission "intentionally targeted immigrants from African countries who were especially vulnerable, exploiting shared ancestry and religious affiliations to generate 'investments.' To make the scheme even more legitimate, one of the [scammers] even rented office space to give the appearance of an authentic company . . . [M]ore than $27 million was defrauded."[3] This example goes to show you that scams are not always that obvious, so you must really be vigilant.

Nobody is immune to scams; they can sometimes catch even the savviest of people. The most famous example is the Bernie Madoff scandal, where a seemingly rich and powerful investor savant stole billions of dollars from some of the wealthiest of Americans in New York and all over the country, including numerous well-known celebrities. Scams catch highly successful people for many reasons. One is that people who are smart in one area of life tend to think they are smart in *all* areas of life, including, of course, investing. In other words, they become overconfident—something we discussed in the last chapter and will again. There is robust research on this topic, and you should take it to heart as best you can. Be humble and admit that you do not know the future, and recognize that slow, steady growth through proper diversification is the path that has the highest probability of success.

Another trap is when people forget the golden rule of investing: "There is no such thing as a free lunch," or that risk and return are always linked. So, when your friend approaches you about a get-rich-quick investment deal that promises you a 25 percent return within a year with "zero risk," your warning signals should be flashing code red. That sounds too good to be true, and it probably is. Do not let yourself fall into that snare. Investments that are low risk and high return simply do not exist. This does not mean that you cannot get lucky and make an investment and get a high return. In that case, however, it was just that the risk that could have materialized did not—you just got lucky. And if it happens to you once, you should take your winnings off the table and think very hard before making a similar investment in the future. With these types of deals, your luck eventually will run out.

When you start saving and accumulating significant amounts of money, people close to you tend to find out. You might have family you haven't spoken to for years come out of the woodwork asking you to invest in their latest business venture. Your answer to this should, for the most part, be "no, thanks." As we discussed, the data are clear on the success rate of new businesses—most of them fail. But even if the business does survive, it does not mean that your investment was sound. Again, you must consider the opportunity costs of what you could have done with that money. If you made a 7 percent return investing in your friend's business but could have earned a 10 percent return in a stock market index fund, then the investment was not too great—you could have earned more return with much less risk elsewhere.

We came across an astute blog post that looked at investing scams and bad deals, which begins with a well-known quote from Warren Buffett: "Only when the tide goes out do you discover who's been swimming naked."[4] It goes on to explain how investing inherently lends itself to scams, as opposed to most other products consumers purchase, because investments are intangible:

> Most consumer goods—apples, hotel rooms, laptop computers—are tangible objects or services that you can see, taste, feel, or experience, so you can judge how much they are worth to you. Investments represent claims about some future probability distribution of monetary outcomes which are not literally verifiable. The best an investor can do is form a reasonable judgment about the uncertainty around those claims, based on historical evidence and details about the mechanics of how those claimed outcomes are generated.[5]

Many investors, the article explains, get duped into believing an investment is "safe" simply because it's contained in a familiar wrapper, like an ETF. While ETFs can be a great choice, especially ones that are passive and low-cost, not all ETFs fit that mold. Many ETFs are active strategies that are high in costs and will most likely underperform a low-cost, passive ETF. Indeed, we've seen many clients believe they are passive investors just because they own ETFs and index funds, which is a necessary condition for passivity, but hardly sufficient. The author lists a few red flags that investors should watch out for:

- ▶ Projected returns far above historical equity returns
- ▶ Claims of returns significantly exceeding bond returns with little or no risk
- ▶ Extrapolation of recent extreme investment performance into the future
- ▶ Overly complex investments with non-transparent sources of return
- ▶ Perverse incentives for the people selling the investment[6]

New technology is especially fertile ground for all sorts of scams and frauds and has likely been so since the beginning of investing itself. That's because investing necessarily involves predicting the future, with the future always bringing promises of new technologies to better our lives. As investors, we usually overreact and overinvest in new technologies to our detriment. For example, the advent of the railroads was one of the greatest leaps forward in technology ever. And investors piled on like almost nothing else before, or since. Most railroad investors, however, lost money—even though, as we all know, railroad technology changed the world in countless ways.

Another tactic used by investment promoters is the use of "anti-establishment language combined with selling something," which is "a common tool used to manipulate ordinary investors who feel left out of Wall Street's riches."[7] We see this now, of course, in the cryptocurrency space ad nauseam.

The previously mentioned blog post concludes with some advice to avoid these scams, frauds, and bad deals, which we repeat here to wrap up:

- ▶ The first step in avoiding being taken for a ride is to recognize that you are a mark for people trying to get rich off your money.
- ▶ Burn the principle into your brain that financial markets are large and competitive and have a lot of smart people in them.
- ▶ Easy money-making opportunities are almost never real; professional mercenaries would have found and exploited them first.
- ▶ High returns with low risk explained away by complicated and nontransparent strategies deserve great scrutiny.
- ▶ Ask questions; be skeptical; do not assume that just because brand-name firms or authority figures are involved that all is well.[8]

◄ 7 ►

Be a Short-Term Pessimist and a Long-Term Optimist

Investing, at its core, is an optimist's game. Whether you know it or not, any time you invest your money, you are making a prediction that the future will be better than today. You must believe this, or else you would not, and should not, invest at all. If you knew that the United States was going to crumble, die on the vine, and become a failed state, then you would never invest in any company doing business there. Why would you? Your money would be better off invested in another country without such a dire future ahead of it. Likewise, if you knew an earth-destroying asteroid was coming within the year, what sense would it make to invest in *any* country? The rational move would be to liquidate all your investments and spend the money today enjoying every second you have doing what you love, with the people you love, until the earth ends.

LONG-TERM OPTIMIST

As an investor, you should try to be optimistic about the future of the United States, as well as the world. You must believe that most people wake up in the morning and go out and try to be productive to make the world a better place. You must believe that companies around the globe are continually trying to be more profitable, adding more value for their customers and clients. You must believe that technology is ever increasing, causing our lives to be enriched, be more prosperous, and yes again, be more productive. In essence, you must believe that trend of increasing global productivity will continue, just as it has in the past.

If you are like most and regularly consume social media and the daily news, you might not *feel* like today is the best time to be alive in human history. You might look back nostalgically to some other decade, or even century, as a time when they had it better. But regardless of how you feel, the objective facts say otherwise. One reason, as the noted author and Harvard psychologist Steven Pinker points out, is that we take much of present-day life for granted:

> [N]ewborns who will live more than eight decades, markets overflowing with food, clean water that appears with a flick of a finger and waste that disappears with another, pills that erase a painful infection, sons who are not sent off to war, daughters who can walk the streets in safety, critics of the powerful who are not jailed or shot, the world's knowledge and culture available in a shirt pocket.[1]

The trend over the last two hundred years on myriad quality of life metrics has been noticeably upward. A quick rundown of a few, compiled by Matt Ridley in his book *The Rational Optimist: How Prosperity Evolves*, helps prove the point:

> Since 1800, the population of the world has multiplied six times, yet average life expectancy has more than doubled and real income has risen more than nine times. Taking a shorter perspective, in

2005, compared with 1955, the average human being on Planet Earth earned nearly three times as much money (corrected for inflation), ate one-third more calories of food, lived one-third longer. She was less likely to die as a result of war, murder, childbirth, accidents, tornadoes, flooding, famine, whooping cough, tuberculosis, malaria, diphtheria, typhus, typhoid, measles, smallpox, scurvy, or polio. She was less likely, at any given age, to get cancer, heart disease, or stroke. She was more likely to be literate and to have finished school. She was more likely to own a telephone, a flush toilet, a refrigerator, and a bicycle. All this during a half-century when the world population has more than doubled, so that far from being rationed by population pressure, the goods and services available to the people of the world have expanded.[2]

Despite all this, we tend to be stubbornly pessimistic, thinking the best times are behind us. This pessimism is not new, however. Indeed, Ridley quotes the 1800s British politician Thomas Babington Macaulay, who wrote: "On what principle is it, that when we see nothing but improvement behind us, we are to expect nothing but deterioration before us?"[3] As investors, we need simply to believe that these positive trends will continue, both in the United States and globally. If you believe this to be so, you should put your money to work, sit back, and watch it grow over time.

Importantly, however, this does not mean there won't be bumps in the road. The business cycle, it seems, is an unavoidable part of modern life and markets. And that means manias, bubbles, crashes, and recessions are too. It also seems that our markets only grow, and incremental improvements in daily life only accrue, through a process called "creative destruction."

CREATIVE DESTRUCTION

One of the best sources on this topic comes from Philippe Aghion, Céline Antonin, and Simon Bunel's wonderful book, *The Power of Creative Destruction: Economic Upheaval and the Wealth of Nations*. There, they write that

[c]reative destruction is the process by which new innovations continually emerge and render existing technologies obsolete, new firms continually arrive to compete with existing firms, and new jobs and activities arise and replace existing jobs and activities. Creative destruction is the driving force of capitalism, ensuring its perpetual renewal and reproduction, but at the same time generating risks and upheaval that must be managed and regulated.[4]

The process of creative destruction is what drives long-term economic growth, in the United States and worldwide, which only happens because of innovation. Innovation, in turn, comes from investment, most especially in research and development by entrepreneurs motivated by returns on their money. Progressive innovation inevitably leads to newer and better products, making older products obsolete, creating a never-ending conflict between old and new. Because of this, old firms will try to push out the new entrants through a variety of ways, including political lobbying and monopolistic activities. Therefore, for example, a properly functioning capitalist system must have antitrust laws to prevent monopolies. Monopolies do not innovate because they don't have to compete.

Assuming the stage is correctly set, creative destruction will inevitably lead to new companies entering markets, displacing the old. This is one reason why picking individual stocks is so hard: the best performing companies change *all the time*. The firms on top ten, twenty, or thirty years ago are not the same as the ones on top today. Thus, if history is our guide, we should expect that the top companies of today will not be the same as tomorrow. So, instead of trying to continually pick and choose which companies will falter and which will rise, the data suggest you are better off riding the wave of creative destruction by taking the returns the market is freely handing out. By doing this, in the cheapest and most efficient way possible, you will get to enjoy the fruits of creative destruction: things like rising economies, markets, and investments. Moreover, you will not have to endure creative destruction's pitfalls, like losing money investing in a company that gets replaced by a newer, nimbler innovator. And, as an investor, you will have a front-row seat to creative destruction playing out over time since "financial markets make it possible to mobilize resources and capital to finance daring ideas."[5]

Being a long-term optimist, however, does not mean you should be naïve. Instead, you must realize that the path toward increased productivity and prosperity for mankind is not a straight line. There will be ups, and downs—you can bet on that. Nobody, and we mean *nobody*, knows how the future will play out. We cannot tell you that the stock market will go up tomorrow, this month, this year, or even the next couple of years. Indeed, there have been times in the past where markets have floundered for many years on end. But, if you are patient enough, and have the right plan, you can take advantage of the trend of long-term productivity and prosperity growth. You can ride the upward trend that has been so strong over the last 150-plus years. And the best part is that you can ride that trend without having to make any predictions, without having to "beat the market," and without having to speculate or bet. You can simply ride the coattails of the market, resting assured that, over time, the trend is upward. Therefore, your mindset should be pessimism for the short term, but optimism for the long term.

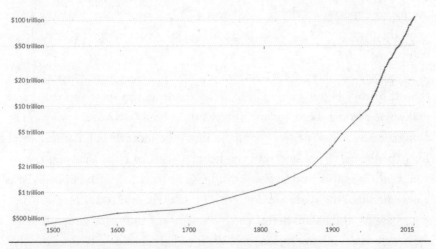

Figure 9. World GDP over the Last Two Millennia. Total output of the world economy; adjusted for inflation and expressed in international-$ in 2011 prices. CC BY. Source: Our World in Data based on World Bank & Maddison (2017). OurWorldinData.org/economic-growth

SHORT-TERM PESSIMIST

You should be a short-term pessimist because the world breaks, on average, every ten years or so. And it never breaks in the way anyone thinks it will. Rather, it breaks in unexpected ways. And it is the surprises that really throw us—and markets—into a tailspin. One need only look very recently at the COVID-19 pandemic. If you go back and read any "market forecast" from all the "experts" on Wall Street and beyond for the year 2020, you would be hard pressed to find "global pandemic that shuts down the world" as a prediction. It was what former U.S. Secretary of Defense Donald Rumsfeld famously referred to as an "unknown unknown." Or a "black swan" event, per the book of the same title by Nassim Taleb.

Even if one of those prognosticators had had a crystal ball, they likely still would not have been able to correctly predict how markets would *react* to COVID. They probably would not have guessed an over 30 percent crash, but a quick recovery leading to an 18 percent *gain* for the year. Utterly unpredictable. And there will be other unpredictable black swan events in our investment lifetimes. Maybe two or three, or more. They are to be expected and you need to be prepared for them if you want your investments to survive long enough to experience the miracle of compound growth.

Just because these events will occur, however, does not change the fact that, if history is our guide, humans will continue to solve problems and make the world a better place, increasing productivity and profitability along the way. While being pessimistic about the short term is natural—and likely beneficial, since it makes you keenly aware of risks that might hurt you, both in nature and in modern life—it is hard to justify a pessimistic view when looking with a wider lens. While the world today certainly has its problems, things are better today than at any point in human history, even if the daily news sometimes makes it feel otherwise. War is rarer today than almost any time in human history, and when it does happen it is less deadly. Same goes for genocides and other mass killings. Life expectancy, literacy, and global standards of living are at all-time highs.[6] Hunger, child mortality, and poverty are likewise all in decline.

One reason you may not have noticed these advances is because good things tend to compound slowly, bit by bit, year by year. So slowly and gradually that, on an annual basis, the gains are not necessarily "newsworthy." For example, death from heart disease has declined each year by about 2 percent.[7] But a 2 percent drop does not make the headlines—it's too small for that. But 2 percent, every year for many years and counting, is an incredible achievement.

Another is that we tend to recognize and attach ourselves to the most recent news of the day—what is called "recency bias." Recency bias, which we will discuss again in chapter eighteen, causes us to latch onto the latest negative headline and then extrapolate that negativity to our current view on the state of the world. So, a mass shooting that makes headlines makes us believe we are living in the most violent of times, even when the opposite is true. This bias likewise makes us forget the bad news of the more distant past. For example, most people look back upon the 1990s as a time of unprecedented peace and prosperity—certainly most think the world was "safer" back then. But the 1990s was objectively more violent and terrible than today, where we saw "genocides in Rwanda and Bosnia. Years of war in Europe amid Yugoslavia's collapse. Devastating famines in Sudan, Somalia and North Korea. Civil wars in over a dozen countries. Crackdowns and coups too numerous to mention."[8] Decades further back were even worse, including, of course, two devasting world wars during the first half of the twentieth century.

Our collective historical memory is similarly flawed on economic measures. Many people believe that the 1950s was an unabashed decade of economic growth. Indeed, when most think of the "good ole' days," the *Leave It to Beaver* 1950s is usually what comes to mind. But the 1950s saw two significant recessions![9] And let's not forget that the 1950s saw fewer rights for women, minorities, and other marginalized groups.

As you can see, on numerous objective measures of well-being, economic or otherwise, we are better off today. Do not let the incessant burr of the daily news make you believe differently. In fact, turning off the news will only help you as an investor. The talking heads on television do not know the future of markets but are simply there to entertain you, whether through fear or greed. Do not fall prey to the bait. *Nothing* they say should affect how you invest your money. You would be better off reading books about history and upward trends that show how things have steadily gotten better, day by day, year by year. Maybe slowly at times, and, yes, sometimes in fits and starts and backwards, but things really do trend upward. It is reasonable to expect that trend to continue.

◄ 8 ►

Know When You Have Enough

We have seen countless investors claim they will be happy when they reach "X" amount, only to say they now want "2X" to finally be content. Then, when they reach "2X," they say they need 3X, 4X, and beyond. This is usually a recipe for unhappiness. You should think long and hard about why you want to save and invest money in the first place. What are you saving up for? What are your goals? What is your view on how money can better your and your family's life? While this might sound trite and cliché, money does not always buy happiness. While studies have shown that money does lead to happiness up to about $75,000 a year in annual income, the gains in happiness above that point are minimal or nonexistent.* Studies have likewise shown that the best way to achieve happiness through money is by using it to buy time and experiences, not things.

---

* More recent studies have suggested that incomes above the $75,000 threshold may, in fact, contribute to more well-being, but those studies recognize that there is no doubt an upper limit to more income contributing to more happiness.

Most of us know intuitively that money alone is not a surefire path to happiness. Just think of all the rich celebrities that check into rehab every year, for one. But most of us also fall into the trap of thinking along the lines of "when I have X amount of money, or when I get that job paying me X amount, *then* I will be happy." We can tell you from experience that rarely happens. Instead, your problems remain and are sometimes even compounded by the additional dollars coming in the door.

So, think long and hard about your money and your life. We have found, and studies back it up, that people who use money to buy freedom and time tend to be the most content with their life. They do not incessantly buy up material things because they know that any happiness those things may bring is fleeting. They also tend to save for saving's sake—not to buy any one thing. Instead, they seek to build a protective barrier from life's unknowns, which helps them sleep well at night.

They also usually have a set number in mind where they know they can be content money-wise in life. A number that will allow them to do the things they love, in perpetuity: To travel. To start a business. To spend quality time with family, without having to strive for a happier tomorrow that may never come. They live in the here and now and are content with what they have—because they have *enough*.

The late Jack Bogle, founder of Vanguard, wrote an entire book on this subject, aptly titled *Enough: True Measures of Money, Business, and Life*. Bogle recaps a study published in the *American Psychologist* magazine detailing the relationship between money and happiness:

[I]t's not money that determines our happiness, but the presence of some combination of these three attributes: (1) autonomy, the extent to which we have the ability to control our own lives, "to do our own thing"; (2) maintaining connectiveness with other human beings, in the form of love of our families, our pleasure in friends and colleagues, and an openness with those we meet in all walks of life; and (3) exercising competence, using our God-given and self-motivated talents, inspired and striving to learn.[1]

Going by these metrics, one can see that it is not money for money's sake that can "buy" happiness, but how you *use* that money. If you use it for freedom to do what you love, with the people you love, then you have a very high chance for true contentment in your life. If you use it to buy things to "keep up with the Joneses," well, good luck. That is not to say that it is wrong to want nice things. But it will behoove you to try and figure out why you want those nice things. Do you want a nice car to show off to your friends and neighbors, or do you spend a lot of time in the car and want to have the convenience and comfort a luxury vehicle can provide? Do you want a big house just to boast, or do you want to live in a nice part of town so your family can be safe, and you can send your kids to better schools? It is not the ownership of nice things that will trip you up, it's the reason for *why* you're owning those things. If it is to impress other people, or to fill a void in your life caused by something else, that shiny object will not do the trick. Fix the problem in ways that do not involve money.

MOVING THE GOALPOSTS

One reason many people do not become happier upon making more and more money is that they are always "moving the goalposts," a term with which you are likely familiar. We all know the feeling. You think that once you reach a certain level of income or saved wealth that then, and only then, will you be happy, only to reach that level to find out that there is now *another* level that must be reached for you to feel content. Rinse and repeat each time a new level is reached. Morgan Housel astutely observes that "[a]n addiction to the process of making money is a version of never having enough and never being satiated. It's a game that can't be won but offers the illusion of a finish line right around the corner."[2]

In his bestselling book, *The Psychology of Money*, Housel touches on this topic with great acumen. He notes that "the hardest financial skill is getting the goalpost to stop moving."[3] Sound familiar? He goes on to say that modern capitalism is great at "generating wealth and generating envy."[4] It is the old "keeping up with the Joneses" cliché. While keeping up with your new friends and neighbors might be a good source of fuel to motivate you to work harder, it is usually a recipe for a dissatisfied life, because someone will surely always have more than you. If you are always comparing yourself to someone else, what you have will never be enough. There are stories of billionaires feeling inadequate because they only have one or two billion, and nowhere near the wealth of Bill Gates or Elon Musk. The comparisons never stop for some people, no matter how far up the ladder they go.

While it is not an easy skill to master, you should try your best to learn what enough is for you. Housel, again, has some relevant wisdom here:

> The idea of having "enough" might look like conservatism, leaving opportunity and potential on the table. I don't think that's right. "Enough" is realizing that the opposite—an insatiable appetite for more—will push you to the point of regret. The only way to know how much food you can eat is to eat until you're sick. Few try this because vomiting hurts more than any meal is good. For some reason the same logic doesn't translate to business and investing, and many will only stop reaching for more when they break and are forced to. This can be as innocent as burning out at work or a risky investment allocation you can't maintain. On the other end there's the Rajat Guptas and Bernie Madoffs in the world, who resort to stealing because every dollar is worth reaching for regardless of consequence. Whatever it is, the inability to deny a potential dollar will eventually catch up to you.[5]

As humans, we are hardwired for moving the goalposts, probably because, in most cases, it is beneficial to our progress. If everyone were content with their station in life, lacking ambition to improve, then most of us would never get anything done. So, it's probably unavoidable, and beneficial, for us to always be working toward some goal, no matter how big or small. And so long as we are accomplishing those goals and moving forward, we are typically content.

However, with money and investing, things are trickier because your invested wealth will never move steadily upward in a straight line. Housel writes that "[w]hat feels great is being on an upward path. That's when dopamine takes over. That's when you can extrapolate it and assume it goes on forever, and compare yourself to where you were before, and feel like nothing can stop you. When that path declines—even if it happens when you have a level of wealth you couldn't fathom a few years ago—the whole sensation shatters."[6]

We are here to tell you now that your investments *will* go backwards (i.e., down), sometimes greatly. You can count on it. In fact, your investments not going backwards should be a huge red flag. Only frauds and Ponzi schemes never go backwards.

If you understand and accept that your wealth accumulation will not always grow upward in a straight line, you'll be better equipped for the investment journey. You will know that stocks, for example, have higher expected returns compared with safer assets because they regularly go down, sometimes drastically. But instead of fretting, stressing, and making a poor decision, you will realize going backwards is just the price of admission for higher returns. You might even relish the down times as an opportunity to buy more at cheaper prices.

You should likewise try your best to find your "enough number"—the amount of money that objectively is enough *for you*, knowing that the wealth accumulation game can never really be won. And while at first that might sound defeatist, we believe that, upon further reflection, it can be liberating. Because once you achieve that number, you really can take yourself out of the game altogether. You can then start focusing on what's important to you in life. You will have security and freedom like you never dreamed.

◄ PART II ►

Investing: Theory and Practice

◄ INTRODUCTION TO PART II ►

In Part I, we gave you some "big picture" concepts of certain viewpoints we believe will not serve you well as an investor in the contemporary United States. We explored certain worldviews that you might have from your home countries, or even the U.S. if you were born and raised here. Here in Part II, we want to dive deeper into the "meat and potatoes" of investing. We will begin by exploring what a market is, and why you're unlikely to beat it. After that, we will look at the specific components of the global market. Then, we'll look at what risk and return are and how to determine your risk tolerance. We will next examine what a "Global Market Portfolio" is and explain why we believe it should be the starting point for most investors, followed by how you can deviate from such a portfolio if you are risk tolerant and want higher expected returns. Finally, we will go into some "nuts and bolts" details about the various account types, custodians, tax considerations, and other housekeeping items with which you should be familiar.

◄ 9 ►

What a Market Is (and Why You Are Unlikely to Beat It)

If you know anything at all about investing, chances are you've heard the term "the market." But what does it mean? For many immigrants, the stock market might as well be synonymous with a casino. Maybe, in your home country, you wouldn't dream of putting in more money into the stock market than you're prepared to lose. We understand the reticence. The lessons you learned back in your home country were probably wise ones, given how unstable many countries' stock markets have been historically. But when you're investing in the United States, the picture looks a bit different. We'd like to invite you to hit "pause" on your reservations and hear us out. "The market" doesn't have to be as scary as you think. And it certainly shouldn't be viewed as a casino if you do it right.

WHAT IS A MARKET?

When you hear the term "stock market," what comes to mind? If you're like most in the U.S., maybe you're thinking of the S&P 500, the Dow Jones Industrial Average, or the NASDAQ. While these are all types of markets, they don't really get to the heart of what a market is. That's because each of these market indices is a tiny sliver of the pie. And by the "pie," we mean the global market of investable assets, which includes many more stocks, along with bonds, real estate, and commodities. So, next time you hear someone say "the market," you need to ask yourself what market they are talking about. All the stocks in the United States? Or just the top five hundred by market capitalization (e.g., the S&P 500)? All the bonds in the world? Or just European sovereign bonds? Or maybe just a specific sector, like energy or telecommunications? Understanding what a market is, and which market you're concerned with, is paramount for your investing success.

Conversely, misunderstanding what a market is can have dire consequences, especially for immigrants who come from countries where stock investing is uncommon. We've seen many people make erratic and risky decisions because they didn't fully appreciate the concept of a market. For example, one Mexican friend thought he could quickly make a killing day trading. He invested $30,000 and lost $7,000 almost immediately. He didn't understand the market in which he was investing and the risks it entailed. So, let's make sure you don't make the same mistake!

By definition, a financial market is a place—whether it be physical, or now more commonly digital—where parties come together to buy and sell financial assets. A market comprises all the assets available for purchase or sale, and typically involves thousands of participants. For example, if we're talking about the stock market, that doesn't mean just the stocks that make up the S&P 500, or even the larger New York Stock Exchange. When we refer to the "stock market," it really means every single publicly traded stock in the entire world—over 41,000 individual companies!

However, to really get to what *the* market is, we must expand our definition further. The stock market isn't the only market in the world. As you might have guessed, we also must include bonds, commodities, and real estate. Therefore, the bond market includes all the bonds in the world, the commodities market includes all the commodities in the world, and the real estate market includes all the real estate *in the world*. And when you put all these assets in the world together, you get "*the* market," or what we refer to as the "global market of investable assets" or the "global market" for short.

Note the phrase "investable assets." There are many assets in the world that you and I cannot reasonably invest in, like someone's private residence, for example. While you might be able to get some exposure, say if you have a mortgage that becomes part of a portfolio of mortgage-backed securities, I can't easily go and buy your specific mortgage. And if your house doesn't have a mortgage because you own it fully outright, I cannot have any exposure to it at all.

Also pay attention to the "global" part—it's important. While the United States is the largest market in the world, it's certainly not the only one. And just because you live in the United States doesn't mean you're limited to investing just there; actually, it's important you don't! You can, and should, invest in the rest of the world, including Europe, Latin America, and emerging markets like Africa and parts of Asia. Fortunately, this is simple for U.S.-based investors to accomplish. One reason is that the United States offers an abundance of cheap, readily available funds that invest in the world's markets. For example, the Vanguard Total World Stock ETF gives investors exposure to all the world's stocks, for a fee of just 0.07 percent per year.

MARKET CAP–WEIGHTED INVESTING

Let's suppose you want to invest $500 in the S&P 500. What would you do? Would you invest $1 into each company and call it a day? While this might seem tempting, this is the wrong way to go about it. That's because each company in the S&P 500 is not the same size by market capitalization. Market capitalization, or "market cap" for short, is how investors measure the size of a company and is defined as the total value of all the company's outstanding shares of stock. Thus, if a company has one million shares of stock and each share is currently worth $2, the market cap of that company would be $2,000,000. Currently, Apple is the largest company in the S&P 500 by market cap, comprising approximately 6.2 percent of the S&P. Compare that to company number 500, which currently comprises approximately 0.000005 percent of the index. If your goal is to invest in the S&P 500 to receive its market performance, you'd want to give 6.2 percent of your money to Apple and only 0.000005 percent of your money to company number 500. You'd want to do this exercise for all five hundred companies in the S&P, which, after Apple, would currently include Microsoft (5.7 percent), Amazon (3.5 percent), Tesla (2.1 percent), and so on down the list. Luckily, you don't have to do this work, since there are ready-made ETFs and index funds available that do just that. Just make sure they are "market cap weighted" and not equally weighted. Now, let's break down *why* investing via market cap is the best strategy for your long-term financial success.

Imagine there are only two companies in the world, and the total value of the world's economy is $100. Company A has a value of $80, and Company B is worth $20. If you invested equally, you'd split your money 50:50 and invest $50 in each company. But if you do that, you're making an active bet *against* the market. Since the market says Company A is worth $80, it should get 80 percent of your money ($80). If you split it 50:50, you're instead saying, "I know Company A is worth $80, but I'm putting only $50 into it because I think Company A and B will one day both be worth $50." That bet could pay off, but if Company A keeps chugging along at its normal pace, you stand to lose money or see a lower rate of return than that of the whole market.

Since we know that, over the long run, 97 percent of active fund managers fail to outperform the market, the most reliable way to invest would be to *mirror the market*. Put 80 percent of your money into Company A and 20 percent into Company B. That way, if Company B does well, you'll experience proportional growth. If they don't, your investment will still reflect the reality of the market, and you'll maximize the returns you're getting from Company A.

Also note that if you invest according to market cap and the market changes—say Company B performs well and takes market share from Company A so that each is now worth $50—you'll get to experience that change in your portfolio *without you having to do anything*. That's because if Company B increases from $20 to $50, the value of your shares in Company B will likewise increase, while the value of Company A will decrease. You don't have to buy or sell any shares whatsoever. And if the entire market increases so that both companies are now worth more money, you'll get to enjoy those gains, too, since the price of the stocks should increase in tandem with the value of the companies.

Unfortunately, most people invest by ignoring a company's market cap; instead, they try to beat the market by figuring out which stocks will outperform their current position. They fall victim to many of the biases we will discuss later and make risky decisions. Unless luck is on their side, they lose.

This tendency to try to outperform the market is why so many people— and so many immigrants in particular—consider intangible investments inherently risky. Investing in intangible assets only seems like a gamble because so many investors have internalized the idea that they're looking for a long shot, so they can beat the odds and cash in quickly. Stocks, bonds, and other financial instruments aren't fundamentally riskier than material investments, but the way most people use them are. If you want to minimize your risk and maximize your investments' growth, you must understand what a market is, why investors aren't likely to outperform the market, and how the market ought to inform your investment strategy.

Remember, the only way to reliably replicate the global market with Company A and Company B was to do it proportionally, according to their market share. The same principle applies to any investment you make. Your goal should be—as closely as possible—to mirror the market or, in other words, to invest in all possible asset classes, globally, in the proper proportion.

WHY OUTPERFORMING THE MARKET IS SO UNLIKELY

One of our clients is a very smart Latino man who made his money in the real estate business in Mexico. In 2008, when everyone was scared about the global economy, he bought land in Cancún, and he made a fortune by developing and selling the land, and then buying more land. From 2008 to 2018, he multiplied his money thousands of times. Finally, he sold a big chunk of his assets and called us to help him invest the money.

Before he became our client, we talked a lot about the global market, and we showed him the economic data behind our methodology. We explained that this isn't our opinion. There are thousands of academic researchers saying the same thing: outperforming the market, in the long run, is like winning the lottery. We aren't saying that it *can't* happen, but you certainly don't want to bank on it. Plus, even if you're lucky enough to hit the jackpot, it would be foolish to think you could win a second or third time. Yet, that's how many investors approach the stock market. In the long run, it's highly unlikely that such investors will keep winning and outperform the market.

After seeing the data, our client became more convinced. One day, he quietly admitted, "If I believed what you're saying now, I wouldn't be rich." And he was right. He would never have taken the risks with real estate that garnered him so much money. "Do you think you could repeat the same thing right now?" we asked. "No, of course not," he replied. And, again, he was right.

Yes, this man is smart. Yes, he worked hard. But luck played a huge factor in his success. He took a risky bet, and his timing was perfect. But if chance hadn't been on his side, things could have turned out the opposite way. He might have lost everything he owned. That's what we mean when we say that it's hard to outperform the market. It's not impossible, but it's also not likely.

To explain why it's so hard, let's look at a simple example. Imagine you're watching a single market—the restaurant market—in a very small town with only three restaurants. You've invested in every restaurant, proportional to its market share. Seventy percent of your money is invested in McDonald's since they get 70 percent of the townspeople's business. Twenty percent goes to the local pizzeria, and 10 percent is dedicated to the mom-and-pop taqueria. After a year, the total growth of the restaurant market in the town is 4 percent. Because you invested proportionally, you would receive the same rate of return on your investment: 4 percent.

If you were trying to outperform the market, you'd have to choose a restaurant that you thought would give you a *better* return. For example, you'd say, "I think the mom-and-pop restaurant will take off, so I'll invest 40 percent of my money there." If you're right, you might be able to outperform the 4 percent market returns; but if you're wrong, you'll earn less.

Crucially, you'd have to *keep* being right to continue to outperform the market. Everyone can make a lucky guess once, but your chances of doing so over and over again are infinitesimally small. When you're trying to outperform the market, you are always vulnerable. Don't leave your investment strategy open to those wild fluctuations. The key to growing wealth involves a healthy dose of time and patience—not taking huge risks that will likely make you worse off.

THE DATA ARE CLEAR: HOW SCIENCE TELLS US TO INVEST

Economists like Eugene Fama, William Sharpe, Harry Markowitz, and James Tobin have provided scientific and empirical evidence that there is one thing investors must do to increase their probability of positive returns:

diversify by investing in the global market. The global market is not overly concentrated in one asset class or one geographic location, but holds its assets proportionally based on their size globally.

Perhaps the best way to think about the global market is to compare it to a balloon. If you squeeze one part of a balloon, what happens? The air rushes to another part of the balloon, and it bulges. Then, when you release your grip, the air rushes back. This is how the cycles of the global economy work. When you diversify as broadly as possible, and as proportionally as possible, you have the highest probability of getting positive returns. If you own a piece of everything, you'll always be seeing returns somewhere, even when some of your assets are down. In fact, your returns will be very close to the global GDP (gross domestic product) because, by definition, global GDP is the return of all the world's economies.

We understand that this may sound overwhelming. How can you invest in every country, technology, company, product, and so on—and not only that, how can you do it proportionally? We'll explain in future chapters how to invest with the whole market in mind, particularly via our "Three Buckets Approach" mentioned earlier. For now, it's enough to see *why* you need to take a wider perspective on the market. If you don't consider the market in its entirety—global stocks, bonds, real estate, and commodities—you will miss out on vital opportunities and leave yourself open to greater risk.

◄ 10 ►

Components of the
Global Market

When it comes to wealth, most people like to have a clear grasp of the things they own. All the clothing, appliances, and possessions that fill your home—these are concrete manifestations of the wealth you've earned. If you own your home, you have walls, a roof, and a front door you can use to let people in or lock them out. These assets are *yours*, through and through. They are also easy to understand—you can touch and feel them to your heart's desire. Indeed, they may be so important and valuable to you that you go to great expense to protect them, such as with insurance, or a safe.

It's understandable, then, why so many immigrants would gravitate toward these kinds of physical assets. In many cases, they are coming from places where the things they can see and touch are their *only* opportunities for wealth. For example, years of political conflicts and violence, power struggles, and growing economic disparity have taught Latin Americans to place their trust only in assets they can experience firsthand. When you

107

can't place your trust in the government or financial institutions—or when you've witnessed multiple, major stock market crashes or hyper-inflationary spikes—there's something reassuring about a piece of land, a house, or even a stockpile of cash or precious metals (e.g., gold and silver).

But even these most concrete, basic assets aren't as simple as they seem. For example, that pile of money in the closet? It may seem stable, but rising inflation means that its value shrinks with each passing year.* That piece of land you bought in your home country? You may have made payments, but chances are, it's not yet *yours*; you probably still owe a monthly mortgage to a lender, for one. And even if you've paid off the mortgage, the value hinges on factors you can't control, like depreciation due to wear and tear. You could also lose your home if you fail to pay property taxes on it.

It may seem like your business or house value will never "crash" the way a stock market crashes, but that's a psychological trick. Just consider the effects that COVID had on the profitability of certain businesses (e.g., restaurants and others in the service industry). The safety of an asset has nothing to do with whether it's material, like a house, or immaterial, like a stock. In fact, you'd be much better off ridding yourself of any preconceptions you might have about "material" and "immaterial" assets in the first place. To begin growing your wealth, you must first understand what kinds of assets are available to you. In this chapter, we'll explain the difference between real and financial assets, and show you why you should be less concerned with those categories than with your assets' relationship to debt and equity.

FINANCIAL AND REAL ASSETS

Broadly speaking, there are two types of assets: real and financial. Real assets are physical assets with intrinsic value linked to their physical properties.

---

* Recent concerns about high inflation are just that: concerns about *high* inflation. Moderate inflation of 2 to 3 percent is normal in the United States (and other countries) and will always be around, as we covered in chapter two.

These include precious metals, like gold and silver; commodities, like wheat and lumber; capital assets, like land and equipment; and natural resources, like oil and natural gas. These are things you can see, touch, smell, and taste. They get their value from people or businesses being able to do things with them in the real world.

On the other hand, financial assets get their value from a contractual right or a claim to ownership. These include things like cash, stocks, bonds, mutual funds, and bank deposits. These assets don't have inherent physical worth, and some of them don't even have a physical form, yet they are every much as valuable and "real" as real assets.

You may be saying, "Hold up! What do you mean cash doesn't have inherent physical worth?" But think about it. The piece of paper a dollar bill is printed on is almost worthless. The thing that has value is the *contract behind it*. As a society, we've all agreed that a dollar is worth a dollar. Its value is further supported by the United States government—if the United States ceased to exist, the dollar's value would too. And not only that, but we've also agreed that the value of a dollar can fluctuate—a dollar won't go as far in 2021 as it did in 1911.

But be careful. Don't discount financial assets just because they aren't "real." The values you see on the stock market every day are tied to very real assets that exist somewhere in the world. When you buy stock in a company, that company physically *exists*. It owns, or leases, offices and things inside those offices, like computers, desks, and chairs. It might own land, vehicles, and equipment, or valuable data existing on physical servers and computers like software code and customer lists. Stock is simply a financial asset a company uses to finance its operations.

That means you can own real assets *through* financial assets. Here's another example. When you buy a futures contract on a commodity like oil, the oil physically exists somewhere. You're just not buying the actual barrels of oil; you're using a financial asset—a contract—to lay claim to the value of that oil. The value of a financial asset comes from your contractual claim *on the underlying asset.*

Many immigrants avoid financial assets because they assume they are riskier. But what's safer: stashing a bar of gold under your bed—where it could be stolen or damaged—or owning that gold through a financial asset with exposure to gold where it cannot be stolen from you by a thief in the night? And risk-wise, what's the difference between owning a barrel of oil and owning a contract that says you own a barrel of oil?

The risk of an investment has nothing to do with whether it's a real asset or a financial asset, but this pernicious misconception has led many to miss out on valuable opportunities for growing their wealth. The Federal Reserve noted that as of 2019, 98.7 percent of U.S. families owned some type of financial asset, including a checking or savings account. But be careful—that number is deceptively high. There's a sharp drop-off between the percentage of people who own bank accounts and those with other types of financial assets. Only 52.1 percent of people own retirement accounts, while only 13.9 percent of American families directly participate in the stock market. A mere 1.2 percent own bonds.

Compared to native-born populations, immigrants are even less likely to participate in financial markets, and their median investments are significantly lower. Consequently, they're missing out on crucial opportunities to grow their wealth because of a misconception that financial assets are riskier. By limiting their investment options at the get-go, immigrants often close themselves off from viable financial alternatives.

DEBT AND EQUITY

An asset consists of debt and equity, which can be represented as follows: Asset = Debt + Equity. Real assets make up the left side of the equation, while financial assets make up the right. For example, the value of a House = Mortgage (debt) + Equity. The value of a Business = Bonds (debt) + Stocks (equity).

Every investment you make should be thought of in terms of debt and equity. Debt is the amount you owe to someone else. It is, therefore, a liability to you, the borrower, and an asset to the lender. Equity is the value of an asset, minus any debt. Homeownership is a familiar example of how debt and equity work. Investors tend to buy real estate because they like the idea of having equity in a property.

When you buy a $500,000 house and take out a mortgage, you are taking on debt. If you have a 20 percent down payment, you have $100,000 of equity in the house right from the start, while the bank still has a claim to 80 percent of the house's equity. Every month, you as a homeowner gain equity and move closer to eliminating your debt. More specifically, you gain equity in two ways. First, each mortgage payment you make will partially pay down the interest on the debt, as well as part of the principal—or the amount that you borrowed. Second, if the value of your house goes up, your equity in the house will too.*

While no one loves being in debt, most people in the U.S. are quite accustomed to it. They take out student loans, house loans, car loans—all kinds of loans. And they're comfortable doing so. In some other countries, like Mexico, for example, dramatic economic cycles have made people wary of taking on debt. They've watched their government take on a lot of debt, default on it, and cause crises that ripple throughout the country. As a result, the fear of debt is stronger there. While large amounts of debt are no doubt ruinous to one's financial health, the right kind of debt (e.g., mortgage debt) can be a smart move that increases your long-term financial well-being.

The fear of debt makes many people in Mexico desperate to become homeowners, all for the security that they believe equity will bring them. There's a popular idiom, "You need to have your ceiling first," meaning you should buy a house before doing anything else with your money. Unfortunately, one of our close Mexican friends is taking that advice to heart, and

---

* This would not be true if you have an interest-only mortgage where you are only required to pay the interest every month.

instead of investing, he's saving so he can pay off his entire mortgage as quickly as possible.

What he's not considering, however, is that every investment is a combination of debt and equity, and a house may not be the best way to grow his money. Let us explain. When you live in a house, you tend to think of the asset as relatively stable. Meanwhile, on the news, you hear about investments that surge and dip daily. Little wonder, then, that real estate seems safer than the capricious world of "the market." Unfortunately, this is a gross misconception.

The value of any asset, whether it's real or financial, follows the same basic principles of debt and equity. For example, there are real companies behind the elusive figures floating around on your stock ticker, just as there are financial instruments like mortgages that make homeownership possible. When an investor buys stock in Apple, they aren't buying an intangible slice of computer-generated numbers; they are buying *equity in a company.*

When a company "goes public"—or opens itself up to public investors—the ownership of the corporation is split into shares. Those shares are collectively known as stock. If you own stock in a company, that means you are a partial owner of that company. When the company succeeds, the stock owner shares in that success by seeing the price of their shares rise, getting dividends (cash in their account), or both. If, on the other hand, the company experiences losses, or fails, as a partial owner in that company you also see a decline in the company's value. That's what is happening when stock prices drop.

In other words, when you own stock, you have equity in a company, in the same way you have equity in your home or your business. It doesn't matter that your home is a real asset while the stock is a financial asset; they work the exact same way.

Just as equity plus debt equals the value of your home, the value of a company is determined by combining the company's equity and debt. That means that stocks (equity) are only one part of the equation. It is also possible to trade in a company's debts. This is referred to as the bond market.

When you buy a bond, you're making a loan to a company or government so they can pay off their debts or finance new growth. Bonds are fixed-income investments, which means that they have a fixed interest rate and a fixed amount of time for repayment (e.g., "We'll repay your $10,000 in five years, with an interest rate of 5 percent per year, paid annually"). Because of these fixed terms, bonds are often considered to be safer than stocks. That's because a bond is a contract promising that the borrower will repay the lender a fixed amount. The borrower must pay this amount or else they will be in breach of the bond contract. The only way to get out of it would be to file for bankruptcy, or to face a lawsuit. Bonds, however, don't have the potential to multiply in value the way stocks do. You know from the beginning of the bond investment the maximum amount of money you'll make (assuming the borrower doesn't default). Stocks, however, have unlimited upside. A lower risk typically means a lower reward. Indeed, in bankruptcy the bondholders are paid first, and any money left over goes to the stockholders.

Because every asset is composed of equity and debt, one is not inherently more secure than the other; they're both equally worthy of your investment attention. Our house-hungry friend could probably earn more equity by renting his residence and investing his money in the stock market than he could by owning the house outright, constantly maintaining it, and missing out on other investment opportunities.

To make this clear, let's look at the example again and assume you bought a $500,000 house and put down a 20 percent down payment of $100,000. Let's further assume the interest on the $400,000 mortgage is 3 percent per year. You have a choice. Choice one is that you take all your excess money and work on paying down the mortgage as quickly as possible. All your funds go to that, and you have no funds left over to invest. Over the next twenty years, you pay down the mortgage and you now own your $500,000 home outright. Maybe it even appreciated in value and your equity is now worth more—say $600,000. Another choice would be to make the minimum payment every month on the mortgage and use any excess funds to invest in the markets. Let's assume you make this choice, and you invest in the markets for the next twenty years earning an average annual return of 8 percent. You're now ahead by 5 percent per year (8 percent return minus 3 percent interest payment on the mortgage). You've now built considerable wealth with your investments over and above what you could have done paying down your mortgage. What's more is that you'll still get to participate in any market gains on your house—say, if the value went up from $500,000 to $600,000—because *you* own the equity, not the bank. Choice two makes more financial sense, even though you'll still have that mortgage debt at the end of twenty years. Again, not all debt is bad. Many supremely wealthy people that could no doubt pay off their house in full still carry sizable mortgages because they know their money can be put to better use in the markets.

REPLICATING THE GLOBAL MARKET

If your goal is to replicate the global market as closely as possible and ride its coattails to growth, you must invest in both debt and equity. Think of it this way: If you want to mirror the value of all the companies in the world, you cannot simply buy their stock. While that would be mirroring the *equity* of all the companies in the world, their value is also contingent upon their debts. Therefore, you must also buy bonds proportionate to what those companies owe.

To put it in more concrete terms, let's return to the example of a house. You have $100,000 in equity, and you owe the bank $400,000. Now, let's say that your friend wants to invest $100 in your house. She couldn't just take your equity into account. She would also have to consider your debt. Mirroring the market of your house would mean putting $20 into your house's imaginary stock and buying an $80 bond to support the bank. She would earn equity if your house's value went up, and she would also earn interest from the bond. Her investment would be an accurate representation of the value of your house.

The reason investing proportionally in both debt and equity is so important is that you need both to adequately mitigate your risk. If your friend only invested in your equity and you stopped paying your loan, she would lose all her money. If, on the other hand, she only invested in your debt, she wouldn't share in your success if your house saw soaring property values. You're not fully invested unless you're investing in both equity and debt.

◄ 11 ►

The Global Market Portfolio

To be fully and properly diversified, every investor should start with what we call a "Global Market Portfolio" as the centerpiece of their investment portfolio. With the Global Market Portfolio as the starting place, investors can then shift their investments to either add or subtract risk to suit their needs.

As we've seen, academic research and real-world data prove that investors cannot consistently outperform the market. So, given that, investors should simply attempt to replicate the market as efficiently and cheaply as possible. The market we are referring to is the entire global market of investable assets, which includes global stocks, bonds, real estate, and commodities. This is what we mean when we say Global Market Portfolio.

THE THEORETICAL GLOBAL MARKET PORTFOLIO

The Global Market Portfolio was first proposed in 1952 by Harry Markowitz, who won a Nobel Prize in economics for his work and is known as the "father of modern portfolio theory." Markowitz earned a PhD from the University of Chicago, where he focused on applying mathematical and statistical rigor to the stock market.[1] At that time, many investors understood the benefit of diversification and that it was risky to put all your money in one stock, for example. However, nobody had yet proven the benefits of diversification mathematically and how to measure overall portfolio risk.[2]

Markowitz studied different portfolios of stocks and other assets as either efficient or inefficient combinations of risk and return. Those combinations that were deemed efficient, on a risk-and-return basis, were later said to sit on what is known as the "efficient frontier,"[3] which is depicted in Figure 10.

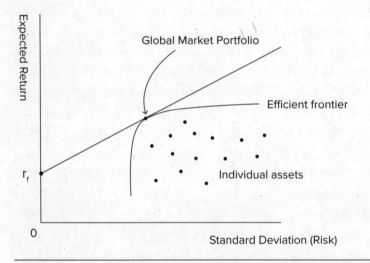

Figure 10. CC BY-SA 3.0. Source: ShuBraque (https://en.wikibooks.org/wiki/Portfolio_theory_and_mathematical_models/Tobin's_theorem)

As you can see, the Y-axis shows the expected return of an investment while the X-axis shows the risk. While risk is multivariable, our concern here is the variability of returns, also known as volatility or standard deviation.* The more volatile an asset, the riskier it is and, therefore, the more toward the right it will sit on the graph. What Markowitz discovered was that for any portfolio of assets (i.e., more than one), the volatility would be *less* than the weighted average of each individual asset in the portfolio. This mathematical truth showed that, through diversification, you could reduce the amount of risk relative to the expected return. In other words, by adding more and more assets to the portfolio, you could bring down the risk, or volatility, without reducing expected return.

The key to beneficial diversification, Markowitz found, was figuring out the correlation, or "covariance," between the different assets in a portfolio. Assets that are highly correlated, say two large energy companies, will tend to move together. Assets that are not highly correlated, say a biotech company and a U.S. Treasury Bond, will tend not to move together, and are said to be uncorrelated, or have a low covariance. Markowitz found that "each efficient portfolio had the highest expected return for a given level of risk as measured by the variance or, conversely, the lowest amount of risk for a given level of expected return."[4] Markowitz imagined there might be numerous efficient portfolios that sit on the efficient frontier, while individual assets and less efficient portfolios would sit below the frontier line.

A few years later, Nobel laureate James Tobin proved there was only one super-efficient portfolio that is incredibly hard to improve upon. Then, in 1964, William Sharpe, another Nobel Prize winner, proved that Tobin's super-efficient portfolio was none other than the Global Market Portfolio.

William Sharpe is famous in investing circles for developing the capital asset pricing model (CAPM). For our purposes, it's important to understand that through Sharpe's work with the CAPM, he showed that investors should be rewarded for bearing systematic risk. And the more systematic risk one bears, the more one should expect to receive in return. His major finding was that investors are only rewarded for risks that cannot be diversified

---

* For example, high inflation could negatively affect the return of an asset without necessarily causing any volatility.

away (i.e., systematic risks). Therefore, investors should hold a diversified portfolio—like the Global Market Portfolio—because it is maximally diversified and gives you the highest expected return for the risk taken. Indeed, according to Sharpe, while "[t]he three principles in real estate are location, location, and location; in some ways in investments it's diversify, diversify, diversify."[5] The Global Market Portfolio ensures maximum diversification.

In addition to diversification, Sharpe posited that investors should also try to keep investment costs as low as possible. Investment costs include things like the management fees you are paying to the funds you're investing in, the advisory fees you're paying for professional advice, and transaction costs when buying and selling your investments. Other cost-type items include taxes you must pay on certain investments if you hold them in a taxable account. This would include things like capital gains taxes and ordinary income taxes paid on stock dividends and bond coupon (interest) payments. "The average investor cannot beat the average investor before costs; and if you are trying to find hot stocks or the best new growth fund manager or listening to Jim Cramer . . . you are going to end up bearing extra risk, on average, and not getting any reward for it, and spending a lot of money in the bargain."[6]

Sharpe also spoke about risk and reward, saying that "if you take more, let's call it market risk, economic risk—in other words if you put yourself in a position to do really bad in bad times . . . then in some sense you should 'expect'—and that's a mathematical or statistical concept—to do better; or another way of saying it is in the very long run maybe you will do better."[7] Here again, we can see the concept of risk and return. If you are well diversified, so that you are exposed mainly to systematic and not idiosyncratic risk, you should expect to be compensated for bearing that risk. The fact that you could have diversified the risk away, say by investing in the energy sector as a whole instead of ExxonMobil by itself, means that you shouldn't be expected to be compensated based on the idiosyncratic risk of ExxonMobil alone.

Sharpe had valuable insight on whether investors should try to outperform the Global Market Portfolio through active management (i.e., trying to beat the index benchmark), echoing many of the themes we've already discussed:

> Of course, many active managers will beat the market and their passive brethren before costs in any given period. And a substantial minority will beat the market and the index funds after costs. The trick is to identify the winners in advance. While it would be tempting to say that this only requires looking for those that have won in the past, the evidence is not very supportive of this assertion. To some extent this is since many past winners were simply lucky. In other cases, competition among professional investors results in prices adjusting so previously winning methods no longer work.[8]

Our last investment-theory titan is perhaps the most famous of all: Eugene Fama. Fama, who is a professor at the University of Chicago and is widely known as the "father of modern finance," is recognized for coming up with the efficient market hypothesis (EMH). In a nutshell, EMH says that asset prices reflect all available information and that it's virtually impossible to outperform a market over time. In other words, the price of any asset—whether it be a stock, bond, commodity, or otherwise—reflects the market's collective best guess as to the true value of that asset. "What you see is what you get."[9] This is important because, if assets are priced fairly at any given moment, then it doesn't make sense to spend time and money trying to outperform the market by picking stocks or other assets. Picking stocks or timing the market won't lead to outperformance. You're better off simply taking the market return as cheaply and efficiently as possible. Investors can only earn higher returns than the market provides over time by taking more risk.

According to Fama:

> [O]n the average, competition will cause the full effects of new information on intrinsic value to be reflected instantaneously in actual prices. An efficient market was one where there are large

numbers of rational profit-maximizers actively competing, with each trying to predict future market values of individual securities, and where important current information is almost freely available to all participants . . . Actual prices of individual securities already reflect the effects of information based on events that have already occurred . . . *In other words, in an efficient market at any point in time the actual price of a security will be a good estimate of its intrinsic value.*[10]

The consequences of EMH cannot be overstated. If the price of a security reflects the market's best estimate of its value, it means that security analysis, both technical and fundamental, is worthless. It means that there's no such thing as a "cheap" or "expensive" stock—the price is always right based on all the currently known information. Same goes for markets being "overvalued" or "undervalued"—there's no such thing.

It's key to understand that, while EMH has been around a long time and is supported by robust evidence, it is still just a theory and does not purport to explain the full picture of asset prices. Nevertheless, it is the authors' opinion that EMH is likely mostly right. This doesn't mean that prices will not change over time—they obviously change every trading hour and minute. But, according to EMH, these changes are due to markets synthesizing *new* information and coming up with a new price.

In chapter sixteen we will look at a newer branch of economics called "behavioral economics." The behavioralists maintain that, while EMH is robust and helpful as a model, it is by no means always right. For example, it doesn't give us the full picture of what's going on because markets are made up of human beings making decisions every day. As such, human biases and emotions play a prominent role in the pricing of assets; therefore, assets can indeed be under- or overvalued. And markets can be wrong—sometimes very wrong.

For now, the best advice we can give on this topic is that we believe markets are efficient most of the time and are highly efficient over the long term. And while we do think that the behavioralists have something to add, especially when looking at short-term prices, trying to exploit any market inefficiencies caused by bad human behavior on a regular basis is almost impossible. The evidence for this can be seen in numerous ways, including that there are few professional asset managers that outperform markets regularly year in and year out. While many will outperform in a single year or two, almost zero can do so repeatedly for five- or ten-plus years. Markets are so competitive and efficient that even if a trader has a good strategy, it's unlikely that strategy will persist over time. In sum, it's best to treat markets as if they are perfectly efficient, even if sometimes they are maybe not.

THE GLOBAL MARKET PORTFOLIO— FROM THEORY TO REALITY

While Markowitz, Tobin, Sharpe, and Fama theorized the concept of the Global Market Portfolio in the 1950s and '60s, investing in one then was virtually impossible. Most investors bought individual stocks and bonds from their stockbrokers and paid hefty transaction costs. Or they purchased actively managed mutual funds, also at very high costs. Moreover, the concept of investing in "the market" to get the "market return" was anathema to most Americans. Indeed, many thought—and some still do—that settling for the "average" market return was *un-American*! Few thought, we surmise, that "average" market returns over one's investment lifetime would put an investor in the top 97th percentile of all investors, but we digress.

The Global Market Portfolio didn't become a viable option to most investors until Jack Bogle created the first index fund, The First Index Investment Trust, through his company, the Vanguard Group, in 1975. That first index fund started with $11 million in assets; today, the Vanguard Group has over $7.2 trillion in assets under management and growing. For this, Bogle has been called "the greatest investor advocate to ever grace the fund industry."[11]

Through diligent research, Bogle discovered that the "average [actively managed, or one that is trying to outperform the market] fund underperformed the S&P 500 index by about 1.5 percent annually, without accounting for index costs. Accounting for turnover costs (but not sales) charges, he estimated average annual fund returns of 9.6 percent compared to index funds of 11.1 percent."[12] In other words, costs matter. A lot. And while a percent or two each year may not sound like much, costs multiply and compound over time. "Do not allow the tyranny of compounding costs to overwhelm the magic of compounding returns," Bogle said.[13] So, his idea was to provide access to market returns at a very low cost. Today, you can buy a typical Vanguard index fund for around 0.03 percent in fees per year—almost for free! Bogle had much sage advice, too much to list here, but a few of our favorites include:

- ► "Rely on simplicity; own American or global business in broadly diversified, low-cost funds."
- ► "Stop trying to find the needle. Invest in the haystack."
- ► "[T]here are four key elements to investing: reward, risk, time, and cost. There is only one element we cannot control: reward. But we can control the other three."
- ► "Ignore the short-term noise of emotions reflected in our financial markets and focus on the productive long-term economics of our corporate businesses."
- ► "Are you an investor, or are you a speculator? If you're going to keep changing things, you are speculating."
- ► "If we're going to have lower returns, well, the worst thing you can do is reach for more yield. You just have to save more."
- ► "[T]he simplest solution is often the best. Time dramatically enhances capital accumulation, given the magic of compounding. Diversification is key to any investment."
- ► "When you hear news that moves the market and your broker calls up and says, 'Do something,' just tell him my rule is 'don't do something, just stand there.'"

► "The secret to investing is that there is no secret . . . There is only the majesty of simplicity. When you own the entire stock market through a broad index fund, all the while balancing your portfolio with an allocation to an all-bond market index fund, you create the optimal investment strategy . . . Owning index funds, with their cost-efficiency, their tax-efficiency, and their assurance that you will earn your fair share of the markets' returns, is, by definition, a winning strategy . . . Stay the course!"[14]

THE GLOBAL MARKET PORTFOLIO— ASSET ALLOCATION

Since Jack Bogle's introduction of the first index fund in 1975, there are now thousands of funds of all shapes and stripes to choose from. You can buy funds for specific sectors, countries, asset classes (e.g., bonds, commodities, stocks, and real estate), and other makeups. But beware: not all index funds are created equal. Some cannot even be called index funds in the strict sense. First, you'll want to choose a fund that is market capitalization weighted. As we've discussed, a market cap–weighted fund will own each individual asset, say an individual company's stock, in the percentage that that company's market cap represents in the overall market. So, if you were to buy an S&P 500 index fund that is market cap weighted, as of this writing, about 6.5 percent would go to Apple, 5.8 percent to Microsoft, and 2.7 percent to Amazon, on down the list to 500 where the five-hundredth company would barely be given any money at all. Contrast that with an equal cap weighted index fund, where each company is equally owned. Although it's called an "index fund," it's not actually replicating the market and should be largely avoided.

Now that we have our building blocks—low-cost, passive index funds or ETFs that replicate the market—let's look at the overall asset allocation of the Global Market Portfolio. To build one, we must start with the size of each of the four major asset classes in the world. Note that the United States is at the top of the list, but that isn't due to any bias; it's simply because the United States is the largest economy in the world, which is reflected in the global market of investable assets. If another country were to one day overtake the U.S., these figures would change to reflect that new reality. As of this writing, the world's publicly traded asset classes are approximately sized as follows (see Figure 11):

- Bonds—61.49%
  - United States—33.96%
  - Non-U.S.—27.53%
- Equities—28.51%
  - United States—18.22%
  - Developed Markets (excluding U.S.)—7.56%
  - Emerging Markets—2.73%
- Commodities—10%
  - Includes oil, gold, silver, platinum, agricultural products, and many others.

You may be surprised to see that bonds are by far the largest asset class. It's not surprising, however, when you consider that most bonds are sovereign (i.e., government) bonds. For example, in the United States, Treasury, or government, bonds represent 35 percent of the total bond market, with mortgage-backed bonds and corporate bonds both coming in second at around 22 percent each. So, while the financial media squawk about stocks all day long, most of the world's capital can actually be found in boring old bonds.

Also note that while we represent real estate as a separate asset class here, it's for simplicity. In truth, real estate is simply a combination of debt and equity, like a company. You can own a company's equity and participate in its upside but with the downside risk, or you can own its debt and only be entitled to the coupon payments and return of principal. We wouldn't say that a corporation is its own "asset class." The same with real

een said that capital is never truly destroyed; it just moves around.*
hat balloon again where the air moves from one side to the other
eezed. Global capital can be viewed the same way. For example,
y flow out of stocks, causing their value to decline, and sub-
flow into bonds, causing their value to increase. If you own a
rket Portfolio of all the world's assets, you'll own "the balloon,"
t have to worry about your capital permanently going away; it'll
rom one asset to another. So, if global capital flows out of United
ks and into European stocks, you're covered, because you own
also not have to do anything to benefit from these capital flows.
or selling. That's because if such a move happens, the value of
cks will go down, while the value of your European stocks will
out you lifting a finger!

ame vein, different asset classes might also perform differently
n the economic environment. If you own a Global Market Port-
e well positioned to own the asset that's performing the best
ar economic scenario. Importantly, asset classes do not always
xpected." So, it's not enough to rely on simple "rules" that may
out in the past. For example, many people used to think that
portfolio was sufficiently diversified because, typically, when
, bonds increase. However, the year 2022 saw both stocks and
together, while commodities have done better. If you only
and bonds, you experienced some real pain.

these capital flows do not happen overnight. They could take
or even years, to fully play out. In addition, during times of
mic stress and uncertainty, all assets could drop as investors
be sure, this is a painful time for most diversified portfolios,
emporary since investors will want to convert their cash to

nes complicated, however, when leverage is introduced. That's because
d cause permanent destruction of capital when it goes against the
Capital can also be destroyed in other ways, such as war.

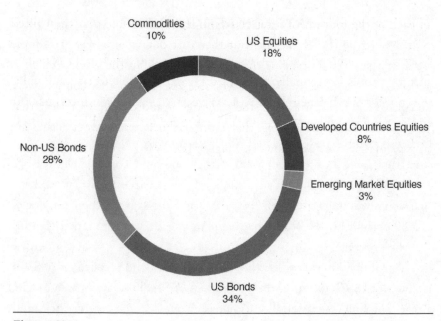

Figure 11

estate. When you invest in real estate, you can either invest in its debt, or
in its equity. But since many people think of real estate as its own separate asset class, we've broken it out here. Just know that when you buy a
well-diversified index fund of stocks, you'll notice that within that fund
are real estate companies that own real assets across the country and world.
Furthermore, when you buy a company's stock, you're buying ownership in
its asset base, which usually includes some real estate, such as land and any
leases it may be a party to.

Finally, you can build the Global Market Portfolio with approximately
ten low-cost index funds, or ETFs. With approximately ten funds, which
are widely available and blessedly cheap, you can replicate the Global Market Portfolio with sufficient accuracy. The only trick is buying them at the
right proportions to match the current global market, which, of course, is
always changing. If you are interested in owning a Global Market Portfolio,
you should contact a trusted advisor to help you build one that best fits
your needs.

A NOTE ON REBALANCING

Once you have created the Global Market Portfolio, you'll need to rebalance the funds occasionally. Let's start with an example to try and make the concept of rebalancing as simple as we can. Let's say you invest $1,000 and create a portfolio of two index funds: a stock fund and a bond fund. Let's also assume you've allocated 70 percent of your money, or $700, to the stock fund, and 30 percent, or $300, to the bond fund. For whatever reason, but usually it is to maintain a certain level of risk exposure, you've decided that you always want to keep that allocation the same: 70 percent stocks and 30 percent bonds. Well, what happens when the stock market goes up and the bond market goes down? In that case, say after a year, your stock investment of $700 is now worth $900, and your bond investment of $300 is now worth $250. Your entire investment of $1,000 is now worth $1,150. Great! But now your asset allocation has changed to 78 percent stocks and 22 percent bonds. What do you do if you want to keep your 70/30 stock/bond allocation? The answer is that you would need to "rebalance" the portfolio by selling some of your stocks and then buying more bonds to bring the asset allocation back to the 70/30 target.

The rub here, however, is that, in a taxable account, when you sell your winning stocks, you're going to have to pay capital gains taxes, so it's smart to only rebalance sparingly when things really get out of whack. If you're holding assets inside a tax-deferred account, however, like an IRA, then you don't have to worry about any tax consequences.

Rebalancing is an important concept to keep in mind because, when your asset allocation strays too much from what you originally intended, you could be taking on much more risk than you anticipated. It may be great that your stocks went from 70 to 90 percent of your portfolio in a bull market, but you may not be comfortable with a 90 percent stock allocation when that bear market eventually comes. Therefore, smart investors always have an eye on rebalancing and smartly deploy it when needed.

WHY OWN A GLOBAL MARK

Now that we've shown you what the Global its theoretical underpinnings and practical tion is to ask why you should own one in th ing it better than simply owning a simple st bother with owning ten funds, when an S do? Why do I need to worry about rebala plications and taxes?

The short answer is because we cann J. Bernstein famously said:

> When all is said and done, there ar those who don't know where the m don't know that they don't know. T those who know they don't know, b *appearing* to know.[15]

Nobody can safely predict whi sectors, assets, or anything of the sort predict it; you cannot either. The qu mental truth of investing, the better lio, however, ensures that you will well, whether it be commodities in Jack Bogle quipped, "Stop trying to The Global Market Portfolio is the

---

* While we can say that stocks should because stocks are typically riskier tha premium" that should give higher ret ever, that stocks will outperform bon

It's b
Imagine
when squ
capital m
sequently
Global M
and will n
just move f
States stoc
both. You'l
No buying
your U.S. st
go up—with

In that
depending o
folio, you'll
in a particul
perform "as
have worked
a stock/bond
stocks declin
bonds declin
owned stocks
Note that
many months,
extreme econo
"run to cash." T
but is usually t

---

* This point becon
leverage can inde
leveraged investor.

assets to avoid the value of their cash depreciating due to inflation. So remain patient and something in your portfolio should come back before too long.

Speaking of inflation, another reason to own a Global Market Portfolio is so you can earn a return sufficiently above and beyond the inflation rate to maintain your purchasing power far into the future. Remember that inflation is just the increase in the price of goods and services over time. And since the Global Market Portfolio owns all the world's assets—both goods and service related—its value should also rise with inflation. Indeed, this is the primary reason to invest at all. While inflation is a dirty word in the zeitgeist, we have shown how it is necessary for our market-based, capitalist economy to fully function, so don't expect it to go anywhere.

Another reason to own a Global Market Portfolio is that it removes the need to predict anything, because, as we know, predictions are futile. You don't have to pick winning stocks, sectors, countries, or assets. You don't have to try and time the market. You don't have to incur excessive trading costs, fees, and taxes, which we know, over time, erode returns by about 2 percent or more per year. You don't have to incur high active management fees, either. You'll also be less tempted to give in to your emotional biases because there are really no decisions to be made except staying the course.

By owning a Global Market Portfolio, you will capture the main driver of real economic returns over time: global productivity growth (i.e., global GDP). If global GDP continues to increase over time, which we wager it will, the Global Market Portfolio should likewise increase and outperform cash, retaining its purchasing power.

Finally, the main reason to own a Global Market Portfolio is that, out of all the investment options available, it has the highest probability of achieving its expected return over the long run. While nothing is certain in investing, owning a Global Market Portfolio is one of the safest ways to ensure that you'll earn a decent return that outpaces inflation, which allows you to maintain your purchasing power well into the future. While it's by no means a straight upward line, it will be a significantly less bumpy ride than many individual assets and other types of investment portfolios. In other words, it's a very safe investment. But again, you should look at the Global Market Portfolio as your starting point and adjust from there if it doesn't fully meet your needs.

WHY DOESN'T EVERYONE OWN A GLOBAL MARKET PORTFOLIO?

Most investors do not own a Global Market Portfolio because the returns are "too low." That's because it's so safe and diversified. Remember, risk and return are related. The safer the investment, the lower the expected return. Assuming inflation is close to its 2 percent target, the Global Market portfolio has an expected return of about 3 to 5 percent per year. This might be sufficient for investors who want to preserve wealth, but for most investors these returns are much too low.

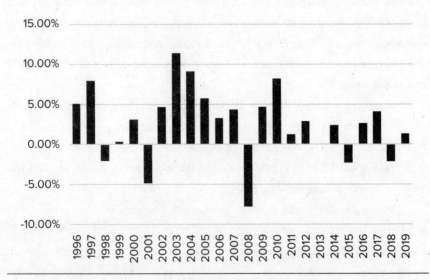

Figure 12. Global Market Portfolio Historical Performance

To earn more return, most investors change their asset allocation from the highly diversified and safe but low-return Global Market Portfolio to an asset allocation that is heavily weighted to riskier assets, like stocks—something akin to a typical 60/40 stock/bond portfolio. Many investors believe that a 60/40 portfolio is sufficient diversification. The problem, however, is that it delivers far too little return per unit of risk. While a 60/40 portfolio may have 60 percent of its *cash* allocated to stocks, it has more like 80 to 90 percent of its *risk* allocated to stocks. The movement of the portfolio is almost entirely dependent on the gyrations of the stock market. This single issue dwarfs all others that investors face—by giving up diversification, investors are taking on too much risk and are literally leaving hundreds of basis points (2 to 3 percent or more) of return on the table. This means that most investors are more exposed to stocks than they even realize. This may be fine during good times, but it spells disaster when the bad times come, especially if they have not planned for such a disaster, are cash poor, and must sell their stock positions when they are down, missing out on the miracle of compound interest that only occurs after a very long holding period. In the next chapter, we'll look at how to best increase returns over and above what the Global Market Portfolio can reasonably offer.

12

Increasing Returns Above a Global Market Portfolio

A client came to us once who considered himself risk averse. Most of his wealth was in the Mexican real estate market, and he had made a good amount of money that way. Once we introduced him to our methodology, he realized that, in fact, he wasn't risk averse at all; he just hadn't been aware of the risks he was taking. We explained to him that if he wanted a higher rate of return, he needed to tolerate more volatility in his portfolio, but all in all, the investments he would make with us would be less risky than the ones he already had going in Mexican real estate.

During the COVID-19 pandemic, we encouraged him to concentrate his money in stocks because prices had dropped so much, and he could buy them at a discount. In the wake of that success, he felt like he could weather even more risk, so we worked with him to build a portfolio that would yield even higher returns. But here's the crucial point: we were able to increase both his risk and return, while still avoiding the exorbitantly high risks his real estate investments would have had during that same volatile period.

Let's say you're in this client's position, have evaluated your risk tolerance, and you're ready to take on more risk. That doesn't mean you should run out and hand your money to the edgiest new company, buy $100,000 worth of lottery tickets, or buy a luxury property in southern France. Even the greatest risk-takers know that some risks are more sensible than others. Remember, investors are not compensated for taking on idiosyncratic risks; they're only compensated for taking on systematic risks. So, what should you do?

Suppose you understand and appreciate the value and benefits that the Global Market Portfolio offers but cannot meet your intended goals with an annual average expected return of 3 to 5 percent. Let's further suppose that you understand and believe that stock picking, market timing, and the like will probably leave you even *worse* off than a well-diversified portfolio and you are, therefore, interested in ways to increase return while maintaining some level of diversification. Supposing all this is true, you have a few options to increase return over and above what the Global Market Portfolio has to offer.

If you're looking to increase your exposure to risk and potentially see higher returns, there are three primary ways of doing so: (1) tilt the Global Market Portfolio toward a riskier asset class, (2) use "factors," or (3) use leverage. Your probability of success is much higher with any of these three options than picking stocks or trying to time the market.

INVEST MORE CASH INTO RISKIER ASSETS

The Global Market Portfolio is safe because it's maximally diversified. By decreasing diversification, you can add risk, and hopefully higher returns, to the portfolio. As we've said before, however, not all risks are created equal. It is not enough to simply take "more risk"; you must, instead, try to take on more systematic risk and not idiosyncratic risk, like picking stocks.

The first option to increase returns, which is the most common, is to change the Global Market Portfolio's asset allocation by adding a diversified mix of riskier assets. If you're risk tolerant, one way to do this is to invest a larger proportion of your money—or to invest solely—in a riskier asset class like stocks, private equity, venture capital, or real estate. If you're trying to determine what a "riskier" asset class is, remember that the higher the possible rate of return, the higher the risk. So, since bonds have a low rate of return, that means they're a more stable asset class. And since stocks have more exposure to systematic risk, that means they carry greater potential for returns. Investing a larger proportion of your money in a riskier asset class will immediately expose you to more risk and give you a chance for higher returns.

For example, assume that the Global Market Portfolio holds 50 percent bonds, 35 percent stocks, 10 percent real estate, and 5 percent commodities. An investor could increase the risk and expected returns by adding more stocks, so the portfolio holds 65 percent stocks, 20 percent bonds, 10 percent real estate, and 5 percent commodities. By adding more stocks, the risk in the portfolio has been increased, but so have the expected returns. So, instead of expecting 3 to 5 percent average, annual returns, this 65 percent stock portfolio might be expected to return 6 to 8 percent. The problem with this approach, however, is that you are essentially betting against bonds in favor of stocks; you are "over-exposed" to stocks. Consequently, if the stock market does poorly for a prolonged period, this portfolio will suffer. If you cannot withstand the volatility that additional stocks will bring, this approach may not be for you. Likewise, if you cannot be patient and ride out a potentially extended period of low to no returns, investing in riskier assets might not be good for you.

If you choose this strategy, it's important to try and have a clear-eyed view of your reasons for doing so, and to be keenly aware of the current market environment. Are you tilting toward more stocks because the stock market has been rising for the last few years and, therefore, you think it will continue to do so forever? Ask yourself what happens if it doesn't. What happens if we go into a bear market or a recession the day after your investment and your portfolio drops 40 percent? Will you stick with the plan, or lose confidence? It's very easy to increase your stock allocation when the stock market is going up, but we've seen many investors get into trouble when things aren't all butterflies and rainbows. Riskier assets, like stocks, have higher long-term expected returns because they are just that: riskier. You must be prepared to weather the coming storm if you increase your exposure to them; there's no free lunch. However, if you've internalized this fact and are prepared for bouts of choppy waters, then this might be a good strategy to pursue.

FACTOR INVESTING

Factor investing is a strategy where investors choose securities based on specific attributes, known as "factors," which have historically been shown to generate higher returns. Over the last decade or more, factors have been a hot topic in the investment world, with many seeing them as a panacea. Huge asset managers, like BlackRock, tout factors as a strategy that "can help improve portfolio outcomes, reduce volatility and enhance diversification."[1] Per BlackRock:

> Global markets are made up of dozens of asset classes and millions of individual securities . . . making it challenging to understand what really matters for your portfolio. But there are few important drivers that can help explain returns across asset classes. These "factors" are broad, persistent drivers of returns that are critical to helping investors seek a range of goals from generating returns, reducing risks, to improving diversification.[2]

With factor investing, the goal is to find specific segments of the stock market that you expect to yield a higher return than other stocks. Many of these segments also carry higher risk. For example, you could single out new companies—which might have a faster growth rate, but also are more likely to fail.

Investment factors typically fall into two major categories: (1) macroeconomic factors, which focus on broad economic drivers, and (2) style factors, which help explain risks and returns. Some key macroeconomic factors include: the pace of economic growth, the rate of inflation, interest-rate movement, liquidity, credit, and emerging markets. Such broad factors can explain the rates of return an investor will see across *different* asset classes. Style factors, on the other hand, can help explain the specific risks and returns within *specific* asset classes. For example, style factors include the size and growth rate of companies, as well as their momentum, volatility, and value. Other style factors include quality, or the financial health of a company, and "carry" the return obtained from holding an asset. For example, some food products have a negative carry because they spoil when they're stored too long.

Knowing which factors drive returns in your portfolio can help you identify segments of the stock market that may provide higher rates of returns. For example, you could buy only "value" stocks, which refers to stocks with lower prices compared to their market competitors. Or you could buy stocks in companies with a higher "momentum" factor, which means they have upward price trends. Let's look at some popular factors in more detail to make the point clearer.

The value factor is one of the oldest and most studied factors around. Every stock can be systematically analyzed based on a company's fundamentals. Things like book value, earnings, and cash flows can be compared to the company's stock price and then one can say whether they believe that stock is under- or overvalued. If it's undervalued, then it should be a good buy—or a good value.

Momentum, or trend, is another popular factor, which basically rests on the idea that assets that have recently gone up will continue to go up, and vice versa. Another one is the defensive factor, which identifies assets that are seen to be low risk or stable. Defensive stocks, for example, should do well on earnings quality and profitability and rank low on volatility. Think companies that tend to do well no matter the economic environment, like utilities and consumer staples, but have limited upside growth potential.

While factor investing can be beneficial, we find that many sellers of factor-based products overstate their benefits while understating their risks. At the end of the day, factors are simply a tool for identifying certain historical characteristics that are believed to drive returns. As such, they tend to look at what has worked in *hindsight*. And as we've stated many times before, what works in hindsight doesn't always work going forward. If some investors find a factor that works and generates outsized returns, other investors will surely follow onto the trend and the outperformance will disappear. Any strategy, rule, or system that works for a while runs the risk of no longer working when everyone starts doing it. Such is the way of investing. More importantly, factor investing can generate greater returns simply because it is riskier. More risk should mean more return, not because there's anything magic about factors. If you understand factors, they can be a useful addition to a portfolio to try to generate higher returns, but just beware that they are not a panacea.

USE LEVERAGE

One problem with the first two approaches is that they add idiosyncratic risks to your portfolio. With the first, you're adding riskier assets like stocks and dumping safer assets like bonds. Consequently, you're betting that stocks will outperform bonds and are thus increasing your exposure to the idiosyncratic risks of stocks. With factor investing, you're focusing on specific traits, most of which are specific to the assets selected—thus they are, by definition, idiosyncratic.

The only way to avoid this and still increase your systematic risks—the risks you should be compensated for taking—is to adopt a method commonly applied in real estate: leverage. Most people who own a home have a mortgage, and most people who invest in real estate have some sort of financing through a bank. When investors calculate their expected returns from those real estate investments, they calculate them with leverage. "Leverage" refers to the practice of borrowing money to increase the potential return of an investment. Leverage is synonymous with debt.

The idea of using leverage, or debt, as part of an investment strategy scares most investors. Most of us are cautious about debt, and for good reason. High student loan debt is currently preventing many young people from saving for the future. Another form of debt, the home mortgage, is the pathway to homeownership for many people; however, our memory of the 2008 financial crisis reminds us that home mortgages can go terribly wrong.

Most of us are even more skeptical about using debt for investment purposes. The stock market crash of 1929 was fueled in part by speculation and investors buying stocks on margin. The more recent 2008 crisis was fueled by an over-leveraged housing market. But it's important not to throw the baby out with the bathwater. Leverage is a tool, and like any tool, it can be used responsibly. Let's remember that debt finances much of our economy. When the government wants to finance a big public works project, they typically do so by issuing bonds—a debt instrument. Corporations use debt financing to fund acquisitions, research and development, and many other types of activities. In general, the wealthy aren't afraid of debt; they just call it "leverage." If you want to take on substantial systematic risk and give yourself the chance to earn high returns, you should consider using leverage, so let's look at an example to help assuage any fears you might have.

Imagine you buy a home worth $100,000. You put $50,000 of your own money as a down payment and a bank lends you the other half, so you've got $50,000 of equity. For the sake of simplicity, let's say you also got an incredible 0 percent interest rate. Almost immediately, luck strikes and your house appreciates 50 percent in value ($50,000). That means you've made a whopping 100 percent return on your investment—*not* a 50 percent return. That's because you only put $50,000 in, and you've now got an additional $50,000 of value. That means you got a 100 percent return on your money, thanks to leverage.

On the flip side, if the home goes down 50 percent in value, you've now lost your entire investment. Your home will only be worth $50,000, but you're still on the hook for $50,000 with the bank, so all your equity has been wiped out. Just like any other kind of risk, leverage is a two-sided coin.

As we mentioned, the wealthy are typically unafraid to use leverage. For example, although he publicly warns against the use of leverage, Warren Buffett has made strategic use of it at times. When he was just starting out as an investor, he borrowed 25 percent of his net worth to invest in the stock market. A few of his bets didn't work out, but most did. Moreover, his company, Berkshire Hathaway, has also occasionally used short-term loans to free up the necessary cash to take advantage of investment opportunities.

Some have even claimed that smart use of leverage can decrease risk. Early in the 2008 financial crisis, two Yale economists, Ian Ayres and Barry Nalebuff, published a study making the case that young people should use debt to buy stocks. The study, *Life-Cycle Investing and Leverage: Buying Stock on Margin Can Reduce Retirement Risk*, was later expanded into a book. While it wasn't great timing to make that argument, it does raise some valuable questions about risk and diversification.

We normally think of diversification in terms of assets. We want to spread our investments across multiple assets and asset classes, so we don't, as the saying goes, "have all our eggs in one basket." But what about time diversification? Don't we also want to spread our investments across time?

As the authors point out in an interview, if you invested in the stock market in only one year, it could be disastrous if you invested right before the peak of a market bubble. That's why most experts suggest a regular schedule of investments over many years—called "dollar cost averaging," which typically means you invest on a regular schedule as you get paid. But many young workers don't have a lot of discretionary cash and end up making most of their investments in a single decade later in their careers. If the market performs badly that decade, it will have real negative consequences for their retirement.

The solution, the authors say, is for young people to borrow money in their twenties and early thirties and use that debt to significantly increase their investments in the stock market. In other words, you take on strategic risk when you're young and can afford it but decrease the overall lifetime risk of your portfolio. As an extensive critique of the book points out, the authors make an important contribution to investment theory by raising the issue of time diversification. But in practice there are simply too many things that can go wrong with this approach.

A better idea is to use leverage for low-risk assets. One of the problems with the life-cycle investing theory is that it uses leverage to purchase risky assets, like stocks, that are already leveraged. For example, the average debt-to-equity ratio for a company in the S&P 500 is 1:1; therefore, for every dollar of equity in the company there is a dollar of debt. Famed hedge fund investor Ray Dalio, of Bridgewater Associates, has a sounder, more conservative approach to using leverage—and identifies a common blind spot in the typical approach to diversification and risk.

In a letter to Bridgewater's investors, Dalio points out that the typical portfolio of 60 percent stocks and 40 percent bonds isn't nearly as diversified as it appears to be. Even a slightly more conservative 50/50 portfolio is divided evenly when it comes to assets, but not evenly when it comes to risk—because stocks are much more volatile than bonds, so that most of the portfolio's risk is in stocks. And the overall return on the portfolio is 98 percent correlated to stocks. With their more modest returns, bonds are not really an effective hedge against a significant downturn in stocks. Moreover, as we saw in 2022, there is no ironclad rule that bonds go up when stocks go down—both were down significantly for the year.

Traditionally, the only way to balance a portfolio in terms of risk and create what Dalio calls "risk parity" would be to take money out of stocks and put it into bonds: to change the asset mix to about 25 percent stocks and 75 percent bonds. But this would also mean accepting a significantly lower return. Dalio's solution is to maintain, for the sake of example, a 50/50 portfolio, but to "lever up" the bond or fixed-income component. Leverage of 2:1 would allow you to substantially increase your exposure in the non-stock half of your portfolio. You would be taking on a small amount of additional, strategic risk. But this portfolio would be less risky and more diversified because the risk would be evenly split between two asset classes instead of concentrated in one.

Dalio's methods are geared mainly to institutional investors and professional managers. Leverage requires constant monitoring and the use of investment instruments not typically available to the average individual investor. A paper published by J.P. Morgan offers some useful advice for investors looking to put Dalio's principles into practice.[3]

First and foremost, get a complete picture of your finances and holdings, and not just your investment portfolio. Thoroughly evaluate assets, liabilities, and cash flow. Use leverage to free up cash for high-conviction, low-risk investment opportunities. That can include leveraged fixed-income investments through vehicles such as bond futures. Generally, you are looking for investments with 1) lower volatility, 2) shorter maturities, and 3) higher liquidity.

Avoid using leverage for investments with lower liquidity and higher risk. Higher-risk assets like stocks already have leverage "embedded" within them. As a *New York Times* column on the dos and don'ts of leverage puts it, "Leverage on leverage never ends well."[4] Using leverage is a tricky business that requires careful monitoring. Seek the guidance of a trusted professional who has experience managing leverage.

Also know that the portfolio Dalio recommends will often underperform a more concentrated, less diverse portfolio. In an environment favorable to stocks, you may lag "hot" index funds and experience FOMO. But your portfolio will be better protected on the downside, and you should come out ahead in the long run. Patience and prudence win out in the end.

So far, we've mentioned the possibility of borrowing money from the bank to get leverage. The second way to use leverage is through a financial instrument called a futures contract. A futures contract is a legal contract between two parties in which one party has the obligation to buy an asset in the future at a predetermined price while the other party agrees to sell the asset for that price at a specific point in the future. In less technical terms, it basically works like borrowing money.

Here's what a futures contract looks like in action. Let's say you enter a futures contract with a one-year term to buy crude oil at $50 per barrel. You don't know what the price of oil will be one year from now, but you're banking on, or at least hoping, that by the time you must buy the oil, it will be worth more. That way, you can buy your barrel at the contractually agreed price of $50 and sell it for $100 to the market. If you borrowed money from the bank to pay for the futures contract, you can pay the bank back $50, and you still make $50 without putting in any money. Futures contracts function like leverage because you're not putting all the money up front, and you will either make money if the value rises or lose money if it drops.

In the meantime, you're basically able to invest with other people's money. Like a mortgage, you get the appreciation of the entire value of the asset, even though you only put a percentage of your own money into the contract. If you have the money to pay back the futures contract, you essentially get to borrow money at a "risk-free" rate.

If you don't know what you're doing, futures contracts can be very risky, given that entering one is equivalent to taking out a large loan on something you're not sure will appreciate. There is, however, a huge misconception around the futures market. Many people avoid it because they do not understand how it works. Futures, however, are no different from taking out a mortgage on a home. In fact, the futures market is much larger than the stock market, which means that it's *less* risky if you know what you're doing, since there's more liquidity.

Futures do have one barrier to entry, though: the buy-in cost is typically quite high. One futures contract on the S&P 500, for example, has a value of $100,000. For individuals who can't meet that minimum, it's possible to invest in a futures fund, which would give them some exposure to the futures market at a lower price point. Nevertheless, futures aren't for everyone. For someone who doesn't have a lot of savings, the better option would be to use factor investing or tilt their portfolios to riskier assets like stocks.

SUMMARY OF INCREASING RETURNS

If you want higher returns than what is expected from the Global Market Portfolio, you should consider increasing your exposure to the right kinds of risk—which usually means adding exposure to systematic risk, while avoiding idiosyncratic risk. While seeking returns through idiosyncratic risk may be tempting, because the rewards are high, the chances you will receive those rewards are slim. Instead, if you want to give yourself the highest probability of increasing your investment returns, stick to the three main options we presented: (1) adding riskier assets in a diversified manner, such as by owning more stocks through a diversified index fund; (2) investing in factors; or (3) using leverage. No matter which path, or combination of paths, you choose, know that there is no free lunch. If you want to try and earn higher returns, you will have to take on more risk, namely volatility risk. This means that you could temporarily lose a large portion of your money—maybe for years on end. Nevertheless, if you are taking the right risks and are patient, you should be rewarded over the long term.

◄ 13 ►

Risk and Return—Why
It's Inescapable

Great investing requires understanding and accepting the relationship between risk and return. And by accepting it, we really mean it. You must internalize it and make it a part of you. Even so, understanding risk and *experiencing* it are two completely different things. Indeed, it's been said that imagining and "being okay with" a huge drawdown in your investment portfolio, like 30 to 50 percent, versus experiencing that drawdown in real time, is like crashing a plane in a flight simulator versus the real thing: there's just no substitute for the actual experience.

You'll only truly know your risk tolerance when things get rough. You must live it to know it, as the saying goes. Unfortunately, any investment decision you make hinges on two fundamental components: the randomness of returns, which is also known as "volatility," and your own individual risk tolerance. And while you can't truly know your risk tolerance beforehand, understanding volatility and the history of markets can help you when times get tough.

Volatility refers to the "statistical measure of the dispersion of returns for a given [asset] or market index. In most cases, the higher the volatility, the riskier the [asset]."[1] The volatility, or randomness, of markets is a given; it cannot be avoided. You can't do anything about the fact that some businesses will boom, while others will flop. You also can't change the rate of return you get from any particular investment any more than you can single-handedly change interest rates or inflation. The randomness of the market simply is what it is, and you must accept it.

You do, however, have control over the second part of the equation: your risk tolerance. Every investment decision you make should be informed by how much risk you can handle. Many investors fail to realize that their potential to achieve their desired returns is directly proportional to the risks they take. Risk and reward are two sides of the same coin. You cannot have one without the other. So, how should investors think about risk and return? One way is through the Random Walk Theory.

THE RANDOM WALK THEORY

The Random Walk Theory was popularized by Professor Burton Malkiel of Princeton University in his seminal book *A Random Walk Down Wall Street*, which was first published in 1973 and is widely recognized as one of the best investment books ever written. Malkiel describes a random walk as:

[O]ne in which future steps or directions cannot be predicted on the basis of past history. When the term is applied to the stock market, it means that short-run changes in stock prices are unpredictable. Investment advisory services, earnings forecasts, and chart patterns are useless. In Wall Street, the term "random walk" is an obscenity. It is an epithet coined by the academic world and hurled insultingly at the professional soothsayers. Taken to its logical extreme, it means that a blindfolded monkey throwing darts at the stock listings could select a portfolio that would do as well as one selected by the experts.[2]

This is not welcome news to the so-called chartists and technical analysts who spend their days trying to predict future stock market movements based on past movements, but the Random Walk Theory is supported by all the available evidence.

The Random Walk Theory says that it's largely impossible for anyone to outperform the stock market without taking additional risk. Malkiel agrees that using technical analysis is useless, as is market timing. By market timing, we mean attempting to outperform the market by being out of it in the bad times and in it for the good. Trying to time the market is especially risky because the best returns usually happen on only a few days. What's more, those days are usually very close to the very *worst* market days—times of extreme volatility when most market timers are probably out of the market and sitting in cash. Malkiel, quoting a major study, states:

> [Ninety-five] percent of the significant market gains over a thirty-year period came on 90 of the roughly 7,500 trading days. If you happened to miss those days, just over 1 percent of the total, the generous long-run stock-market returns of the period would have been wiped out. [Another study] has calculated that a buy-and-hold investor would have seen one dollar invested in the Dow Jones Industrial Average in 1900 grow to $290 by the start of 2013. Had that investor missed the best five days each year, however, that dollar invested would have been worth less than a penny in 2013.[3]

As we showed in chapter three, Figure 7, market timing simply does not work and should not be relied upon for increasing your investment returns. The Random Walk Theory can be helpful in seeing the forest for the trees on this point. Let's look at an example to explain.

The stock market can be compared to a man walking his dog on a very long leash in New York City's Central Park. The dog walker starts at Columbus Circle, on the lower left side of the park, and plans on walking to the top right corner of the park. His dog, on that very long leash, runs wildly and unpredictably this way and that. Maybe a smell catches the dog's nose, and he darts left; then he sees a squirrel, and darts right. Perhaps he sees another dog and runs backwards for a bit, only to be yanked forward again by his owner. Whatever the case, the dog's movements are unpredictable and random, but the man's movement is different. The man is slowly but steadily making his way up to the top right corner of the park, seemingly undisturbed by the dog's erratic behavior. Unless something truly unfortunate happens to the man, we can rest assured he'll make it to his destination.

As you might have guessed, the dog represents the random, short-term fluctuations of the market—unpredictable; without rhyme or reason. It's best not to try and guess which direction it will go, because nobody really knows. Anyone who can accurately predict its next move once is probably lucky and won't be able to do it again. The dog walker represents the long-term trend of the stock market, which, if history is our guide, tends to increase over time. Successful investors know to ignore the dog and focus on the dog walker, because stock returns are volatile, erratic, and unpredictable in the short term, but have been generous over the long term. Let's now take a closer look at the volatility of returns and what that means for your investing success.

VOLATILITY OF ASSET RETURNS

As noted before, volatility is the statistical measure of the dispersion of returns for a given asset's value over time. Typically, the higher the volatility, the riskier the asset. For example, a stock that's highly volatile might have large swings in its daily price—gaining 5 percent one day and losing 5 percent the next. Another stock might have lower volatility, moving 1 percent up or down on any given day. If both stocks have the same average return over time, a rational investor should choose the second stock, because it has lower volatility. Its daily returns are more predictable and, therefore, less risky.

Historically, the S&P 500 has had a volatility of around 20 percent. The chart shows the S&P's annual returns since 1980, along with each year's maximum drawdown in red. The average, annual return from 1980–2021 was just above 10.5 percent, and was positive for thirty-two of forty-two years, or 76 percent of the time. However, the average annual drawdown for each year was 14 percent. As you can see in Figure 13, drawdowns and volatility are a given when investing in risky assets like stocks. Again, if you want high returns, you're going to have to deal with volatility.

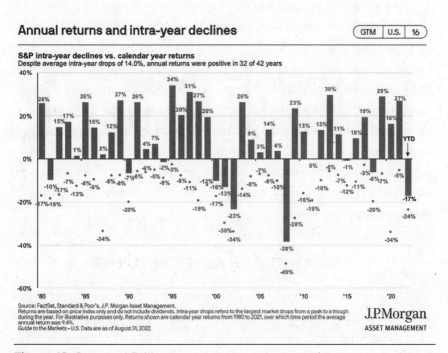

Figure 13. Source: J.P. Morgan

As we saw earlier, bonds are less risky by nature and, therefore, have lower expected returns compared to stocks. They also have lower volatility. The next chart shows the return of the United States' bond market, along with the average intra-year decline. In Figure 14, the volatility is much lower than in the stock market, with an average yearly drawdown of only 3.1 percent. So, once again, it all comes down to risk and return. If you don't like volatility, then you'll have to invest in less volatile assets, like bonds. Just know that you'll probably receive lower returns over time.

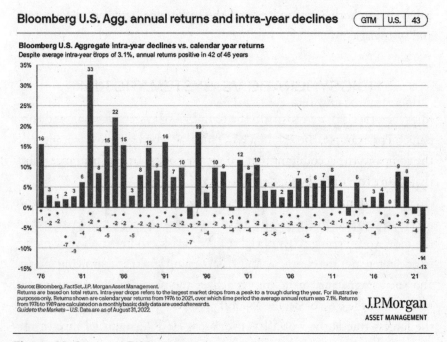

Bloomberg U.S. Agg. annual returns and intra-year declines GTM | U.S. | 43

Bloomberg U.S. Aggregate intra-year declines vs. calendar year returns
Despite average intra-year drops of 3.1%, annual returns positive in 42 of 46 years

Source: Bloomberg, FactSet, J.P. Morgan Asset Management.
Returns are based on total return. Intra-year drops refers to the largest market drops from a peak to a trough during the year. For illustrative purposes only. Returns shown are calendar year returns from 1976 to 2021, over which time period the average annual return was 7.1%. Returns from 1976 to 1989 are calculated on a monthly basis; daily data are used afterwards.
Guide to the Markets – U.S. Data are as of August 31, 2022.

J.P.Morgan
ASSET MANAGEMENT

Figure 14. Source J.P. Morgan

THERE'S NO SUCH THING AS A FREE LUNCH

For many years, Julio believed he could pick the best stocks and find great investments without taking any risk. And, in fact, he made a lot of money treating the stock market that way—but he lost a lot of money too. When you first hear that everything you've believed about the stock market for years is misguided, you might be skeptical or feel reluctant to give up those long-held beliefs. But everything we're telling you comes not only from personal experience, but also from empirical data. When it comes to investing, there is no such thing as a free lunch. If you want high returns, you must take a lot of risk. If you want low risk, you must settle for low returns. There's no way around it. Many investors insist they understand this basic concept, but when they're presented with tantalizing opportunities, they quickly forget. One way to try and keep your risk-taking behavior in check is to understand the difference between idiosyncratic and systematic risk.

IDIOSYNCRATIC VS. SYSTEMATIC RISK

Idiosyncratic risks are those specific to individual assets, regions, and companies. For example, the risk of a CEO making a bad decision that imperils the company, the accountant that "cooks the books," or the insurance policy that didn't cover the damage.

Let's imagine you see a company you believe will do well in the future and consider pouring all your money into its stock. The more you put in, the more you're going to gain, right? But it's risky to invest all your money in one company. The company is at risk of going bankrupt, growing too fast and then stagnating, or failing to deliver the products they've promised. Just look at the case of Bernie Madoff, a former billionaire who ran one of the largest frauds the world has ever seen. He sold financial investments to smart, wealthy people, promising huge returns. Most of his victims will likely never be fully repaid. To reduce your exposure to these kinds of idiosyncratic risks, you should invest in multiple companies. When you diversify, you lessen the potential blow of any single negative outcome.

Since idiosyncratic risks are a type of risk, you might think you'll earn high returns by taking them on, because "risk and return are linked." But remember that not all risks are created equal, and that not all risks have positive expected returns. Idiosyncratic risks are one such risk: on average, you should not expect to be compensated for taking them. The reason is that you can eliminate most, if not all, idiosyncratic risks by owning a properly diversified portfolio. And if you can eliminate a risk through diversification, you should not expect to be compensated for taking the risk. Let's see why.

You can eliminate the risk of ABC Co. having a bad CEO by investing in other companies within ABC Co.'s sector. So, if ABC Co. shutters, other companies in its industry sector will absorb its market share. And if the market cap of the sector goes up, your investment in the sector will too. You didn't need to concentrate all your money in ABC Co. to obtain the sector's return. You took on risk that you could've diversified; therefore, that risk should not be expected to be rewarded. Now, ABC Co. could have instead had a great CEO, and outperformed its competitors in the sector and made you a nice return. However, this excess return was due to luck and not for a risk that was being compensated for pre-investment. The risk that the CEO would be bad always existed; it just never materialized. While you made a good return, you should not have expected to outperform the sector's return before the investment was made.

On the other hand, systematic risks are ones that affect the entire market and that cannot be eliminated through diversification. Examples include recessions, pandemics, and wars. These are risks you should expect to be compensated for because you can't diversify them away, since they tend to affect entire economies and asset classes. Over the long run, unless you are very lucky, most of your returns will come from taking on systematic risks instead of idiosyncratic risks. While you will certainly realize returns based on idiosyncratic risks, they will likely wash out over time. What you'll be left with, therefore, are returns from the systematic risks that you take.

It's important to understand the difference between *expected* return and *realized* return. Expected return is what you should expect to receive from your investment based on the risks you are taking. You should expect to be compensated for taking systematic risks. You should *not* expect to be compensated for taking idiosyncratic risks. Realized return is what you actually receive from your investment, including speculative or luck-based returns.

You can unexpectedly realize an outsized return because of luck, but banking on continuous luck over the many decades you will be an investor is usually not a winning strategy. If you play that game, you should expect to underperform the market.

Your goal should be to have the highest probability of achieving a given expected return based on your risk tolerance and financial goals. Because most people have too much idiosyncratic risk in their businesses, private investments, and day-to-day lives, and since you are not compensated for taking more idiosyncratic risk, you should only focus on how much *systematic* risk you are willing to take.

Idiosyncratic risk goes down as diversification goes up; therefore, a maximally diversified portfolio of all publicly available asset classes, from all regions, countries, sectors, and industries, will virtually eliminate idiosyncratic risk. This can all be accomplished by owning a market portfolio of all asset classes, also called a Global Market Portfolio, which we covered in chapter eleven.

YOU ONLY GET COMPENSATED FOR SYSTEMATIC RISKS

Any company you invest in will have many idiosyncratic risks. The CEO may be bad at his job, the board might make a misguided decision, or the product quality might decline because the company is trying to cut corners.

As an investor, you can diversify to mitigate those risks. You can invest in other companies that specialize in the same area, say crude oil. Or, if you're worried that something's going to happen to crude oil, but you still like the energy sector, you could diversify to other non–crude oil energy companies. If you're worried that something's going to happen to the old-line energy sector, you could diversify to new green tech companies. Or, if you're worried that the United States won't perform well in the energy sector, you could invest in global energy companies.

Not all risks are created equal, so when you take risks, it's worth knowing which risks can help you achieve the returns you want and which to avoid. And, as we discussed in chapter twelve, if you want more risk than the Global Market Portfolio, you have a few options, all of which focus on increasing the systematic risks in the portfolio.

THE RISKS OF ENTREPRENEURSHIP

Some people thrive on risk. They get a thrill out of beating the odds, and sometimes they even get adrenaline rushes from failure because they know another opportunity is just around the corner. Entrepreneurs often fall into this category. They tend to be more risk tolerant, in large part because they've given in to the illusions created by survivorship bias and the mythology of success. If this sounds like you, here's our warning: acknowledge that sharks can kill you. In other words, don't just blindly leap into the pool. Make as accurate an assessment of your risks as possible before you decide to jump.

Per capita, immigrants start twice as many businesses as native-born Americans. They see gas stations, nail salons, grocery stores, restaurants, and other needs-oriented businesses as safe bets. "There will always be a need for a dry cleaner," they tell themselves. So, they invest their life's savings into their small businesses, in the hopes of building a better future for their families. Unfortunately, a fifth of all new businesses fold within the first year, and that number rises to 70 percent within the first ten years.

When you consider the relationship between risk and reward, the stakes of starting a business become even clearer: the entrepreneurial path that seems so stable to thousands of immigrants is anything but. Yes, the returns on entrepreneurship could potentially be significant, but to give it a shot, you must lay your life savings on the line. That's a steep price to pay for what is, essentially, a financial lottery ticket. Instead of focusing on entrepreneurship, most immigrants would find more financial stability by focusing on lower-risk investment choices.

SWIMMING WITH SHARKS—RISKS THAT NEVER MATERIALIZED

Imagine there's a pool of sharks. A person walks to the edge, and they have no idea that sharks can kill you. So, they jump into the pool and swim to the other side. They get lucky, and they make it across with no problem. Another person walks to the edge of the pool. They have watched *Jaws* and are avid fans of Shark Week, so they know sharks can kill you. That person would never dream of jumping into the pool because they know the risks.

If you don't know the risks of a situation, you are more likely to take them. So, if you decide to swim with the sharks because you don't know that they'll kill you, you might be like the first person, who was lucky and escaped unscathed. But you might just as easily meet a messy, painful demise.

Many investors take on much more risk than they should, simply because they're unaware they're taking any risks at all. That's why it's so important to have a clear understanding of how risk and reward function. If you're fully aware of all the risks that exist, you can make a better decision about whether it's worth it to take your chances with the sharks.

Risk is finnicky. That's because, many times, the risks that *could have* happened . . . didn't. The CEO was the savant you hoped for and turned the company around, beyond all expectations. Your speculative stock pick paid off handsomely. Investing is easy! The real estate play that was never supposed to pan out because of the "flooding issues" on the lot did, in fact, get the necessary permits to proceed—major upside coming your way! The moon-shot business that was supposed to fail, succeeded. Big-time. Where are all the haters now?

Many times, because of luck, skill, or a combination of both, risky, low-probability-of-success investments turn out great. The risks that you contemplated, and the ones you didn't, never materialized. However, to be a great investor, it will serve you well to appreciate all the things that *didn't* go wrong.

The shark example, however implausible, is meant to showcase how people take risks, often unknowingly, and don't suffer the consequences. The bad thing never happened. The sharks were all napping. Or maybe they were just full from another swimmer that came through an hour before. The problem with risks that don't materialize is that people start to think they don't exist. They see pristine pools everywhere providing shortcuts to riches. And because they haven't yet gotten eaten, they continue to swim across. But the funny thing about risk is that, while it may not appear for a long time, eventually the odds will likely catch up with you. It only takes one shark on the next swim to kill you. That you made it across twenty times unscathed doesn't matter.

Investment risk is strikingly similar. You can avoid the odds for a long time, but one misguided investment decision can ruin you forever. For example, bull markets can make many investors forget about the risks of their investments. When everything's going up, it seems like you can't lose. Maybe, because of your stock picking prowess, you believe you have some real skill. This investing thing is easy. If only I had more money. What's this? Someone's offering me money on loan to invest even more? I can double my returns? Triple? Why not!

Sadly, this is what happens to many investors. They think the good times will always last and they get overextended. They buy stocks on margin debt or make bigger moves with their retirement portfolio than they otherwise should, and then the market tanks 50 percent and they get wiped out. Zero. Nada. Zilch. Nothing left. They wiped out ten years of stellar performance in an afternoon. The sharks finally arrived, and they were hungry for blood.

Some investors might get bitten by the sharks and survive, but they've now been forever scarred. The result of many investment meltdowns is that the investor oftentimes is so battered and bruised he swears off risky investments forever. Instead of picking stocks, he buys government bonds until he dies because he can't relive another crash. Indeed, this is exactly what happened to many investors during the Great Depression, when the stock market crashed and lost 90 percent of its value. A whole generation of investors swore off stocks for life. And who could blame them? Anything close to that carnage today would likely affect most of us the same.

Taking risks unknowingly, and getting shark-bit when they eventually materialize, can wreak havoc on your investment journey in two major ways. First, you'll obviously lose a lot of your money and miss out on the miracle of long-term compounding growth. You'll have to start over later in life and simply won't have enough time to make it back. Second, you may swear off *any* risk forever, further compounding the problem. That's because if you aren't willing to take on smart risks (i.e., the systematic risks that you should get compensated for), you'll never earn the returns you need. The math simply won't work out for you. Most of us can't get where we need to be by only investing in bonds for thirty years. Most of us need to take some calculated risks.

So, if you want to be a savvy investor, don't take unnecessary risks. Further, when you take the necessary risks, understand them. If you invest all your money in a single company's stock, you're exposing yourself to a lot of unnecessary, idiosyncratic risk. When that stock tanks 40 percent, there's no good reason to think that it will *ever* come back. You might sell to stop the bleeding—maybe rightly so—and take the loss. However, if you invested your money in a well-diversified stock fund, say a fund that owns all the public companies in the world, your risk outlook should be considerably different. If that world-stock index fund drops 40 percent, we can say with reasonable confidence that it should, one day, come back. In that scenario, just be patient and wait it out. You took the right risk—one day it should pay off.

DETERMINE HOW MUCH RISK IS IN
ANY GIVEN INVESTMENT

Even if you're unaware of which specific risks are attached to a particular investment, it is still possible to get a feel for the risk. To do so, use truly risk-free investments as your baseline. United States Treasury Bills are a great example. Treasury Bills, or "T-Bills," are short-term government debt. The U.S. government can print dollars, so if you loan the government money for a year by buying a bond, they'll never default. Yet, because those bonds are risk free, you won't make much return; at the time we write this, they're paying about 3 percent. So, if someone offers you a "risk-free" investment around 3 percent, you can assume that it's relatively low risk. But if the promised return is 10 percent, know that you're signing on to a lot of risk—whether you know it or not.

Note that all U.S. government bonds are low risk because the government has little to no risk of defaulting. However, the longer the term of the bond, the more inflation-related risk you are taking on. That's why the "risk-free" rate is pegged at T-Bills because they are only four-week obligations; inflation will not affect them much, if at all. A thirty-year government bond, however, carries serious inflation risk. If you buy a thirty-year bond paying 3 percent and inflation comes in at 10 percent for years on end, your real rate of return will be negative 7 percent.

The amount of risk you can bear also depends on your unique financial circumstances. For example, if you have worked with a financial advisor to come up with an investment plan like the "Three Buckets Approach" we will present in chapter nineteen, you might have ample cash reserves and lower, "middle-risk" investments, like the Global Market Portfolio, that will allow you to survive major drawdowns on your high-risk investments. Similarly, if you are very wealthy and have myriad investments and assets, you might be okay with taking on more risk. You might even take risks that could result in a total loss compared with someone saving for retirement that cannot afford for their retirement account to go to zero.

Things like your job and income security will obviously play a role too. Is your paycheck from a cyclical industry, like oil and gas, or from a more stable industry, like government, education, or healthcare? If your job and industry are stable, maybe you can afford to have a smaller cash safety net and to take on riskier investments. But if your job is highly cyclical, then maybe you need more of a cash cushion than most before you can take on substantial risk. Figuring out how much risk you can bear is admittedly more art than science. A good financial advisor can help you figure this all out, but in the end, you must be comfortable and knowledgeable about the risks you're taking.

In our own advisory practice, we've noticed that the better investors understand their investments, the less scared they are when temporary drawdowns occur. While you don't need to be experts like us, it pays to have some basic knowledge. We liken it to driving a car. While you don't have to know about the details of the engine and how to fix every problem that arises, you must still know a few things to get down the road—things like filling the tank with gas, making sure the oil level is sufficient, and checking that the tires have enough air in them. Without knowing these simple things, you'll either not go anywhere, or you'll risk catastrophe at the worst possible time. Same with investing. While you don't need to know all the details of your investments, understanding what you own, why you own it, the historical trends of what it does and doesn't do, and what it can be expected to do in the future will serve you greatly. Again, a good financial advisor should be ready and willing to explain as much or as little as you want.

◄ 14 ►

How to Determine Your Risk Tolerance

If knowing your true risk tolerance requires "crashing the plane" instead of mimicking one using a "flight simulator," how can you determine yours without risking your financial life and limb? While it's not easy, there are things you can do to plan for risk and judge how much you'll likely be able to withstand. Keep in mind, however, that you'll never truly understand your risk tolerance until you experience the excruciating drawdowns and crashes that markets will inevitably throw your way.

A few years ago, a professor friend of Julio's was at a meeting with a multimillionaire—someone who had *hundreds* of millions of dollars. He turned to Julio's friend and said, "If you're so smart, tell me one thing. You're giving me advice on the perfect way to invest, and you claim to have all the answers. So, why am I a multimillionaire, and you're not?"

The multimillionaire was flabbergasted by the professor's candid response: "Because I know the risks that were involved to do what you did building and selling your company, and I chose not to take those risks. You had no clue they were risks when you took them, but I clearly see them as risks I'm not willing to take. It's like I decided not to play the roulette wheel. I won't be able to win if I don't play, but I also won't lose." The professor knew about the sharks. The fact that the multimillionaire didn't get bit was immaterial.

You can strike it rich on a business and become a billionaire, but realistically, what's the probability of that happening? Let us tell you: miniscule. In March 2020, there were only 2,095 billionaires worldwide, out of a total population of nearly 7.6 billion people—or .000027 percent of the population. Many try to follow in the footsteps of billionaires, but statistically speaking, almost 100 percent fail. There are better ways to have a good life than to risk everything you own, time and time again.

Still, it's hard to know where to draw the line. Maybe you don't want to risk everything you own, but you still want to risk *something*. After all, risk and reward are two sides of the same coin, and everyone needs some reward to live well. So how do you determine what an appropriate amount of risk—and its contingent reward—is?

The answer is different for every person, and it's based on their unique level of risk tolerance. One thing we know, however, is that if you want high expected returns, you need to have a lot of exposure to systematic risk. In the next sections we'll help you understand more fully what risk tolerance is, how to figure out yours, and how it should guide your investment decisions.

DEFINING RISK TOLERANCE

Risk tolerance is, on the surface, a simple concept. It refers to how much risk, or volatility of returns, you can tolerate. On a deeper level, though, it's about how much *loss—temporary or permanent*—you can handle. If you invested your money into something and lost it all, could you handle it? Would you be destitute, or would you still have plenty to pay your bills? And, psychologically, could you cope with the loss? Could you make another risky investment again? Or will you avoid risk for the rest of your life? Risk tolerance isn't just about your aversion to or embracement of risk; it's about the financial and emotional effects of a potential loss, whether temporary or permanent.

Many immigrants care for their extended families, which might make them more risk averse. When you have a large group of people dependent on you, you may opt for safer investments. Or, if you come from a wealthy family, you might be inclined to take on more risk, which is a trait we've observed in many of our well-off Mexican clients. If you're worth a hundred million dollars, you can stand to lose a million on a risky investment. If you're worth a million total, then . . . not so much.

Let's assume I was able to accurately predict the future, and I made you the following offer: "I'm going to put all your money in the S&P 500, and you'll make 10 percent compounded returns over the next thirty years." If you gave me $100,000, in thirty years you would have close to $2 million without lifting a finger. You'd probably jump at the chance.

When it comes to investing, though, "not lifting a finger" can be excruciating. What if I told you that over the course of that thirty-year run, you would have to stomach at least seven moments where your investment dropped by 50 percent? So, that $100,000 might drop to $50,000 right off the bat, and you would just have to sit calmly by and ride the roller coaster. Most clients would say, "No problem. I can handle that," but when their investments plummet, they can't. For example, when March 2020 rolled around, and COVID drove the stock market down by 40 percent, many of our clients called to say, "Get me the hell out! This is my retirement. This is my life savings." It's easy to say in the abstract you can weather risk, but the real test of risk tolerance comes when panic sets in.

That's what you really need to understand about risk tolerance. We're not simply asking what you can stand to lose financially; we're also asking what you can *personally* weather. Instead of making 10 percent returns off the S&P 500, some people might feel better making 5 percent through a less volatile combination of stocks and bonds. Their $100,000 wouldn't result in $2 million at retirement, but they also won't suffer any intense financial scares. And if those scares on the 10 percent track would make you get out of the market for good with a realized loss, you'd be much better off with the less risky 5 percent path anyway. The choice is personal to you.

This is also why it's important to try and take the right kind of risk—namely, systematic risk. As we saw earlier, a well-diversified portfolio containing low-cost index funds that are market cap weighted will be high on systematic risk, and low on idiosyncratic risk. When that portfolio is down, like during a recession or some other crisis, we can say with a high degree of confidence that it should come back in the future. Indeed, properly constructed, such a portfolio should track global gross domestic product (GDP), and if the trend of increasing global GDP continues, you should be fine. On the other hand, if you own a portfolio containing a handful of individual stocks, there is no guarantee they'll ever come back after a big drawdown. In that case, it might make sense to get nervous and jump ship. But if you follow our advice, all you need to do is be patient and wait for the good times to eventually come back again.

USE THE PAST TO IMAGINE THE FUTURE

One way to get a feel for your risk tolerance is to try and remember how you felt during past market meltdowns. Maybe you're old enough to remember a few; maybe not. Perhaps you were even invested during a crash or two. Most of you probably remember the most recent market scare: COVID-19. So, let's recall the COVID-19 stock market crash in March of 2020. Try to remember where you were and what you were doing. Try very hard to visualize yourself, your family, your schooling, your business—whatever you were doing at the time. Do you remember when the world shut down and the stock market crashed 7 percent in a single day? Do you remember being scared, or did you relish the opportunity to buy assets at lower prices?

In January of 2020, Cole and his family closed on a new house that they planned to extensively remodel. They moved out of their old house

166

that same month and broke ground on the renovation in late February 2020. A few weeks later, after the new house was sufficiently demolished to make it unlivable, the world seemed to be ending. The stock market was crashing—not good for Cole's investment advisory business. People braced themselves for the worst, putting off big decisions like buying a house—not good for Cole's wife's residential real estate business. Luckily, the markets quickly recovered, real estate boomed, and the renovation was finished. But looking back at that time, remembering his mental state, Cole can tell you it was pretty scary for a bit. Almost everyone seemed to be worried about their jobs, income, and livelihood.

Try to remember how you felt in March and April of 2020. Or, as we write this, during the year 2022 with high inflation and down markets. Do you remember? What were your thoughts about your future—whether they be career, investment, or otherwise? Did you wish you had more money to invest when things were scary? Or were you thankful you didn't have too much exposure? Were you checking your investments every day? Every minute? Or were you ignoring them with the thought that "they'll come back eventually"? Try to remember how you felt, without judgment. What you felt during that tumultuous time could go a long way in predicting how you'll feel during the next downturn.

Regardless of how you felt during past market drawdowns—and regardless of how you think you'll feel during the next one—your feelings aren't necessarily the be-all and end-all. Instead, it's your *actions* that count. If you felt anxious, wanted to sell everything and go to cash, but didn't—then well done, maybe you're more risk tolerant than you think because you have control over your emotions. On the flip side, if you didn't really get anxious, but decided to sell in a spontaneous moment, and locked in some painful losses—well, maybe you *can* control your emotions, but your *actions* are the problem. A lot of self-reflection is needed to figure out your true risk tolerance. A good financial advisor can also help with this. Indeed, the best ones act like counselors, helping you through the thick and thin times. More on that in chapter twenty.

DETERMINING YOUR RISK PROFILE

Whenever we acquire a new client, we give them a questionnaire to help evaluate their risk tolerance. This questionnaire helps us to accurately gauge our clients' future behavior. For example, if a forty-year-old client earns $300,000 a year and is a successful executive with a 401(k) and $500,000 in the bank, we immediately know that person should be willing to take more risk than a sixty-five-year-old client approaching retirement with only $100,000 in savings.

Notice, we wrote "*should* be willing to take," not "*will* be willing to take." Every person has a different threshold for risk. Just because their bank account says they could weather the rough seas of high-risk, high-returns investments doesn't mean they will be comfortable doing so. That's why this questionnaire is a starting place for assessing our clients' risk tolerance.

We find that a lot of people are more risk averse than they initially state. Younger people tend to take fewer risks than they should, as do many immigrants. When you have savings for possibly the first time in your life, you're far less willing to risk parting with them, even temporarily. Moreover, in the case of immigrant families, they've already risked a great deal by moving to a foreign country, so they may not be eager to jeopardize their hard-won resources acquired here in the U.S.

Conversely, we see clients, both young and old, who are comfortable taking too much risk, in our opinion. Many might have never seen a nasty bear market as investors. But others are just more risk tolerant than average. And that's okay. As advisors, our job is to try to steer them to the right risky investments and not ones that can leave them with nothing. At the end of the day, only you know which risks are going to make you comfortable and which will create unendurable bouts of nausea and sleepless nights.

And you never really know until you're in the thick of it. What's more, your risk tolerance will likely change over time. Maybe your income goes down and you use up more of your cash, so you're less risky now. Or maybe you just grow older, get closer to retirement, and don't want to deal with volatility anymore. Or perhaps you had a bad investment experience that swears you off risky assets for life. These things can happen, so it's prudent to revisit your risk tolerance from time to time, preferably writing it down somewhere so it's clear to you, and potentially to others.

HOW YOUR RISK TOLERANCE GUIDES YOUR INVESTMENTS

Having a clear handle on your risk tolerance will help you look at risk realistically, so you can develop an investment profile that suits your needs. Without any gauge of your personal risk tolerance, it's far too easy to be carried along by the shifting tides of impulse, particularly when you're facing volatile markets.

Many investors make the mistake of thinking risk only means volatility. Risk, as we've described, refers to an investment that carries with it the potential for pain. If you risk your money, you fully acknowledge that you may lose it. Volatility describes the day-to-day, or moment-to-moment, price movement of an asset. Think of the exchange rate of currency, which can be extremely volatile in the wrong circumstances. For example, in 1994, the Mexican Central Bank devalued the peso, igniting a series of economic crises that rippled across the globe. The U.S. and the International Monetary Fund ultimately propped the currency up with a $50 billion bailout, but not before the value of the peso dropped by roughly 50 percent, causing prices in Mexico to soar.

The more volatile an asset is, the riskier it tends to be, but that doesn't mean that risk and volatility are identical. Remember our earlier example of the S&P 500? To receive your $2 million payout, you would have had to weather periods of extreme volatility, with precipitous drops and climbs. Yet, in our hypothetical, I could accurately predict the future, so you knew you'd eventually get the $2 million. There was no risk involved.

Volatility is a good indicator of risk, but it doesn't mean that investors must avoid volatile investments. If you have a firm grasp on your risk tolerance, it's easier to assess how that volatility fits into your overall risk profile. If you've opted for a high-risk portfolio, you must expect volatility. If you want a low-risk portfolio, but notice a lot of volatility in your portfolio, you may want to reallocate your investments.

When you seek to lower your risk, the easiest method is to use diversification to eliminate idiosyncratic risk. When you're as diversified as possible, you'll only have exposure to systematic risks. This is another reason that the Global Market Portfolio is a good option—it removes the need to worry about idiosyncratic risks.

◄ 15 ►

Investing Nuts & Bolts

Often, the choice of what to invest in is relatively simple, but the logistics of where to make the investment—which account type, custodian, and more—is not. Moreover, if you are an immigrant, access to certain financial institutions, accounts, custodians, and the like may be more challenging, or forbidden altogether. Luckily, with the advent of greater technology and the work of some pioneering firms, these problems for some "un-banked" immigrants may be slowly receding. But, regardless of whether you are an immigrant with banking challenges or a longtime U.S. resident, opening the right kinds of accounts with the right custodians is always important.

CUSTODIANS

A financial custodian is a type of company, typically a large financial institution, that holds your financial assets on your behalf. They are responsible for maintaining and keeping your assets safe from loss. Most custodians will also serve as your broker-dealer for when you want to buy or sell your financial assets. The custodian will receive dividends and deposit them into your account or will reinvest those dividends if you choose. Custodians keep records of your accounts and will keep track of all your transactions for tax and other purposes. If you work with an independent financial advisor, they will typically arrange a custodian for you. Some large custodians will have financial advisors in-house that you may choose to use as well. Individual financial advisors that choose a third-party custodian should never take possession, also called "custody," of your assets and cash money. They should only have supervisory authority over the account and be able to transact on your behalf under your strict instructions. You should never give money directly to your advisor or anyone else who does not have custodial authority and responsibility.

ACCOUNT TYPES

While deciding which type of accounts to open might be an afterthought for most, it is important to know about the different investment vehicles available to you, along with their pros and cons. First, let's distinguish investment accounts from some that you might be more familiar with: checking and savings accounts. Checking accounts rarely provide any type of return for your deposits—at least not enough to get you anywhere close to outpacing inflation. While savings accounts do provide more return than checking accounts, the return is typically lower than what you can get in other investment accounts. Savings accounts also usually have limitations on the number of withdrawals you can make within a year. Moreover, most savings accounts will not offer rates as high as those you can earn in an investment brokerage account. For this reason, we typically advise clients to use a checking account for their everyday needs and to move any excess funds over into investment accounts.

BROKERAGE ACCOUNTS

The most basic investment account is called a brokerage account. Individuals can open brokerage accounts in their own name, or they can be opened jointly with another person, such as a spouse. Corporations and the like (e.g., LLCs) can also open brokerage accounts, as well as trusts. Brokerage accounts give you the flexibility of owning many different types of assets, whether they be stocks, bonds, commodities, or various funds holding similar assets, like exchange traded funds (ETFs), mutual funds, and index funds. You can also hold alternative assets inside a brokerage account, like hedge funds or limited partnership (LP) funds. There are no limits on the amount of money you can hold in a brokerage account—the sky is the limit. The drawback, however, is that a brokerage account has no tax advantages. Any income, like stock dividends or bond interest, or capital gains that are realized in your brokerage account, will be taxed in that tax year. Therefore, you will want to first utilize as many tax-deferred accounts as you can before investing through a taxable brokerage account.

TAX-DEFERRED ACCOUNTS

Tax-deferred accounts come in many shapes and sizes, and the types available to you will depend on your employment status, income, and other considerations. For example, a 401(k) plan is a retirement savings plan typically offered by your employer. Your investment options in a 401(k) will have been chosen by the employer, or someone, like an investment consultant, acting on its behalf. That means that you will be limited to the investment options chosen by the employer. Money goes into a 401(k) plan tax free, which means that if you contribute $20,500 in a year (the maximum amount allowed in 2022), then your taxable income will be reduced by $20,500. So, if you made $100,000 a year in 2022 and contributed $20,500 to a 401(k) plan, according to the IRS, you only made $79,500, and will only be taxed on that amount. The money then gets to grow tax-free until you retire.

Then, when you retire and start to withdraw the money, the withdrawals will be taxed as ordinary income for each tax year in which withdrawals occur. In the meantime, any dividends, interest income, or capital gains realized inside the 401(k) or other tax-deferred accounts are not taxed.

Obviously, tax deferment is a huge deal and you should try to maximize your investments in these favored accounts. Other tax-deferred accounts include Individual Retirement Accounts (IRAs), Simplified Employee Pension IRAs (SEP-IRAs), and defined benefit pension plans, along with many others. You should consult with a tax professional to go over all your tax-deferred account options. However, just know that investments made in most tax-deferred accounts should be viewed as long-term investments. That's because, many times, you cannot withdraw money from them until you reach a certain age (e.g., 59 ½) or else you will have to pay a steep penalty. This restriction makes it easier to "set and forget" your investments. You will not need to worry about temporary drawdowns that will occur with regularity.

Although increasingly rare, some employers will match a certain percentage of employee contributions to 401(k) or other retirement savings plans. Obviously, if an employer provides you with this generous option, you should not hesitate to contribute funds at least up until the match percentage. For example, although you may be entitled by law to contribute $20,500 to a 401(k) plan, your employer may provide a match of up to $5,000 per year. If this is the case, you should try your best to contribute at least $5,000 so you can get the money your employer is graciously offering. It is literally "free money," after all. Whether you should contribute more than the free match would depend on the quality of the fund options provided in your specific plan, however. Most 401(k) plans should have basic index fund options available and, if that is the case, you should strive to max out your contributions to enjoy the tax savings today. Contributing to a tax-deferred account, like a 401(k) or an IRA, will also let you enjoy many years of tax savings and result in more money being compounded over time.

You should also be aware that, even though a 401(k) plan is sponsored by an employer, the money is yours and yours alone. If you leave your employment, you can take your money with you, usually by "rolling it over" to an IRA, which we highly recommend doing. An IRA rollover, done properly, will not be considered a taxable event by the IRS. Additionally, once the money is in an IRA, you will no longer be limited by the list of funds in the 401(k) chosen by your former employer. You will now be free to invest in almost anything you would like, with some limitations.

COLLEGE SAVINGS PLANS

Another tax-advantaged account is what's known as a "529 College Savings Plan," again after a section of the U.S. Tax Code. These plans allow you to save money for a child's higher education. In fact, recent changes in the tax law now allow you to use 529 funds to pay for private elementary, middle, and high schools, as well as other expenses. Importantly, you can only use after-tax dollars in a 529 Plan—meaning that you will not get a deduction from your income for the year in which you contribute. The key benefit, however, is that any income or gains realized inside of the account are *never* taxed, so long as the money withdrawn from the account is used for a permitted purpose—such as someone's education, like your child. While you can now use 529 funds for schooling other than college, their best use, we think, is for educational expenses decently far enough in the future for the account to have time to realize some substantial capital gains. For example, opening a 529 plan for your newborn child and contributing regularly to it over time should lead to a substantial tax savings when the investments grow over the eighteen to twenty years in which they will be needed. Given enough time, you should have the chance to compound some significant gains that will never be taxed whatsoever if used for educational purposes. If it is money you plan to spend for a child's college education anyway, why not get some tax advantages out of it? A financial advisor can assist you with finding the right 529 plan for you and will work with you on how much you should contribute.

INSURANCE & ANNUITIES

We turn now to a topic that you may be familiar with: insurance. Once you start accumulating significant amounts of money, you will want to ensure that you protect it. Insurance helps you do that, so it is wise to carry the proper amount of insurance on anything valuable that you may own, like a car, house, boat, and jewelry. Of course, you are required by law to carry insurance for certain items, like cars, and you are likewise required to carry insurance on your home if you have a mortgage from a bank.

If you are working and receiving an income and have others that depend on that income to live, like a spouse or children, you should also protect that income if something were to happen to you. This is where life insurance comes in. Just as it sounds, life insurance is insurance that you purchase on a person's life. If you are the primary earner for the family and you pass away, life insurance will pay your family a lump sum benefit to replace that lost income. For most people, term life insurance is the best option. Term insurance means that the life insurance company will cover your life for a specified term, usually ten, twenty, or thirty years. For example, let's say you are thirty-five years old, you make $150,000 a year, and you want to buy term life insurance for thirty years. Let's further assume that you choose a policy that will pay your family $2,000,000—called a "death benefit"—if you pass away during the thirty-year term (i.e., before you turn sixty-five). If you were to meet an early death within that term, the insurer would pay your family the entire $2,000,000. What's more, that money is not taxed to your family, so they get to keep the entire $2,000,000 free and clear. If you make it to age sixty-five and the term ends, then the insurance goes away. If you were to die at age sixty-six, your family would get nothing. At that point, you can decide to renew, which will be more expensive because you are older, or not carry insurance at all. Maybe your kids are grown and self-sufficient, so you don't have to worry about supporting them.

Another type of life insurance is called "whole life." There are many different types of whole life insurance, but the gist is that, so long as you pay the monthly premiums, the insurance will cover you for life so that one day when you die, your beneficiaries will get the death benefit. Moreover, whole life policies build up a cash value over time. The way it typically works is that you pay monthly premiums to the insurance company. Some of those premiums go to the company to cover their costs of insuring you, while another chunk is yours to invest inside of the policy. You can pick different funds and watch the cash value of the policy grow over time. Many whole life policies carry significant tax and estate planning advantages and are, therefore, routinely used by the wealthy.

There are many different types of whole life policies out there, some of which can get very complicated and confusing. And we must warn you that there are also many salespeople who will try and get you to buy a whole life policy. That's because the salespeople make a very nice commission from selling you these products. They will try and convince you of all the reasons you should buy one, usually for the tax advantages. But since they are so much more expensive than term life policies, we recommend speaking to a professional advisor before purchasing one. While whole life policies make sense for some people, term life insurance is a fine choice for most people who simply want to protect their family if they were to meet an unexpected demise. And while you won't get the cash value built up with term as you do with whole, you can take the savings from using term and invest it yourself.

The final insurance products we want to cover here are annuities. An annuity is an insurance contract whereby the insurer promises to pay the insured a fixed sum of money per year or month, for the rest of that person's life. The insured person gives the life insurance company a lump sum of money. The insurance company takes that money up front and, depending on age and the company's estimate of life expectancy, promises to pay a fixed sum of money every year until the insured dies. Many people like annuities because they provide peace of mind. If the insurance company does not fail, the investor should receive a monthly check until death.

While we are not always opposed to annuities, we want people to understand the game that is being played here. Let's imagine a forty-year-old person who has $1,000,000 and decides to give it all to the insurance company for a monthly annuity until the day he dies. Let's further assume that the man is in good health and that he lives until he is eighty-five years old. We'll even further assume that he will receive a 5 percent annuity per year, so that he gets $50,000 a year, or just over $4,166 a month. Was the annuity a good deal? It depends. You must realize that the insurer can only promise to pay the 5 percent annual annuity because it feels it can earn more than 5 percent by investing the $1,000,000 into something else. For example, the insurer could take the $1,000,000 and invest it in the stock market and expect to get a 9 percent average annual return based on the historical returns of the U.S. market. The company then pays the man 5 percent and pockets the 4 percent difference. Moreover, the insurer is earning hefty fees and commissions on the annuity contract as well. On the other hand, if the man invested that $1,000,000 himself and likewise received a 9 percent annual return, he would have been better off foregoing the annuity altogether. Finally, under our example, the man would have received a total annuity payout of $2,250,000 by the time he died at eighty-five ($50,000 per year for forty-five years). Sounds pretty good, right? But if he had invested the $1,000,000 for forty-five years and earned a 9 percent return from the stock market, he would have received over $48,000,000 by the time he died!

To be clear, we are not suggesting that annuities are always a bad option. Some people really cannot stand the volatility of the stock market and would never be able to go through the ups and downs for forty-five years to compound 9 percent annually. And a lot of people like knowing they will receive a fixed amount of money every month or year. Our purpose is to show you how it works and why it is not always the best option if you want to build wealth long term.

PART III

Behavior, and How to Control It

◄ INTRODUCTION TO PART III ►

Recall that the number-one factor that determines investment success is your savings rate. Well, to be completely honest, that's only *mostly* true. That's because you can skimp, pinch, and save every penny that ever comes your way and still come up short. Very short. You can save every dollar, follow all the investment advice offered in this book, and still fall flat. There's one thing, one very peculiar thing, that can trip you up. That thing is *you*. It's you, it's us, it's everyone. It's your behavior as an individual investor, and it's our collective behavior—the market's behavior—that will also have a huge effect on your long-term investment returns. When we consider our collective behavior, reflected in the behavior of the markets, we call it "behavioral economics." When we refer to our individual behavior, we call it "behavioral biases." At their core, both are simply reflections of two primary human emotions: fear and greed.

Markets routinely cycle between times of "irrational exuberance" and deep, irrational depression. This is common to markets because they're common to all humans. We, along with markets, tend to go through swings of irrational optimism, when we think things only go up and the good times will only get better, followed by irrational pessimism, when we think the world is ending and nothing will ever be good again. If you understand that this will occur in markets, and *within you*, you'll be better equipped to manage it and, hopefully, overcome it.

We'll first consider behavioral economics and how it might help to explain some peculiarities about markets. Next, we'll present some real-deal historical examples of markets behaving badly. We'll look at times when the crowd seems to go mad, and we'll also explore when crowds might help us as investors. We'll then travel inward to understand all the behavioral biases that can affect even the savviest of investors—like overconfidence, hindsight bias, herding, and others, which can make us quite irrational. Finally, we'll dive into two things that can help you manage your behavior: proper financial planning and a sound, fiduciary-based financial advisor.

◄ 16 ►

The Pros and Cons of Behavioral Economics

Behavioral economics is "the study of psychology as it relates to the economic decision-making processes of individuals and institutions."[1] It is a relatively new and exciting field of economics but is somewhat controversial because it turns much of traditional economics on its head. Before behavioral economics, "[t]he core premise of economic theory [wa]s that people choose by optimizing. Of all the goods and services a family could buy, the family chooses the best one that it can afford."[2] In this world, people are thought to be rational, economic maximizers; they do not succumb to behavioral biases, like overconfidence.

A second core tenant of traditional economics is that markets tend to work toward an equilibrium. "In competitive markets where prices are free to move up and down, those prices fluctuate in such a way that supply equals demand."[3] For example, if demand for a good increases over and above the available supply of that good, the good's price will increase, causing demand to go down, and supply and demand to be equal. The human agents in the economy, always acting, of course, as rational, economic maximizers, quickly adjust their behavior to bring supply and demand into equilibrium.

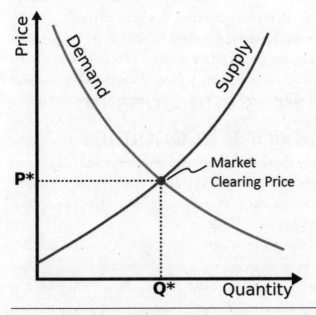

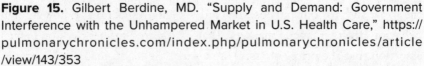

Figure 15. Gilbert Berdine, MD. "Supply and Demand: Government Interference with the Unhampered Market in U.S. Health Care," https://pulmonarychronicles.com/index.php/pulmonarychronicles/article/view/143/353

Traditional economics provides a baseline view of the world as if everyone were a spreadsheet, without human biases, excesses, and emotions. And while it did, and still does, provide useful models for how people interact in complex systems like our market economies, we now know that it probably does not paint a complete picture of reality. Traditional economics is a starting point, whereas behavioral economics can be thought of as an "enriched version of economic theory" that "acknowledges the existence and relevance of humans"—warts and all.[4]

Behavioral economics also contradicts much of Eugene Fama's power-ful efficient market hypothesis (EMH) in the same way. Remember that the EMH posits that the "price is right" at any given time. The price of a stock, bond, or other financial asset reflects all the available information. Prices are not "too high" or "too low"—what you see is what you get. Any changes in price are due only to the markets digesting new information.

Behavioral economics, however, says there is more to the story. It the-orizes that markets are not always efficient—or, in other words, are not always rational. In effect, since markets are made up of the decisions of millions of human investors every day, sometimes human emotions, biases, and other irrational inefficiencies can creep in and affect prices. Most behavioral economics evangelists, however, do not believe EMH should be scrapped. Instead, they think that behavioral economics adds depth and flavor to the traditional viewpoint and can help better explain the reality of markets. They just want a seat at the table, and there is considerable evi-dence that they should be given a chair.

Richard Thaler is a Nobel Prize–winning economist who has spent his career working on behavioral economics. He is considered a leader in the field and is credited with making economics "more human."[5] His book *Mis-behaving: The Making of Behavioral Economics* is a fascinating deep dive on the topic and, for our purposes, includes a lengthy section on how human behavior affects financial markets. Thaler's research pushes back on Fama's assertion that the prices of assets are always "right." Instead, Thaler argues that market prices are formed by a complex dance of what people believe *others* believe an asset is worth. He quotes the beauty contest analogy first raised by the famous economist John Maynard Keynes, which we looked at before. Remember that, under this view, the only thing that matters for asset prices is what everyone thinks everyone else thinks has value.

Thus, according to this perspective, the value of any asset should not depend on one objective internal price based on, for instance, the pres-ent value of a company's forecasted future earnings, but what *other peo-ple* think of it. It does you no good to own a stock that only you think is valuable—other people must also agree if you want to sell it one day for a higher price.* "Buying a stock that the market does not fully appreciate today is fine, as long as the rest of the market comes around to your point of view sooner rather than later!"[6] Even the staunchest EMH proponents would probably agree that market sentiment is important and can affect the price you will receive for any asset you own if you were to sell it.

According to the behavioralists, markets both under- and overreact to the news of the day, becoming either too pessimistic or optimistic. As evidence, Thaler points out that in a world of purely rational, efficient markets, there should not be as much trading volume as there is—the joke being that "no rational agent will want to buy a stock that some other rational agent is willing to sell." If markets were perfectly efficient and every stock price reflected its true, underlying value, then we would not see the staggering daily price changes and trading that regularly occurs. Human biases, such as overconfidence, must be playing a role.[7] "[I]f you assume that some investors are overconfident, high trading volume emerges naturally. Jerry has no trouble doing the trade with Tom, because he thinks that he is smarter than Tom, and Tom thinks he's smarter than Jerry. They happily trade, each feeling a twinge of guilt for taking advantage of his friend's poor judgment."[8]

Thaler and the behavioralists argue that humans might also be reacting to things that are not "news," which then affect stock prices beyond what their intrinsic value says they should be worth, or not worth. While the fictional, rational economic maximizer from the economics textbook may only change their mind based upon "genuine news," "humans might react to something that does not qualify as news, such as seeing an ad for the company behind the investment that made them laugh."[9] One only need

---

* Of course, owning assets like stocks and bonds typically entitles the owner to regular dividend or interest payments, regardless of whether the price of the asset goes up or down. Investors should be concerned with total return, which equals dividend payments plus price appreciation.

look at the "meme stock" mania over the last few years to see this play out. Assets that have little to no value, but which thrive on viral narratives, can do strange and unpredictable things. That does not mean, however, that fundamentals will never come back into play, which we've also seen with the crash of those same meme stocks.

Fama and the EMH crowd respond to these criticisms by pointing out that you can earn higher returns than the market by simply taking on additional risk. This would not prove a violation of EMH, because more risk can lead to higher returns. If that is what is going on, then it's not evidence that the markets are acting inefficiently. Instead, it's just people earning more returns for taking on more risk. It's not "free lunch" when you take on more risk than the market, in other words.

Importantly, even Thaler and the behavioralists do not argue that the typical investor can reliably beat the market over the long term. While they believe markets are not perfectly efficient, finding free lunch and exploiting any such inefficiencies is time consuming, expensive, and risky. Indeed, Thaler explicitly cautions against doing so:

> Investors should be wary of pouring money into markets that are showing signs of being overheated, but also should not expect to be able to get rich by successfully timing the market. It is much easier to detect that we may be in a bubble than it is to say when it will pop, and investors who attempt to make money by timing market turns are rarely successful.[10]

Moreover, Thaler does not want to get rid of EMH, believing it a useful "starting point to organize our thoughts" and that it remains the best one we have. He also thinks that the EMH's tenet of no free lunch is "mostly true," and even acknowledges:

> [W]hen investors know for sure that prices are wrong, these prices can still stay wrong, or even get more wrong. This should rightly scare investors who think they are smart and want to exploit apparent mispricing. It is possible to make money, but it is not

easy. Certainly, investors who accept the EMH gospel and invest in low-cost index funds cannot be faulted for that choice.[11]

Our own working theory, based upon all the available and reliable research, is that markets are not perfectly efficient. The evidence for that is all around us: the GameStop/meme mania, bubbles, crashes, and the like. But even as Thaler and others admit, just because markets can be inefficient at times, exploiting those inefficiencies to beat the market is nearly impossible to do over one's lifetime of investing. As we have shown, the evidence for this is overwhelming. Professional investors, who have millions of dollars to spend acquiring the best talent and the most recent technologies and strategies, cannot reliably do it either. Behavioral economics is no doubt a new and exciting field and is rightly deserving of attention, and it provides more nuance and flavor to the investing landscape. While it probably helps explain some peculiarities of markets, especially in the short term, we believe that, over the long term, EMH should still be largely respected by most investors.

◄ 17 ►

The Wisdom and Madness of Markets

Consider whether markets are good at collectively coming up with the right answer (i.e., the correct price of assets), or whether they do the opposite: madly create bubbles, fads, crashes, and meltdowns. For it seems like there is a dichotomy. On the one hand, people routinely speak of the "wisdom of crowds"—think polling the audience on a game show. On the other hand, though, we surely know of the "madness of crowds" too—think every crazed fad that came and went (e.g., Beanie Babies). So, which is it: wisdom or madness? In this chapter we will explore both and attempt to provide you with a framework for analyzing when to join the crowd, and when to stay on the sidelines.

THE WISDOM OF CROWDS

Many investors believe their path to success depends on identifying the best expert. That is why, for example, people spend an inordinate amount of time trying to park their money in hedge funds run by Ivy League graduates who promise to beat the market year after year. There are no doubt thousands of intelligent people working on Wall Street and other investment hubs worldwide. But, as we have shown, no matter how smart someone might be, they are rarely smart enough to beat the market over the long term. True, they may beat the market for a year or two, but hardly anyone can consistently beat it for five, ten, or more years. That's because even the savviest of investors are likely not smarter than the entire market.

In his bestselling book, *The Wisdom of Crowds*, James Surowiecki investigates this issue. He begins by telling a story about a contest at a county fair where 787 people were asked to guess the weight of a live ox *after* it had been slaughtered and dressed. While some of the people in the crowd could be called experts on the matter (e.g., people in the butcher industry), most of them were just regular people from the community attending the fair.

A series of statistical tests was run on the crowd's guesses to where the mean of the group's guesses was established—essentially the "collective wisdom" of the crowd. Much to the shock of the contest's organizer, the crowd guessed that the slaughtered and dressed ox would weigh 1,197 pounds, compared to the actual weight of 1,198 pounds. In other words, the crowd was basically perfect—off by just one pound![1]

Surowiecki's research, laid out extensively in the book, posits that:

> [U]nder the right circumstances, groups are remarkably intelligent, and are often smarter than the smartest people in them. Groups do not need to be dominated by exceptionally intelligent people in order to be smart. Even if most of the people within a group are not especially well-informed or rational, it can still reach a collectively wise decision. This is a good thing, since human beings are not perfectly designed decision makers. Instead, we are what the economist Herbert Simon called "boundedly rational." We generally have less information than we'd like. We have limited foresight

into the future. Most of us lack the ability—and the desire—to make sophisticated cost-benefit calculations. Instead of insisting on finding the best possible decision, we will often accept one that seems good enough. And we often let emotion affect our judgment. Yet despite all these limitations, when our imperfect judgments are aggregated in the right way, our collective intelligence is often excellent.[2]

This is remarkably similar to our overarching thesis in this book: that investors are better off following the wisdom of the market, instead of trying to beat or time it. Surowiecki goes on to say that chasing the experts is a mistake and that we should "stop hunting and ask the crowd (which, of course, includes the geniuses as well as everyone else) instead. Chances are it knows."[3] We could not agree more.

WISE MARKETS

Let's first look at when markets get it right, which is, in fact, most of time. Surowiecki tells the amazing story of how markets reacted to the horrific explosion of the *Challenger* space shuttle, in 1986. Within mere minutes of the explosion the stock market began attempting to evaluate which one of the four main outside contractors was most responsible for the disaster. By the end of the day, three of the four contractors' stock had fallen only around 3 percent. A fourth contractor's stock, Morton Thiokol, however, had its stock price slashed by almost 12 percent by day's end. This meant that the stock market had, within a day, and without any information other than the publicly available video of the crash, assigned blame on Morton Thiokol. Amazingly, six months later, the Presidential Commission on the Space Shuttle *Challenger* Accident submitted its report showing that Morton Thiokol had been primarily responsible. It took six months and countless hours of analysis to come to the same conclusion that the market did within thirty minutes![4]

While it's only one example, the *Challenger* story shows the power of markets when they work correctly. So, when do they work correctly? Surowiecki provides four conditions that must be present for markets to be wise:

1. **Diversity of Opinion**—Each person should have some private information, even if it's just an eccentric interpretation of the known facts.
2. **Independence**—People's opinions are not determined by the opinions of those around them.
3. **Decentralization**—People are able to specialize and draw on local knowledge.
4. **Aggregation**—Some mechanism exists for turning private judgments into a collective decision.[5]

If a market functions with these four conditions present, it will likely be right.

But what about the behavioral biases that we have looked at? If markets are simply a collection of individual investors making decisions, and if we know that individuals are all flawed and biased, doesn't that mean that the market is flawed and biased too? Amazingly, Surowiecki finds that a collection of unwise individuals can come together to create a wise crowd. He explains:

Take overconfidence. There's no doubt it explains why there's so much trading, and no doubt that it hurts individual traders. But what we want to know is whether it systematically skews the market (or the price of particular stocks) in one direction. There's no reason to believe it does, because the fact that investors are overconfident tells us nothing about *what* opinion they're overconfident about. I can be overconfident that the stock I just bought is going to go up, or I can be overconfident that the stock I just sold short is going to go down. But my feeling of certainty will not have a systematic effect on market prices because there's no reason to think that overconfidence is somehow correlated with a particular attitude toward stocks. If it was—if, say, overconfident people all hated technology stocks—then its effect on prices would be severe. But the evidence for a connection is still missing. The same is true of our overvaluation of recent news. Even if investors overvalue recent news about a company, there's no reason to think they will all overvalue it in the same way, because any piece of information will mean different things to different investors.[6]

In other words, a lot of irrational and biased investors, when taken together as a large group, can make a very wise, rational market. This does not mean, however, that the market will always be completely "right," as we will see later. But what it does mean is that the market will usually come up with a better answer than any single individual investor could on their own. Thus, when you as an individual begin second-guessing the market, or the price of any asset for that matter, you need to think long and hard about why you believe you have the superior viewpoint. Is it just a feeling? A hunch? Or do you have some real insight or information that everyone else in the world is missing? What sets you apart from the crowd? If you cannot come up with a well-reasoned answer, then you should consider it a speculative bet, not an investment.

UNWISE MARKETS

Crowds, as you may have guessed, are not always so wise. And for our purposes, nothing exemplifies an unwise crowd better than bubbles and crashes. Surowiecki explores in detail how markets can screw things up. One peculiarity unique to markets compared to, say, polling the audience in *Who Wants to Be a Millionaire*, is that markets never end. They go on and on, forever. There is never a time, like in a game show, where we definitively know the final answer. The market may be down this year, but it could go

CLOSE THE GAP & GET YOUR SHARE

up big tomorrow. It is, therefore, hard to prove whether someone is right or wrong with confidence. We can, nonetheless, look to certain stories and periods where we can say with conviction that an unwise market created a bubble that later crashed and burned.

Surowiecki points to bowling alley stocks as a prime example. Bowling, in its infancy, was a back-alley pastime that relied on "pin boys" to manually set up the pins after each round. Bowling was not very popular for various reasons, one of which was that relying on the pin boys was slow and cumbersome. Eventually, though, someone came up with the idea to automate the setting of pins. This technology was bought by the AMF company that is still around today. Because of this technological advancement, bowling took off in the 1950s. Any company that had anything to do with bowling garnered great attention and their stock prices soared. "Between 1957 and 1958, the stocks of AMF and Brunswick—another bowling equipment manufacturer—doubled. Smaller bowling companies went public, and investors poured money into the industry. If you had a bowling-related idea, people were happy to give you money."[7]

Wall Street analysts then started to project that the growth of bowling would continue at the same pace indefinitely, until almost every American would be bowling some two hours a week! The good roll was not to last, however. As soon as 1963, bowling stocks had lost almost 80 percent of their value and bowling got less popular over time, never reaching the height of the 1950s to this day.[8] In hindsight, bowling was a quintessential market bubble. So, what went wrong? How did the market become so unwise about bowling stocks?

Surowiecki explains that the bowling bubble, like all financial asset bubbles, occurred because at least one, or more, of the four conditions listed above—independence, diversity, decentralization, and aggregation—was not present. With bowling, there was not enough diversity or independence of thought—"everyone was saying that bowling was it, so everyone believed that bowling was it."[9] Bubbles are notoriously difficult to recognize in real time. They are even harder to profit from, since, as the old saying goes, the market can be wrong longer than you can stay solvent. Bubbles typically occur because people all share the same, false narrative. Moreover, the more the price of the asset goes up, the more it attracts follow-on investors believing the upward trend will continue indefinitely. Even investors who do not believe in the narrative and feel they're amid a bubble may participate, in the hopes they can get in, ride the wave, and then sell to a "greater fool" down the road before the bubble pops.

Once the bubble bursts and the crash starts, "investors are similarly uninterested in the 'real' value of a stock, and are similarly obsessed with reselling it." The big difference compared with bubbles, however, is that, in a crash, investors become too pessimistic, believing that the asset will go down forever. This usually causes its price to dip far below its true, intrinsic value. Bubbles and crashes are two sides of the same irrational coin, it seems. And while we do not know the full dynamics of what causes a major crash, one good comparison is "the collapse of a sandpile. As you add grains of sand to a pile, it will keep its shape as it grows bigger. But at some point, one grain of sand too many will send the pile tumbling."[10] This, combined with there being no "greater fools" out there to continue buying the asset at its inflated price, likely explains most bubbles in history. Another problem with bubbles, as Surowiecki points out, is that the longer they go on, the more it seems like they can never end—because that's just the way things are. The housing bubble easily comes to mind. Before 2008, it was "common knowledge" that housing real estate "always went up." All you had to do was get in on the party.

When groupthink grabs hold and there are no real differing opinions, crowds get into trouble. "The problem is that once everyone starts piggybacking on the wisdom of the group, then no one is doing anything to add to the wisdom of the group . . . [T]he beauty contest only has a hope of picking the prettiest girl—which is, after all, what it's there for—if some of the people in it really are thinking about which girl is prettiest . . . [A]s investors start mirroring each other, the wisdom of the group as a whole declines."[11]

At this point, you may be wondering whether following our advice of taking market returns and investing in low-cost index funds is really a smart idea, since it is literally "following the crowd." Admittedly, if everyone followed our advice and the entire market became 100 percent passive, we would have a problem. That's because nobody would be out there making sure that asset prices were reasonable. We surely need active investors for this very reason. But not to worry. While passive investing has grown in popularity over time, it is far from getting to the point of overshadowing active investors.

Many scholars estimate that we could have a much larger percentage of the market dedicated to passive investing than we do today, with only a small percent dedicated to active, and we would be just fine. Moreover, the moment the market becomes *too* passive and begins to fail at its job of "getting the price right," active investing would become especially lucrative. In that scenario, market inefficiencies would become painfully obvious, and smart—and maybe even some not-so-smart—traders would be able to make an easy profit. Currently, however, there is no reason to worry about the market being too passive—we have a long way to go.

PUTTING IT TOGETHER

So, are markets wise or unwise? Are they mad crowds more akin to a mob, constantly going from bubble to crash and back again? Or are they wise groups made up of millions of imperfect people coming together to arrive at the best solution? While we know this answer will be frustrating, the truth is likely somewhere in between. Sometimes it appears that crowds do know best, under certain conditions. At other times, it is obvious that crowds do go mad and go too far in both directions. Fads and bubbles are human nature, and probably unavoidable. But you, the individual, can choose to follow the crowd, or not. So, our advice would be to join the crowd on most of your long-term investments, letting the active investors do the heavy (read: expensive) lifting and riding their coattails. If you remain well diversified, we can say with a high probability that you should do well over time, even if there are significant ups and downs along the way.

On the other hand, you will want to try to avoid the crowd when it comes to investing in the latest and greatest fads, like the hot new company, technology, or asset class (e.g., crypto). While some will no doubt do well, they are usually the first movers, promoters, and their cronies; most follow-on investors will not. Take, for example, the recent craze of Cathie Wood's ARKK funds. They had explosive growth in the beginning years, making the first investors a lot of money quickly. This, as always, attracted bands of follow-on investors without any care about the viability of the underlying funds. The only attractor was that her funds had made money and they hoped they would continue to do so, because why wouldn't they? The narrative soon turned to Cathie Wood being the second coming of Jesus Christ who could do no wrong. She, so the narrative went, had her thumb on the pulse of the next wave of new technologies. If you did not get on board, and quick, you were destined to spend the rest of your life poor. As you can surmise by our tone, things eventually did take a turn for the ARKK funds, which fell a staggering 66 percent in 2022. And the worst part was that most investors lost money because they only got in when prices rose precipitously and there was nowhere else to go but down.

◄ 18 ►

Understanding and Controlling Behavioral Biases

Benjamin Graham famously stated that, "The investor's chief problem—even his worst enemy—is likely to be himself."[1] This is because, as humans, we all come preprogrammed with a laundry list of behavioral biases. The well-known author and Harvard psychologist Steven Pinker succinctly lists many of them, all backed by academic research:

> People are by nature illiterate and innumerate, quantifying the world by "one, two, many" and by rough guestimates. They understand physical things as having hidden essences that obey the laws of sympathetic magic or voodoo rather than physics and biology: objects can reach across time and space to affect things that resemble them or that had been in contact with them in the past . . . They underestimate the prevalence of coincidence. They generalize

from paltry samples, namely their own experience, and they reason by stereotype, projecting the typical traits of the group onto any individual that belongs to it. They infer causation from correlation. They think holistically, in black and white, and physically, treating abstract networks as concrete stuff. They are not so much intuitive scientists as intuitive lawyers and politicians, marshaling evidence that confirms their convictions while dismissing evidence that contradicts them. They overestimate their own knowledge, understanding, rectitude, competence, and luck.[2]

You might recognize these biases as ubiquitous in humans *generally* but fail to accept that they also exist within *you*, to one degree or another. Accepting that they do apply to you, however, will only serve you well as an investor. Because once you start to realize that you are a flawed decision maker, you will come to ignore your "gut" when it comes to making the monumental decisions of where to park your money for decades on end. You will no doubt still have biased thoughts, instincts, and failures, but you will hopefully learn to discount those feelings and not let them affect your investment decisions.

If you follow all the investment advice in this book, you stand a good chance of meeting your reasonable investment goals over the long run. However, that assumes you follow and stick with the plan and do not let your innate, human biases ruin all your hard work. In this chapter, we will go over some of the most common behavioral biases that can affect your investment outcomes.* Once you learn about common biases, you can then take steps to control them, which we will cover here and over the next two chapters.

---

* Recall that we covered one behavioral bias, overconfidence, in chapter four, due to its being so pervasive for most investors.

HINDSIGHT BIAS—"I KNEW IT ALL ALONG"

We crave certainty and abhor uncertainty. In his bestselling book, *The Black Swan*, Nassim Taleb discusses how people create narratives to explain the complex world we've all found ourselves within. This attempt to make sense of the world creates what Taleb calls "narrative fallacies." We continually construct narratives, both individually and as groups, to explain the past. The allure of narratives is that they offer simple, distilled versions of past events. We are very adept at creating narratives to explain past events because we have the benefit of hindsight. Pieces of the past that help to explain and support our chosen narrative are included, while other facts that don't support the narrative, or overly complicate it, are excluded.

Narratives typically assign a larger role to effort, skill, and talent than they do to luck or randomness. They also have the special skill of making an event seem inevitable—the "I knew it all along" phenomenon. Events that occurred purely by luck or random chance are seen, in hindsight, as having always been *certain* to occur. Moreover, the human mind is bad at dealing with events that *didn't* happen; only events that did occur are part of the narrative. Events that could have happened, but did not, are never considered.

Luck, as we've seen, also plays a role. Maybe the good event that did happen only happened because one was lucky. Maybe next time you won't be so lucky. In essence, we believe that we understand the past because our minds are continually building a coherent narrative. Consequently, we believe we can know the future as well. Nobel laureate Daniel Kahneman says that a "[g]eneral limitation of the human mind is its imperfect ability to reconstruct past states of knowledge, or beliefs that have changed. Once you adopt a new view of the world (or any part of it), you immediately lose much of your ability to recall what you used to believe before your mind changed."[3]

What gets us in trouble with investing is when we use narratives based on past events to predict the future. Or, because something didn't happen in the past, it won't ever happen in the future. Let's look at a concrete example to see how this works with investing.

Today we all know that Apple is one of the most successful companies that's ever existed. In hindsight, with the well-known narrative of Apple's story from near-bankruptcy to trillion-dollar-plus company, it's easy to say that one knew all along Apple would be what it is today. Its products, like the iPhone, are ubiquitous. It's a staple of our collective culture. But let's rewind back to the year 1992 and imagine that we purchased shares of Apple then for fifty-three cents—yes, that was really the price. Let's also assume you believed in the company then, were very confident about its future, and planned on holding the stock for many years. Here's what your investment looked like at that moment in 1992:

Jan 10 2023, 4:41PM EST. Powered by YCHARTS

Figure 16. Apple Inc. Price, 1982–1992. Data illustrated by Ycharts.com

Now, fast-forward five years to 1997:

Figure 17. Apple Inc. Price Percent Change, 1992–1997. Data illustrated by Ycharts.com

Do you think you'd have still believed in the company after it dropped 77 percent? Let's say you sold Apple at a 77 percent loss. Amazingly, after that, Apple went on a stupendous run over the next few years:

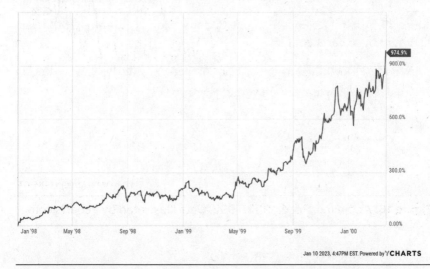

Figure 18. Apple Inc. Price Percent Change, 1998–2000. Data illustrated by Ycharts.com

If you did, in fact, sell when Apple was down 77 percent, you were certainly feeling some terrible regret. And, if you happened to buy Apple when it was down 77 percent, you were now feeling like a genius. So, now that Apple is up 974 percent, maybe you decided to get back in. Here's what happened next:

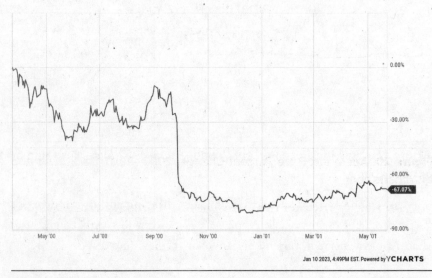

Figure 19. Apple Inc. Price Percent Change, May 2000–May 2001. Data illustrated by Ycharts.com

Whoops! Down again—more than 67 percent. Maybe you sold again and gave up on Apple stock. But wait, there's more!

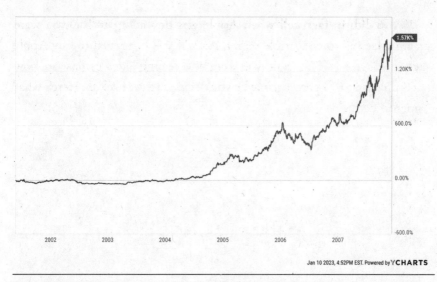

Figure 20. Apple Inc. Price Percent Change, 2002–2007. Data illustrated by Ycharts.com

However, shortly after this incredible run, it dropped again:

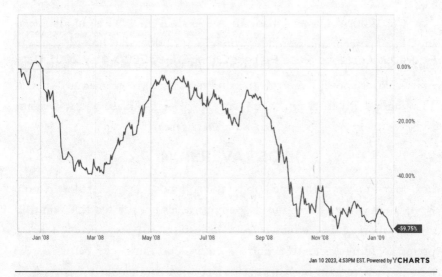

Figure 21. Apple Inc. Price Percent Change, January 2008–January 2009. Data illustrated by Ycharts.com

It then, however, went on another incredible run up until today:

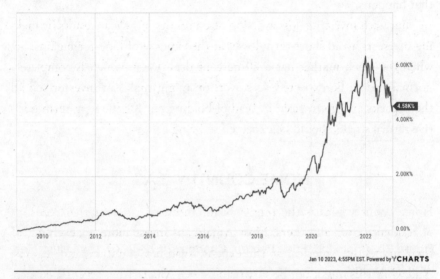

Jan 10 2023, 4:55PM EST. Powered by YCHARTS

Figure 22. Apple Inc. Price Percent Change, 2010–2022. Data illustrated by Ycharts.com

A $10,000 investment made in Apple stock in 1992 is up a stagger-ing 24,620 percent and would be worth $3,462,000 today. But ask yourself: How many people do you think bought in 1992 and held on through the roller coaster above? Keep this in mind next time you think you "knew it all along."

LOSS AVERSION

Loss aversion can be summed up by the common idiom that "losses loom larger than gains." Numerous academic studies have tested this point. In essence, most of us are biased to avoid losses at all costs. People tend to prefer avoiding losses to acquiring equivalent gains—it's better not to lose $5 than to gain $5. This bias is deep-seated and likely has roots in our evolutionary history. It is not hard to imagine how fearing threats is more useful than exploiting opportunities. Threats, like a lion hiding in the bushes, kill. Game over. There won't be any opportunities to exploit if that happens.

But with investing, loss aversion often results in subpar results by making investors avoid short-term losses at the expense of long-term gains. So, when the stock market has a 20 percent drawdown, which is completely normal and to be expected, loss aversion might make an investor sell all their stocks and go to cash, instead of holding out for the long-term positive return stocks should be expected to bring.

HOME COUNTRY BIAS

Home country bias is the tendency for investors to favor their country of residence over all others. Most Americans invest more, or even all, of their money in America, at the expense of other countries and regions. And while this might not be surprising, since America has recently outperformed most every other country economically, the bias extends to foreign investors too. So, Germans invest more, proportionally, in Germany than any other country, including the U.S. Same for Mexicans, Australians, and the Japanese. This bias is by no means unsurprising since people tend to invest in goods and services they find familiar. It may also make you stay with an investment because you are more accustomed to it; maybe you see the local company's products every day or interact with it regularly.

The problem, however, is if your home country underperforms the globe. For example, Japan was an economic juggernaut in the 1980s, and the Japanese people, as well as others, loaded up on Japanese stock, sending its stock market soaring. But as you can see from the Nikkei index in Figure 23, if you were unlucky enough to have bought at the peak of the mania, you still would not have recovered to this day.*[4]

---

* Figure 23 shows the price return of the Nikkei index and does not account for re-invested dividends. Those that re-invested dividends did finally recover after many years.

Figure 23. Japan Level. Data illustrated by Ycharts.com

For this reason, it is best to be well diversified across countries and regions throughout the world. Indeed, as Figure 24 shows, even the U.S. does not always outperform the rest of globe.[5]

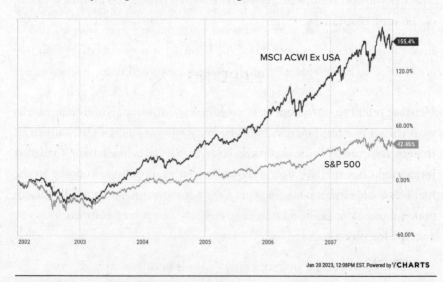

Figure 24. MSCI ACWI Ex USA Total Return vs. S&P 500 Total Return. Data illustrated by. Ycharts.com

SUNK COST FALLACY

A sunk cost refers to our tendency to continue with a course of action if we've already put some time and effort into it, even though continuing down that path would bring no benefit, or maybe even be negative. Traditional economic theory states that rational actors should ignore sunk costs when making decisions in the present. But we all know that is far from how things work in real life. Imagine, for example, that you put a $100, nonrefundable deposit down to go on a vacation in six months. A few months later, when it comes time to book the hotel and flights, you change your mind about the vacation spot and would prefer to go somewhere else. If you are purely rational, you should look at the $100 deposit as gone and go to your preferred destination. But because of the sunk cost fallacy, most people will continue with the original choice because they've already spent the $100.

In investing, sunk costs make people stick with bad investments for far too long. So next time you find yourself doing the same, ask yourself whether you still believe in the investment or whether you are just a victim of the sunk cost fallacy.

HERDING

Herding refers to our propensity to follow what others are doing. Just as with things like fashion, cars, and the latest phones, most of us want to fit in with the crowd. To be accepted. To be liked. But while having the latest jeans might not spell disaster, following what everyone else is doing in the markets could. In his book *The Four Pillars of Investing*, William J. Bernstein makes a prescient point on why following the latest trends in stocks is not a recipe for success:

> [T]he conventional investment wisdom is usually wrong. If everyone believes that stocks are the best investment, what that tells you is that everyone already owns them. This, in turn, means two

things. First, that because everyone has bought them, prices are high and future returns, low. And second, and more important, *that there is no one left to buy these stocks.* For it is only when there is an untapped reservoir of future buyers that prices can rise.[6]

This is one reason why investing is so difficult. We all want to buy the stocks that everyone else is buying because they are popular and likely well known in the zeitgeist. But, as Bernstein points out, if the current price of a stock is too high because the stock is wildly popular, it likely means your future returns will be low. Conversely, if the price of an asset is low because it has done poorly and nobody likes it, it probably will have high future returns. In markets, not following the latest fads will usually pay dividends over time. Not to worry, however. By being well diversified, you can be assured of owning assets that most people currently dislike; one day, you should be smartly rewarded.

ANCHORING

Daniel Kahneman, along with his research partner, Amos Tversky, presented pioneering work about anchoring, which has deep implications for every investor. Anchoring is another bias that causes us to rely much too heavily on the first piece of information—the "anchor"—we receive, resulting in every subsequent piece of information and decision made from the reference point of the anchor. As Kahneman explains in his book *Thinking, Fast and Slow*, anchoring is "one of the most reliable and robust results of experimental psychology." For example, "[i]f you are asked whether Ghandi was more than 114 years old when he died you will end up with a much higher estimate of his age at death than you would if the anchoring question referred to his death at 35." Similarly, when shopping for a home, your offer price will depend heavily on the asking price, which is the anchor.[7]

With investing, the anchoring bias causes many to anchor to an arbitrary number or figure. When you buy a stock for a certain price, for example, your mind will forever anchor to that price, regardless of any new information you receive. Any future decisions about that stock will be highly affected by your anchor price. This usually results in investors holding loser stocks because they believe the price will one day return to the anchor, even when the company is facing large headwinds, or even bankruptcy. We also see this when a stock has reached an all-time high after a staggering upward run, but then falls precipitously. Many then think the low price is a great opportunity to buy because they believe it will surely return to the all-time high (i.e., the "anchor").

If you turn on the financial news, you will commonly see anchors at play. For example, take any amazing success story of a growth stock that fell, such as Netflix. Netflix had a ridiculous run from its IPO in May 2002 until the end of 2021, gaining over 50,000 percent—a truly incredible amount. It then fell 51 percent in 2022, with many calling it an "implosion." Here, the pundits are "anchoring" to the high-water mark. But, even with the drop in 2022, if you take the all-time return of Netflix from inception to the end of 2022, the return is still a stunning 24,000 percent. Many, however, will simply say that Netflix is now a "loser" stock because they anchored to its all-time high number.*

Once you recognize the anchoring bias, it should become easier to spot and curb it. For example, whenever you find yourself focused on a specific price of a stock or other asset, ask yourself why you've chosen that number. Is it based on your research or objective data about its value, or are you simply anchoring? As with all biases, if you know about them beforehand, you'll have a better shot at not letting them trip you up down the road.

---

* No doubt, many Netflix investors likely did lose money, since when an asset has a stratospheric rise it brings follow-on investors, bidding the price up even higher. There were likely vanishingly few investors who bought Netflix and held it through the ups and downs.

AVAILABILITY HEURISTIC

Kahneman also did a lot of groundbreaking research on the availability heuristic, which he defines as "the process of judging frequency by the ease with which instances come to mind." He goes on to describe it as a bias that causes one to "substitute one question for another: you wish to estimate the size of a category or the frequency of an event, but you report an impression of the ease with which instances come to mind." The bias is, admittedly, better explained with examples, of which there are many. Some provided by Kahneman include:

- A salient event that attracts your attention will be easily retrieved from memory. Divorces among Hollywood celebrities and sex scandals among politicians attract much attention, and instances easily come to mind. You are therefore likely to exaggerate the frequency of both Hollywood divorces and political sex scandals.
- A dramatic event temporarily increases the availability of its category. A plane crash that attracts media coverage will temporarily alter your feelings about the safety of flying. Accidents are on your mind, for a while, after you see a car burning on the side of the road, and the world feels like a more dangerous place.
- Personal experiences, pictures, and vivid examples are more available than incidents that happened to others, or mere words, or statistics. A judicial error that affects you will undermine your faith in the justice system more than a similar incident you read about in the newspaper.[8]

The availability bias runs rampant in the investment world, primarily because money is so personal. Every single one of us has money experiences upon which we continuously draw. Our personal money experiences, or those of our loved ones, will forever color our judgment simply because those experience are readily available. Thus, if you had a parent who picked stocks and lost the family fortune, that memory will be especially salient, and might result in you forever shunning stocks, even though the objective data say you should not. Indeed, the generation that lived through the 1929 stock market crash and subsequent Great Depression mostly avoided stocks for the rest of their lives, missing the incredible post-WWII bull market.

Another availability bias problem investors face is the notion that the most easily recalled event—usually the most recent—is either the best or worst possible future scenario. For example, Kahneman writes that "[a]s long ago as pharaonic Egypt, societies have tracked the high-water mark of rivers that periodically flood—and have always prepared accordingly, apparently assuming that floods will not rise higher than the existing high-water mark. Images of a worse disaster do not easily come to mind."[9] We see this play out regularly when investors look at recent crashes as "the worst-case scenarios" and build their portfolios accordingly, forgetting that the future never looks like the past. That's why we tell clients that the worst recession is always in the future.

NEGATIVITY BIAS

Our brains are hardwired to relish the negative over the positive. We can see this at work regularly with the news, especially the financial news. Indeed, if you turn on the financial news you will quickly learn that there is always something to be worried about with your investments. This bias again stems from our evolutionary history, since you have a better chance of surviving in the wild if you focus on all the things that can go wrong. While the negativity bias might be hard to shake, one way to deal with it is to maintain a long-term perspective with an eye toward history. Markets go up over time even with the constant burr of negative news always nagging at investors.

RECENCY BIAS

Recency bias is the tendency for people to favor recent events over more distant, historic ones. With investors, we see this happening when prices go up, as well as down. When prices go up, investors believe that they'll go up forever, because that's what's happened recently. They also believe that their future returns will be higher. Conversely, on the way down, investors believe that the price will go down forever, because that's what has been happening recently. But, in fact, the opposite is true due to simple math.

Imagine you buy Microsoft stock for $100 when Microsoft is a break-out favorite. Imagine again that, a year later, the stock plummets to $50 during a time of deep market upheaval when people fear the future and are negative on return prospects. Your friend buys Microsoft at $50 on a whim. Let's next assume that you both sell five years later for $200. Who made more money? Obviously, your friend who bought at $50 and sold at $200! While we can easily see the folly of this example, most of us find it very difficult to buy stocks during bad times. Yet we are more than happy to buy them up to abundance during the good. When stocks are down, we think they'll go down forever. And when they're up, we think they'll go up forever too.

One way we try to help clients tame the recency bias is to point them to very long-term trends for asset prices. For example, the U.S. stock market has averaged an annual return, including reinvesting dividends, of around 10 percent. Therefore, when the market has years of 20 percent–plus returns, the prudent expectation is for subsequent years to be less rosy when stocks revert to their historical mean. On the flip side, when an asset has had years of historical underperformance and clients want to jump ship, thinking the trend will continue, it helps to show them how the long-term trend has been higher. They should expect returns to revert *up* to the mean. As with anything, a long-term perspective and knowledge of history is useful.

PATTERN SEEKING

We love patterns. Think of seeing animals in the clouds, or the Virgin Mary on a piece of toast. But while rolling around on the green grass debating whether a cloud looks like a puppy or a dinosaur is nothing more than harmless play, trying to find patterns in the movement of stocks is illusory. This doesn't stop people from trying. In fact, there is an entire industry of people that do this every single day. They are called "chartists" and their craft is referred to as "technical analysis."

Technical analysis looks at past price movements, trends, and volume of asset trading to try to predict the future. Pure chartists, for example, will not care about the fundamentals of the company they are tracking—such as price-to-earnings ratios or growth prospects. Instead, they might see patterns in the movement of the stock price that make it a strong buy or sell. As Burton Malkiel writes, "[t]o a chartist, these patterns have the same significance as X-ray plates to a surgeon."[10]

Once you know what to look for, you will start seeing shades of technical analysis everywhere you look. Turn on CNBC and you'll hear about how the market has "support" or is reaching a "resistance" level. Go to any Reddit investing forum and technical analysis runs rampant. You'll read stories about how you sell in certain months and buy in others—because, you know, that's what has worked before. We saw a humorous example recently in an announcement that CNBC personality Jim Cramer was ringing in the bell the next day at the stock market. The commentator noted that the last time Cramer rang the bell, the market fell by such-and-such percent. There is probably someone right now subscribing to the "Cramer rule" of investing.

Once again, Malkiel is astute on the ability of chartists using technical analysis to play the stock market:

> The past history of stock prices cannot be used to predict the future in any meaningful way. Technical strategies are usually amusing, often comforting, but of no real value . . . Technical theories enrich only the people preparing and marketing the technical service or the brokerage firms who hire technicians in the hope that their analyses may help encourage investors to do more in-and-out trading and thus generate more commissions.

Using technical analysis for market timing is especially dangerous. Because there is a long-term uptrend in the stock market it can be very risky to be in cash. An investor who frequently carries a large cash position to avoid periods of market decline is very likely to be out of the market during some periods where it rallies smartly.

The implications are simple. If past prices contain little or no useful information for predicting future prices, there is no point in following technical trading rules.[11]

As Malkiel makes clear with his evidence-based Random Walk Theory, the stock market does not follow any trend or pattern—past performance is not indicative of future results. Do not fall into the trap of believing that you, or anyone else, can predict its movements based on historical patterns, especially in the short run. Your best bet is to ignore any talk from the chartists and pundits and ride the waves up and down to long-term success.

WHAT TO DO ABOUT BIASES

We have listed a small fraction of the myriad biases that can affect your investment success, so now let's briefly answer what to do about them. Recognizing that we all have them is the first step. No matter what you do, a bias is probably lurking in the background. If you do not know about them, however, you cannot manage them. So, try and internalize that you have biases, just like every human that has ever existed. Next, try and figure out which biases you are most susceptible to. Are you more overconfident than most? Maybe you suffer from hindsight bias more than your peers. Whatever they are, try and figure out which ones are likely to rear their heads with you.

Once you know your biases, you can deal with them. So, if you have a fear of missing out and are prone to herding behavior, the next time you start to feel anxious about getting in on the "next big thing," stop, take a breath, and tell yourself that this opportunity likely isn't a great fit for you and that you're just feeling anxious because of your herding bias. Another tactic could be to sleep on it and come back the next day to reevaluate once the emotion has gone away. Or you might reach out to a trusted friend or advisor to get their advice. They will likely not be having the same emotion as you and can be a sounding board of reason.

Apart from understanding your biases, there are other ways to manage them. One is to follow the investment advice in this book—namely, taking a passive approach with most of your funds. Replicating the market by investing in low-cost index funds, and then holding them for as long as possible, will do wonders to combat any innate biases you may have. For instance, you will be less likely to follow the herd when you invest in index funds, because nobody is ever talking up index funds as the "next big thing." Moreover, by owning an index fund, you likely already own a piece of everything, so you are not missing out on the next big thing—you'll at least have a little. Similarly, if you believe in the concept of markets being a "random walk," you will be less likely to succumb to pattern seeking, knowing that patterns are simply illusions that we paste onto the world to try and make sense of it. And if you are more overconfident than most, hewing toward an index-based plan will straitjacket your tendency to take big bets based on your strong opinions of the moment.

Other techniques for combating biases are financial planning and working with a fiduciary financial advisor, which we will discuss over the next two chapters.

◄ 19 ►

Financial Planning Made Easy

et's look at the basics of how to construct a simple financial plan
that fits your needs. Note that this is a basic overview of our typical
approach and your plan should be customized to fit your unique needs.

Many financial planners tout how their system or approach is superior
to the rest. It seems to us that they are selling complexity. The notion that a
solid financial plan is difficult to come up with and must be overly complex
is misguided. While there is no doubt that a good financial plan should be
constructed deliberately and carefully, we believe many people try to make
financial planning seem too complex.

Just as the investment industry makes investing seem complicated, so,
too, does the financial planning industry. Make no mistake: a good financial planner, whether acting as an investment advisor, a certified financial planner (or CFP), or otherwise, can make a world of difference. But a
solid financial plan need not be too complicated. Just having a simple plan
in your head or jotted down on a scrap of paper will put you well ahead
of most. With our own clients, we typically use a simple, straightforward

system to cut through all the complexity and intimidation: the "Three Buckets Approach."

THE THREE BUCKETS APPROACH

A lot of investors think of their investments as one big pile of money. Indeed, if you invest all your money with one custodian, your financial statements will lump everything together and give you one rate of return. Most are usually fixated on this single number. But this is the wrong way to go about it. A good financial plan should split up investments based upon their intended purpose. For example, money invested every month into a 401(k) plan for retirement in thirty years should be thought about much differently than money invested in a short-term emergency fund account. The purpose of each investment is drastically different. For one, the emergency fund is meant for, well, emergencies. For it to serve that purpose, it needs to be invested in something very conservative so you can access it when you need it. It does you no good to have an emergency fund invested in stocks if that investment is down 40 percent when you need it! No, it needs to be in cash or a cash equivalent, like short-term T-Bills that do not fluctuate much. The return on that cash will be low.

Conversely, if you cannot touch your 401(k) account for thirty years, it should be invested with a longer time frame in mind, which usually means in riskier assets. You can afford to have some ups and downs because your time horizon is longer.

So, split up those investments—both in your mind and on paper. Split up your investments into three separate "buckets," going from less risk to more—and from a short time horizon to a long one.

Bucket One

When coming up with your plan, first think about how much cash you'll need on hand for emergencies. An emergency can mean many things and will be unique to you. It includes obvious things like losing your job or an income source. It also includes unexpected expenses, like a house repair or medical bill. A good rule of thumb is to have at least six months to a year of living expenses set aside in case of job or major income loss. We think this is prudent, but it is up to you on whether you need more, or less. Think about your job security and how closely it may be tied to the general economy. For example, if you work for an oil and gas company that experiences regular ups and downs, your job security may be more tenuous than if you worked for the government. You should also consider other sources of money if you were to lose your job. Do you have a spouse who works? Do you come from a wealthy family that will help support you if times get rough? These are all things to consider, and which only you can know.

Bucket One is not just for emergencies, however. It's also for expenses you know you'll incur within a year or two. Are you saving up for a down payment on a new house? Do you have a major trip or purchase planned? Are you having to pay for a wedding soon?

Other considerations include whether you will need cash to comply with capital calls on a private investment (e.g., private equity, real estate). If those are coming due within the next year or two, you'll need cash on hand to meet your commitments.

Once you have your own unique number for Bucket One, invest it in a cash equivalent. We typically suggest short-term Treasury Bills, so you at least earn the "risk-free rate of return." We call it risk-free because the U.S. government will not default on its obligations because it can print money. While all U.S. bonds carry little to no repayment risk for that reason, longer-term government bonds carry interest rate and inflation risk. However, short-term government debt, like T-Bills, does not since the maturity (or time until repayment) is short. That's why we refer to T-Bills as a cash equivalent that has little to no risk.

We recommend investing in T-Bills, or other short-term government debt, because of the low risk, and the chance to earn some return above and beyond that of a savings or checking account. But there is another reason why investing in T-Bills with your cash is prudent, especially if that amount is above $250,000. In the United States, almost every bank that offers checking and savings accounts will have what is called FDIC insurance. FDIC stands for "Federal Deposit Insurance Corporation" and is a government program that insures certain checking and savings accounts from loss, so long as the amount is less than $250,000. So, if your bank or custodian folds and loses the money in your checking or savings account, the United States government will repay you any amount up to $250,000. Therefore, you should never have anything in a checking or savings account over $250,000. But another thing to consider is that even if your deposits are insured by the FDIC, recouping any lost funds could take some time. For this reason, we typically suggest that clients should not hold more money in a checking account than they need for everyday expenses. Anything over and above that should probably be moved to an investment brokerage account and invested in T-Bills or other short-term government debt.

A lot of people balk at holding a lot of cash in Bucket One. They want to be fully invested in risky assets, like stocks, private equity, and real estate. Holding a lot of cash is anathema to them. They will rightly state that they earn little to no return on Bucket One, and maybe even earn a negative real return when inflation is considered. While this is understandable, we suggest looking at your cash reserve with a different perspective. You should instead think of Bucket One as *insurance* for your riskier investments in Buckets Two and Three, which we will cover next.

Imagine the stock market crashes 30 to 40 percent within a year because of fears about the future of the economy. Because of the crash, we can infer investors are fearing a recession or some other negative economic headwinds. You, being a member of that economy, might also be facing some headwinds. Maybe things in your company or industry are feeling uncertain too. Maybe you're worried about earning less income or missing out on a bonus. Maybe you've been laid off or let go. Now let's imagine that you've only invested in risky assets, like stocks, and they are down 30 to 40 percent along with the market.

Now imagine you need cash. What do you do? You'll have to sell your risky assets at a loss. Maybe a steep loss. This will spell disaster for your long-term investments, which need time to grow and compound. You might have to start from the beginning, and you might not have enough time to make it up. You probably will not. However, if you had a substantial amount in your Bucket One, you probably could have weathered the storm. You could have used the cash as a backstop to continue to pay your bills and survive the downturn without having had to touch a single penny in Buckets Two and Three. Those investments would stay untouched and would have the opportunity to rebound when the economy came back. You now get to experience the miracle of compounding returns, and your long-term investment plan and goals remain on track.

So, instead of thinking of your Bucket One cash as a *drag* on your investments, think of it instead as *insurance* for your risky investments. Think of it as allowing you to calmly carry on with those investments during bad times. If you look at it this way—as a backstop, and not as a liability—then you'll have fewer worries about holding too much cash.

Bucket Two

Bucket Two is your middle-of-the-road "Goldilocks investments": not too much risk, not too little, but just right. Bucket Two serves a few distinct purposes. The first is practical, serving as a second tranche of liquidity if you run out of money in Bucket One. If that happens, you can sell assets in Bucket Two and not have to touch your riskiest investments in Bucket Three. Or, if you draw down Bucket One and need to add new money, you can get it from Bucket Two. Bucket Two also serves as a psychological hedge. If markets tank and your Bucket Three investments are doing poorly, it is very unlikely that Bucket Two will be down as much as Three. This will help you sleep better at night, knowing everything is not falling apart.

Bucket Two also acts as a place for medium-term investments. For example, if you are saving for something five to ten years down the road, you might want to think about taking a little bit of risk to try and earn some return. Bucket Two is a good place to put that money to work. Keep in mind that you are taking more risk than Bucket One, and there are no guarantees; however, the longer your time horizon, the less likely this will be an issue.

So, what type of investments should you make in Bucket Two? We advise most clients to start with the Global Market Portfolio (GMP), which we covered in chapter eleven. Remember, the GMP is the "index of indexes" and is a conservative portfolio holding approximately 70 percent global bonds, 20 percent equities, and 10 percent commodities, with real estate exposure through both bonds and equities. You should expect returns somewhere between 3 to 5 percent annually, on average, which we covered in detail in chapter eleven. It is a great portfolio for outpacing inflation and maintaining your purchasing power far into the future. Moreover, the volatility should be lower than stocks, so when the stock market crashes, the GMP will suffer less. But with low volatility and conservative holdings, the returns are lower than some would like.

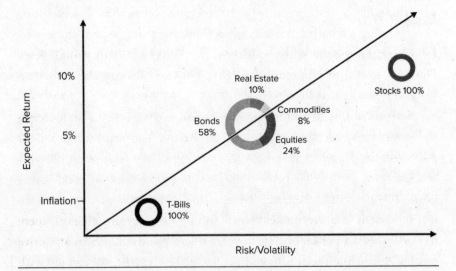

Figure 25. Risk & Expected Return of the Global Market Portfolio

For those seeking higher returns, we recommend tilting the portfolio toward riskier assets, such as adding additional stocks and proportionally removing bonds. If instead you want less risk than the GMP, you can likewise remove stocks and add bonds. Think of the GMP as the starting place that can be dialed up or down depending on your risk tolerance. Moreover, some people might find it beneficial to have multiple portfolios under the Bucket Two umbrella. For example, you might have a savings goal that is ten years out and, therefore, you can consider dialing up the risk a bit, while also having a shorter-term portfolio, say for a five-year investment, that you may want to dial down the risk for.

Bucket Three

The last one, Bucket Three, is meant for long-term, higher-risk, high expected return investments. Here, you want to take calculated risks that should, more than likely, earn you a good return over many years—think fifteen-, twenty-plus years. But remember, not all risks are the same. You'll want to try to have significant exposure to systematic risk, not idiosyncratic. So, something like a well-diversified total stock market fund is a great option here. Holding a handful of stocks is not. Holding a 100 percent stock portfolio might be volatile, with drawdowns that could last many painful years. However, over time horizons longer than ten years, owning the stock market will typically make you money.

The probability of having a positive return in the stock market increases the longer your investment time horizon. Rolling one-year returns for the S&P 500, for example, are positive 75 percent of the time, with five-year returns being positive 87 percent of the time, and ten-year periods being positive 94 percent of the time.[1] While losing money over a ten-year stretch can happen if you are unlucky with timing (a 6 percent chance), there has never been a period of sixteen years where you did not earn a positive return. And while the future will not look like the past, we can say with a high degree of confidence that investing in the market for fifteen- or twenty-plus years should earn you a handsome, compounded return. If we take the historical return of the S&P 500 as being approximately 10 percent, with dividends reinvested, a $100,000 investment left to grow for twenty years would equal over $672,000. Left alone for thirty years, it would return you over $1,700,000.

Yes, it is here, in Bucket Three, where you will make or break your financial future. It is here that the magic of compound interest really takes over. Because the magic of compounding requires, above all, time. Given enough time, a simple, cheap, and well-diversified market index fund or ETF can produce life-changing results. You don't have to start with millions of dollars to end up with millions. Start as soon as you can, and contribute regularly, and your Bucket Three will flourish into something astonishing years down the road.

All your long-term money should be allocated to Bucket Three. Retirement accounts, like 401(k)s and IRAs, are some easy examples, especially if you are young—because you know that you cannot touch them without penalty for many years. But even if you can technically touch the money, because, for example, it is not in a restricted retirement account, you should think of Bucket Three money the same way: restricted. Off limits. No matter what. What is more, if you have followed our advice of having set up Buckets One and Two, you will not have to touch it in an emergency either. You have other sources of funds that you can use for that.

OTHER PLANNING CONSIDERATIONS

Simple is usually better when it comes to planning. However, while we believe this should be the backbone of any plan, there are other considerations depending on your situation. These include, but are not limited to, college savings planning, insurance planning, tax planning, estate planning, retirement planning, withdrawal planning, successor planning, and charitable planning. These topics are beyond the scope of this book, but should be discussed with a financial advisor, financial planner, estate lawyer, or a similar professional if appropriate. Importantly, make sure anyone giving you financial advice is acting as a fiduciary, which means they must put your interests ahead of their own, which we will discuss in the next chapter.

In sum, having a written financial plan along the lines of the Three Buckets Approach will help you in innumerable ways. First, by forcing you to think about investing with different risk parameters, goals, and time horizons, it will go a long way toward making you a better investor. Second, it will help curb many innate biases that you may harbor. Finally, and most importantly, it will serve as an insurance plan to allow your riskiest investments to grow unfettered for hopefully decades on end—letting the miracle of compound interest do its thing.

◄ 20 ►

The Value of Professional Advice

While some might be able to handle their investments completely on their own, we recommend that most consider the help of a professional advisor. Studies have shown that a competent advisor can deliver value of around 2.88 percent per year, which is well above the typical 1 percent fee most advisors charge. That study "arrived at the 2.88 percent figure by calculating the additional returns a human advisor generates across three categories—annual rebalancing of investment portfolios [0.10 percent], correcting behavioral mistakes such as overconfidence and herding [1 percent], and tax-efficient investing [0.66 percent]—and by adding the typical fees charged for basic investment management [0.40 percent] and financial planning and answering questions [0.72 percent]."[1]

Vanguard has likewise studied this, but recognized that quantifying advisor value is not straightforward:

> For some investors without the time, willingness, or ability to confidently handle their financial matters, working with an advisor

may bring peace of mind. They may simply prefer to spend their time doing something—anything—else. Maybe they feel overwhelmed by product proliferation in the fund industry, given, for example, that the number of ETFs in the United States now exceeds 2,000. The value of an advisor in this context is virtually impossible to quantify. Nonetheless, the overwhelming majority of mutual fund assets are advised, indicating that investors strongly value professional investment advice. We don't need to see oxygen to feel its benefits.[2]

Nevertheless, Vanguard has indeed also quantified such value, finding that "advisors can potentially add up to, or even exceed, 3 percent in net returns" by implementing certain strategies, including:

- ► Determining a client's optimal asset allocation;
- ► Cost-effective implementation of investment strategies;
- ► Rebalancing;
- ► Behavioral coaching;
- ► Asset location (i.e., which accounts will hold your investments);
- ► Spending strategy (withdrawal order); and
- ► Total return versus income investing.

Importantly, Vanguard cautions that this 3 percent advantage is unlikely to be recognized equally annually, but rather during times of "market duress or euphoria when clients are tempted to abandon their well-thought-out investment plans."[3]

A well-versed advisor can develop a customized investment plan that fits your unique life situation, risk tolerance, goals, and other factors. This plan should ideally be in writing and revisited as needed. Among the many benefits of a written plan is it ensures you and your advisor are on the same page. Per the Vanguard study, "[w]hen clients are tempted to abandon the markets because performance has been poor or to chase the next 'hot' investment," reference to the plan can do wonders to keep things on track.

Other studies have similarly shown that advisors add value for investors. For example, one paper performed a meta-analysis of numerous studies looking into the issue and concluded that there is "evidence of the added value of financial advice" and that "generally, professionals are associated with better portfolio performance than [non-advised] investors." It also found that "[i]n terms of diversification, advised portfolios perform much better than self-directed portfolio, thus reducing avoidable risk" and that "advisers positively affect diversification." In sum, the paper found that "[i]t is widely known that retail investors make suboptimal portfolio decisions. Although advisers are sometimes subject to similarly biased decision making or have incentives that exacerbate their clients' biases, this paper confirms that advisors do add positive value. They improve portfolio diversification."[4]

Recall that diversification in real time is hard, sometimes very hard. A good advisor, therefore, can help you not only build a well-diversified portfolio, but also stick with it during the tough times. This simple fact alone can add real value over the many years you must hold a diversified portfolio to see its benefits.

A financial advisor can also serve as your "one-stop shop" for all things financial. While this clearly includes long-term investments and planning, your advisor can also provide feedback and wisdom in other areas, like the appropriate mortgage, or whether you need insurance, estate planning, or other professionals to step in and help. You should feel comfortable asking your advisor for their opinion on the recent news of the day, and they should be a sounding board for your thoughts, fears, worries, and aspirations.

Importantly, a financial advisor can help control emotions and biases. "Advisors can act as emotional circuit breakers by circumventing clients' tendencies to chase returns or run for cover in emotionally charged markets. In the process, they may prevent significant wealth destruction and add percentage points—rather than basis points—of value. A single such intervention could more than offset years of advisory fees."[5]

FIDUCIARY, FEE-BASED ADVISORS

Not all advisors are created equal, however. Importantly, you want to make sure you are working with an advisor who is a fiduciary. A fiduciary financial advisor must place your interests ahead of their own, must act with your best interests in mind, and may not receive commissions for products that they sell to you, without proper disclosure.

Most fiduciary advisors will be "fee based," meaning they will only charge a fee based on the amount of work required or on the amount of money invested. For example, if an advisor charges an assets under management (AUM) fee of 1 percent and you invest $100,000 under that advisor, then you would pay the advisor $1,000 a year for their services. Under this arrangement, the advisor is incentivized to grow your account, because the more money you make, the more money the advisor makes. It is always good to have your incentives aligned with those advising you. You should, therefore, mostly avoid advisors who earn commissions from products they sell you because they are only incentivized to get the product sold and have little interest in how suitable that product is for you long term.

There are other investment professionals that hold themselves out as "financial advisors," or something similar, but do not always have to act as fiduciaries. For example, a traditional broker-dealer that is selling you mutual funds, stocks, bonds, and the like does not have to act as a fiduciary. Instead, broker-dealers can act under a lower standard called the "suitability standard," where they can sell clients products so long as those products are "suitable" for the client. They do not, however, have to act in the best interests of the client. Moreover, the suitability rule is so gray and all-encompassing that it basically makes almost all investment recommendations arguably suitable. A broker dealer can sell you a product, collect the commission, and go about their day without a worry or care about the long-term consequences for you. Non-fiduciary advisors should really be avoided as providers of long-term financial advice because their incentives are so poorly aligned. This is not to say that broker-dealers and other non-fiduciary advisors cannot play a role. They provide valuable services to the financial industry in a wide multitude of ways—we just would not recommend working with one as your trusted financial advisor.

One thing to watch out for are professionals acting in a dual capacity under both the suitability and fiduciary standards. Often, these are people working for large financial institutions that offer both broker-dealer and financial advisory services. What happens is that the advisor could be acting as a broker-dealer for some things, like when buying you a stock, under a suitability standard, and then as an advisor for other things, like when coming up with a financial plan, under a fiduciary standard. In other words, they can wear "two hats"—sometimes during the same call or meeting. While some of these advisors may be very good, you should ask which standard they are making recommendations to you under and always be aware of the difference. If they are trying to sell you specific products, including insurance-related products, you should ask how they are getting paid. Is it by commission? If so, then, whether they know it themselves or not, there is an inherent conflict of interest with your long-term prospects and goals—so beware!

Whether an advisor can add value depends on your level of investment sophistication, time constraints, behavioral biases, emotions, and other factors unique to each person. On average, we believe that a competent, fee-based advisor acting in a fiduciary manner can add real value. And even if you are knowledgeable about investments, an advisor might still be worthwhile if they serve in a coaching role, since we all likely need someone to bounce ideas off and speak with during both thick and thin times. Just think, Tiger Woods is arguably the greatest golfer of all time and he has always employed a swing coach. We can all use a little help.

◄ 21 ►

Investing for *You*

In his wonderful book *The Psychology of Money*, Morgan Housel pens a line that we use regularly with our clients: "You're *not* a spreadsheet. You're a person. A screwed up, emotional person."[1] We usually bring it up after we've educated the client about what the academic research says to do and the kind of investment strategy we recommend. So, let's first recapitulate what that is, so it is clear. Then we can get to the you-not-being-a-spreadsheet part. We distill our knowledge here so you can see how we work with clients in the real world.

SAVE AS MUCH AS YOU CAN

The first step for investing success is obvious, but also the hardest for most people: saving money. Housel again points out that:

> [B]uilding wealth has little to do with your income or investment returns, and lots to do with your savings rate . . . Wealth is just the

accumulated leftovers after you spend what you take in. And since you can build wealth without a high income, but have no chance of building wealth without a high savings rate, it's clear which one matters more.[2]

In our own practice, we often hear of people who have high incomes, with little to no investments to show for it. Conversely, we see people with modest incomes with impressive savings rates and investments. Your number-one focus should, therefore, be your savings rate. It is the most important variable you can control.

You should also save for saving's sake. You do not need a "goal." You do not have to save up for that down payment on a house and then stop saving. You also should not view saving money as something you are doing for retirement. Yes, you can max out your retirement savings for the year and keep saving money—nothing is stopping you! We counsel clients that, at some point, if you save enough money and control your spending, you can be financially free. Maybe you reach financial freedom well before your retirement age—great! You can keep working or do something else entirely. Wouldn't you like that choice? It's possible, but only through a robust savings habit. Try to build one and stick with it.

One way to do that is by automating your savings, such as through a weekly or monthly set withdrawal from your checking account to your investment account. You can start with a number that is barely noticeable and build up from there. Most people are shocked at how even small amounts of savings can accumulate over time—especially when the miracle of compounding happens. So, start saving. Save for no reason at all. And do it regularly. The rest should take care of itself.

DETERMINE YOUR OPTIMAL INVESTMENT INFRASTRUCTURE

Once you start saving money, you will next need to invest it. But before you can do that, you need to know *where* to invest it. This constitutes what we sometimes call the "nuts and bolts" of investing. It is tedious and often gets ignored, to most investors' detriment.

You should first pick a custodian, which is the financial institution that will physically—or, more accurately, digitally—hold your money. These include large, well-known institutions such as Charles Schwab, Fidelity, and TD Ameritrade.

After you've picked a custodian, you'll then need to open your investment accounts. You should consider which accounts are right for you based on your specific situation and goals. Work-sponsored retirement plans, like a 401(k), will stay under the control of your employer, but you may also consider opening your own retirement savings account (e.g., an IRA) through your chosen custodian if allowed under current IRS rules.

Next, consider whether you can take advantage of other tax-advantaged accounts, such as 529 College Savings Plans. After you have maxed out your tax-advantaged accounts, you'll then want to open and fund a taxable brokerage account for any excess funds. Depending on your situation, infrastructure planning can be simple or quite complicated. If you lean more toward the latter, we recommend working with a professional advisor to guide you through the process, since optimization here can add real value.

CREATE AN INVESTMENT PLAN

As we've discussed, a written investment plan is ideal, but regardless of whether it's in writing or not, you need something. The "Three Buckets Approach" we revealed in chapter nineteen is one simple solution to consider. Recall that Bucket One is your cash savings emergency account; Bucket Two is your mid-range, mid-risk account; and Bucket Three is your long-range, higher-risk account. We typically recommend clients first max out any tax-advantaged, long-term accounts first, which would include retirement accounts, or Bucket Three money. This is because these types of investments are higher risk and, therefore, need the most time to grow. We next advise clients to fill Bucket One, since running out of cash because of a job loss or other disaster can quickly ruin all the other buckets. After you have maximized Buckets Three and One, you can focus on filling Bucket Two.

Recall that Bucket One investments should aim for maximal safety. Your goal here is not to earn much return on the money, but to have it readily available if needed. You, therefore, cannot afford to take much, if any, risk and should instead try and get the risk-free rate of return to attempt to keep up with inflation. You should invest in short-term government bonds, money-market funds, and the like. Come up with a goal for the amount that you think you need for this account, and once you reach that number, stop. Bucket One is the only bucket that you can fill and then stop once you've reached your number, which is completely unique to you.

Bucket Two investments are not as easy to define, but we usually begin the conversation by considering the Global Market Portfolio from chapter eleven. Remember that a GMP is a market capitalization weighted index of all the world's investable assets and that it has great diversification. Through this portfolio, you own all the world's assets, including global bonds, stocks, real estate, and commodities. Because of the diversification, it is relatively safe and should not have major swings. And if you need money from this account, there should hopefully be some assets that are performing well at any given time that you can draw from.

Finally, Bucket Three is where all your longer-term investments should be housed. Things like retirement savings are an obvious candidate. Anything that you put into this bucket should be thought of as "gone" and unavailable to you—meaning that you cannot touch it for at least ten to fifteen years, preferably longer. If you need money, then you should first go to Bucket One, then Two, but never Three. Since Bucket Three should have the highest expected returns, your long-term investment success will primarily depend on your ability to allow it to grow unfettered. Your Bucket Three investments should be things like a well-diversified global stock portfolio, factors, or a GMP with leverage. The investments will be volatile—so buckle up. But, over time, they should earn you a great return, especially when the miracle of compound interest takes over.

HAVE A PLAN TO DEAL WITH YOUR BEHAVIOR

Now that you've created a plan and begun to implement it, your next focus should be in not screwing it up. Ruminate on your quirks, biases, and misconceptions, accept them, and learn to live with them. We find that many clients do this by following the Three Buckets Approach, since it allows you to see your money as different buckets of risk and utility instead of one blob of money. Thus, when you see your Bucket Three down 25 percent, but your Bucket One is even and earning interest, and your Bucket Two is flat or maybe even up a bit, you don't freak out. So, having a plan is a crucial way to control behavior.

We have also observed that proper diversification itself can be a great tool to curb one's worst impulses. For example, a client told us that his friend said "gold was about to go through the roof" and that he wanted to buy some quickly. Since he had already invested in the Global Market Portfolio, we told him that he already had some exposure to gold. If he were to buy more, he would tilt his portfolio toward a bet on gold. After considering this, he decided that since he already had some exposure, he was fine not buying any additional gold. When you own everything, you are less inclined to rush into the latest fads.

Finally, a fee-based, fiduciary financial advisor that you trust should be able to help curb your worst impulses, adding significant value throughout the years. Just make sure that you agree with and understand whatever financial plan they develop for you.

TWEAK YOUR PLAN TO FIT YOU

Up until now we have discussed a singular investment strategy and philosophy that we believe most investors should follow. Nevertheless, we realize that "you are not a spreadsheet," and even though an investment strategy might be optimal on paper, it may not be optimal for *you*. We, therefore, counsel clients to simply use our recommendations as a starting point from which they can deviate if need be. To make this clear, we will now look at two hypothetical client investors, who have very different life situations and risk tolerances, to show how the strategy can be tweaked for both.

Hypothetical client one is a married, young professional immigrant to the United States, with little debt and high income. He has two small children and great job security. He has no major upcoming expenses like a house down payment or big vacation. Along with his immediate family, he has a large extended family in the U.S. and wants to maximize his wealth so he can provide a better life for everyone. After extensive discussions with this client, we determine that he is risk tolerant, able to withstand substantial volatility, and interested in maximizing his investments' long-term growth potential.

Based on this example, we might normally recommend a client of his income and spending habits needing six months of living expenses in Bucket One, but here, we are comfortable lowering it to three months. We then decide that while we would normally want a client having exposure to the Global Market Portfolio in Bucket Two, this client wants added risk; therefore, we tilt his Bucket Two portfolio toward riskier assets by adding stocks and removing bonds and keeping his commodity exposure the same. Now his Bucket Two is riskier, but the expected returns are also higher. And while many clients should hold global stocks in Bucket Three, this client wants even more risk. We, therefore, recommend that he hold a leveraged Global Market Portfolio, which should earn him higher returns than a 100 percent equity portfolio. Finally, this client has an itch to try and hit a home run through speculative stock picking, and he enjoys researching various up-and-coming companies in his free time. To feed his active appetite, we carve out no more than 5 percent of his overall investment portfolio for active bets, allowing him to play the stock market. We stress to him, however, that he will likely underperform the market and might even lose all this money. Nevertheless, if this allows him to feed his active appetite without blowing up most of his portfolio, then it is a worthwhile tack to take. And if he enjoys it as a source of entertainment, even better. As you can see, this plan is custom-built for him, and he believes in it and will be happy if the plan meets its expected return targets. His risk appetite is satisfied, and he can even play around with some of his money to feed his active investing itch.

Let's look at another hypothetical client example. This time, imagine a middle-aged woman who is a mid-level manager in the oil and gas industry. She leans mostly on her advisor to guide her. Her main goal is to slowly build wealth over time. Most importantly, she hates seeing her accounts in the red—even for a day. Her industry is cyclical and prone to major booms and busts. She has been laid off twice already in her career and fears it could happen again during the next oil downturn. She is married with three kids in private school. She and her husband have a sizable mortgage on their house.

We determine that she is more risk averse than most. Although we explain to her that her investments will not always go upward in a straight line, she cannot bear the thought of being down more than 10 percent during a bad bear market or recession. We first recommend that she have an above-average Bucket One, due to her fears about being laid off in a cyclical industry. Moreover, she has a family relying on her unstable income and a big mortgage to pay. Therefore, instead of the typically advised six months of living expenses, we recommend she have a year-and-a-half of expenses saved. For Bucket Two, we advise that she keep the Global Market Portfolio intact and not tilt toward riskier assets as we did for hypothetical client one. For her retirement accounts in Bucket Three, we discuss the benefits of holding equities, but she still is not convinced she can handle the volatility. Another issue we discuss with this client is her investment exposure to oil and gas stocks. Because her income comes from that sector, any downturn there will doubly affect her if she holds oil and gas assets in her investments.

We, therefore, recommend that instead of holding 100 percent stocks, she try 70 percent global stocks, 20 percent global bonds, and 10 percent commodities, removing oil and gas exposure from all three asset classes. We further assure her that we will be by her side during the good times and bad and we will reevaluate the allocation in a year or two depending on how she handles market volatility.

As these examples show, everyone is different when it comes to money, investing, and risk. Indeed, the risk one should take depends not only on their unique personality, but also their station in life. Warren Buffett can afford to risk a million dollars on a speculative bet—if he loses it all, his life won't change one iota! But our hypothetical client number two probably could not tolerate losing $25,000 on a risky bet—even if she could handle it emotionally. Her income stream and family obligations would make her think twice.

Most importantly, these examples are meant to show that while both clients' planning starts from the same point, we have provided them with different investment plans based on their unique situations. The plans fit their needs and they both believe in them and are willing to let them run their course. But while their plans are different, their strategies are largely the same, both being based on our advice of trying to mostly replicate the market with low-cost, passively managed funds, and creating a financial plan based on the Three Buckets Approach. Similar overarching strategies on paper, but quite different plans in the real world. The most important thing is that you believe in the plan and are willing to stick with it through thick and thin. Nothing will matter more than that.

DETERMINE WHAT YOU NEED AND WHAT IS ENOUGH

Once you have a written plan you believe in, the rest should take care of itself. That's not to say that the plan cannot be tweaked or revisited—far from it. Indeed, you should think of your investment plan as a living document that changes with you. A plan for a young, twenty-something professional will likely look different than the plan for the older professional nearing retirement. As we've shown, two plans can be based on the same philosophy, but look markedly different. The more difficult task now, we think, is knowing when you have enough, as we explored in chapter eight.

There are no easy answers here, but we think most investors should try to determine their "number" as soon as possible. Your number is the amount of money you think you could live off in perpetuity. It's the nest egg that, once reached, in retirement or otherwise, would make you financially free. And because we all have different spending needs and habits, this number will be unique to you. So, while we cannot tell you the exact number for you, we can give some general advice.

A common rule of thumb is that you can safely withdraw 4 percent of your investments every year without having to worry about draining the principal. For example, if you have a $2,000,000 investment portfolio, you should be able to take out $80,000 a year without ever touching the $2,000,000. This assumes, however, that your $2,000,000 portfolio earns, on average, at least 4 percent a year. If it earns less than that, and you continue to take out the $80,000, then you run the risk of depleting your portfolio's principal.

We want to stress that this is simply a back-of-the-envelope, general rule of advice. Many advisors worry that 4 percent might be too much if future returns are lower than their historical average. We should also point out that if you begin withdrawals later in life, such as retirement, you can probably afford to drain some of the principal (e.g., the aforementioned $2,000,000), because you are closer to death than, say, a forty-five-year-old retiring very early. This is more art than science, unfortunately.

Nevertheless, we recommend at least trying to come up with a number that you are comfortable with, which is easiest to do by deciding on what you'd like to spend every year in perpetuity. Is it $50,000? $80,000? $400,000? Once you decide on a spending number, you can back into the amount you need to have for your principal. Finally, determine what kind of return you need to avoid touching that principal. Is it 4 percent;

2 percent; 5 percent? The lower the number, the more confident you should be in meeting your spending goals.

SIT BACK AND LET THE MIRACLE OF COMPOUND GROWTH WORK FOR YOU

Investing is simple, but not easy. If you save enough money and invest in low-cost, diversified funds that replicate the market, you should be able to meet your reasonable wealth accumulation goals. Controlling your behavior and having a solid financial plan that you believe in are critical to a successful investment journey. Do these things and the only thing left is

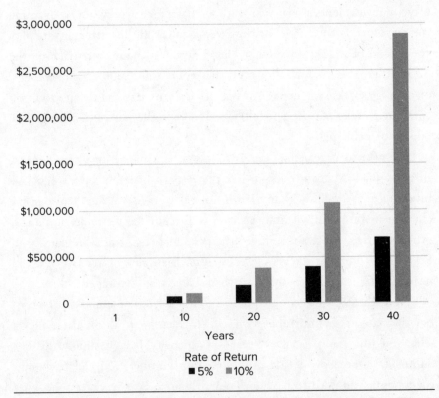

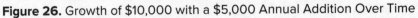

Figure 26. Growth of $10,000 with a $5,000 Annual Addition Over Time

to sit back and let the miracle of compound growth work its magic. In closing, Figure 26 shows the growth of $10,000, adding $5,000 every year, over various time periods and with either a 5 percent or 10 percent average annual return. This is meant to show what the miracle of compounding can do. These figures are modest and should be achievable if you can stick with it. So, don't delay—start saving and investing according to the data and get the market returns that are freely available for the taking. Close the gap and get your share!

◄ ACKNOWLEDGMENTS ►

We would first like to thank our families for supporting us throughout this endeavor. Julio thanks his wife, Claudia, and his children, Julito, Pau, and Rex. Cole thanks his wife, Rachel, and his two daughters, Elle and Lily. Juan Carlos thanks his wife, Hanna, and his daughter, Mathilda. We are grateful for your support. We'd also like to give thanks to our parents for giving us the support and opportunities in life to be where we are today.

Since we are registered investment advisors by day, we could not do our jobs without our wonderful clients. Thanks to all of you for entrusting us with your hard-earned money—we are truly grateful.

The entire editorial team at BenBella Books and Matt Holt Books have been fantastic to work with on this project and we are thankful for their efforts and assistance. Specifically, we'd like to thank Camille Cline for all her help with editing the book to get it to a final product. Thanks also to Katie Dickman, Brigid Pearson, Mallory Hyde, Kerri Stebbins, and Jessika Rieck.

We'd also like to thank our literary agent, Linda Konner, at Linda Konner Literary Agency for representing us and guiding us through this journey.

Thank you to our partners at Inscription Capital, including Brian Bova, Marc Oster, and Leeds Eustis. We are grateful for our partnership and your support in getting this book written.

Thank you to Julio's research assistant, Charlie Zhang, at Rice University for his help with data gathering and research.

Finally, we'd like to thank every reader of this book for taking the time to learn about investing to better yourself and your family's financial future. Whether you are a new immigrant to this country, or have had family here for generations, we hope that this book helps you to *Close the Gap & Get Your Share* of the American Dream.

Julio, Cole & Juan Carlos
January 2023

◄ NOTES ►

INTRODUCTION

1. Dedrick Asante-Muhammad and Sally Sim, "Racial Wealth Snapshot: Immigration and the Racial Wealth Divide," National Community Reinvestment Coalition, September 17, 2020, https://ncrc.org/racial-wealth-snapshot-immigration-and-the-racial-wealth-divide/.

CHAPTER 1

1. Katherine Gustafson, "The Percentage of Businesses That Fail and How to Boost Your Chances of Success," LendingTree, May 2, 2022, https://www.lendingtree.com/business/small/failure-rate/.

CHAPTER 2

1. Robert G. Hagstrom, "What Is the Difference Between Investing and Speculation?" Enterprising Investor, CFA Institute, February 27, 2013, https://blogs.cfainstitute.org/investor/2013/02/27/what-is-the-difference-between-investing-and-speculation-2/.
2. Benjamin Graham, *The Intelligent Investor: A Book of Practical Counsel*, rev. ed. (New York: HarperBusiness Essentials, 2003).
3. Hagstrom, "What Is the Difference Between Investing and Speculation?"
4. John C. Bogle, *Common Sense on Mutual Funds: New Imperatives for the Intelligent Investor*, 10th anniversary ed. (Hoboken, NJ: Wiley, 2010), 54–55.
5. Adam P. Brownlee, "Warren Buffett: Be Fearful When Others Are Greedy," Investopedia, November 30, 2022, https://www.investopedia.com/articles/investing/012116/warren-buffett-be-fearful-when-others-are-greedy.asp.

6. Burton G. Malkiel, *A Random Walk Down Wall Street: The Time-Tested Strategy for Successful Investing* (New York: Norton, 2019), 28.
7. Wayne Duggan, "If You're Day Trading, You Will Probably Lose Money: Here's Why," *Markets Insider*, July 30, 2021, https://markets.businessinsider.com/news/stocks/if-you-re-day-trading-you-will-probably-lose-money-here-s-why-1030667770.
8. Bob Pisani, "Attention Robinhood Power Users: Most Day Traders Lose Money," CNBC, November 20, 2020, https://www.cnbc.com/2020/11/20/attention-robinhood-power-users-most-day-traders-lose-money.html.
9. Ibid.
10. Malkiel, *A Random Walk*, 30.
11. Ibid.
12. Ibid., 33.
13. Ibid., 32–33.
14. Wharton Executive Education, "Active vs. Passive Investing: Which Approach Offers Better Returns?," The Wharton School, The University of Pennsylvania, accessed February 28, 2023, https://executiveeducation.wharton.upenn.edu/thought-leadership/wharton-wealth-management-initiative/wmi-thought-leadership/active-vs-passive-investing-which-approach-offers-better-returns/.

CHAPTER 3

1. Romans 7:15, New International Version.
2. Ulrike Malmendier and Stefan Nagel, "Depression Babies: Do Macroeconomic Experiences Affect Risk Taking?" *Quarterly Journal of Economics* 126, no. 1 (February 2011): 373–416, doi:10.1093/qje/qjq004.
3. Philipp Hillenbrand et al, "Traditional Company, New Businesses: The Pairing That Can Ensure an Incumbent's Survival," McKinsey & Company, accessed January 18, 2023, PDF file, https://www.mckinsey.com/~/media/McKinsey/Industries/Electric%20Power%20and%20Natural%20Gas/Our%20Insights/Traditional%20company%20new%20businesses%20The%20pairing%20that%20can%20ensure%20an%20incumbents%20survival/Traditional-company-new-businesses-VF.pdf.
4. Jody Agius Vallejo and Lisa Keister, "Immigrants and Wealth Attainment: Migration, Inequality, and Integration," *Journal of Ethnic and Migration Studies* 46, no. 18 (2020): 3745–61, doi:10.1080/1369183X.2019.1592872.
5. Marcel Zeelenberg and Rik Pieters, "A Theory of Regret Regulation 1.0," *Journal of Consumer Psychology* 17, no. 1 (January 2007): 3–18, doi:10.1207/s15327663jcp1701_3.
6. Daniel Kahneman, *Thinking, Fast and Slow* (New York: Farrar, Straus and Giroux, 2013), 255.
7. Mark J. Perry, "More Evidence That It's Really Hard to 'Beat the Market' Over Time, 95% of Finance Professionals Can't Do It," American Enterprise Institute, October 18, 2018, https://www.aei.org/carpe-diem/more-evidence-that-its-really-hard-to-beat-the-market-over-time-95-of-finance-professionals-cant-do-it/.

8. William J. Bernstein, *The Four Pillars of Investing: Lessons for Building a Winning Portfolio* (New York: McGraw-Hill, 2010), 167.
9. Ibid., 167–68.
10. Ibid., 169.
11. Ibid., 168.

CHAPTER 4

1. Neil Bhutta, Andrew C. Chang, Lisa J. Dettling, and Joanne W. Hsu, "Disparities in Wealth by Race and Ethnicity in the 2019 Survey of Consumer Finances," FEDS Notes, Washington: Board of Governors of the Federal Reserve System, September 28, 2020, https://doi.org/10.17016/2380-7172.2797.
2. Richard Feloni, "'The Big Short' Author Michael Lewis Tells Us What Scares Him Most About Trump and Wall Street—and Why His New Book Is 'a Love Story Without the Sex,'" *Insider*, December 18, 2016, https://www.businessinsider.com/michael-lewis-talks-about-the-undoing-project-trump-and-wall-street-2016-12.
3. Morgan Housel, *The Psychology of Money: Timeless Lessons on Wealth, Greed, and Happiness* (Hampshire, Great Britain: Harriman House, 2020), 49.
4. Ibid., 50.
5. Robert H. Frank, *Success and Luck: Good Fortune and the Myth of Meritocracy* (Princeton, NJ: Princeton University Press, 2016).
6. Ibid., 7
7. Ibid., 8.
8. Ibid., 11.

CHAPTER 5

1. Kahneman, *Thinking, Fast and Slow*, 256–57.
2. Malkiel, *A Random Walk*, 193.
3. Ibid.
4. Ibid., 193–94.
5. Ibid., 194–95.
6. Ibid., 195.

CHAPTER 6

1. Brian O'Connell, "The True Cost of Investing: Opportunity Cost," *Forbes Advisor*, March 29, 2021, https://www.forbes.com/advisor/investing/opportunity-cost/.
2. Richard Rosen, "Using Benchmarks in Investing," Investopedia, September 28, 2022, https://www.investopedia.com/articles/investing/032516/how-use-benchmark-evaluate-portfolio.asp.

3. "SEC Files Complaint for Investment Fraud," *Norris McLaughlin* (blog), accessed January 18, 2023, https://norrismclaughlin.com/blogs/ib/category/sec-complaint -investment-fraud.

4. Benn Eifert, "On Bullshit in Investing," *Noahpinion* (blog), July 11, 2022, https:// noahpinion.substack.com/p/on-bullshit-in-investing.

5. Ibid.

6. Ibid.

7. Ibid.

8. Ibid.

CHAPTER 7

1. Steven Pinker, *Enlightenment Now: The Case for Reason, Science, Humanism, and Progress* (New York: Viking, 2018), 4.

2. Matt Ridley, *The Rational Optimist: How Prosperity Evolves* (New York: Harper Perennial, 2011), 14.

3. Ibid., 11.

4. Philippe Aghion, Céline Antonin, and Simon Bunel, *The Power of Creative Destruction: Economic Upheaval and the Wealth of Nations* (Cambridge, MA: Belknap Press, 2021), 1.

5. Ibid.

6. Max Fisher, "Is the World Really Falling Apart, or Does It Just Feel That Way?" *New York Times*, July 12, 2022, https://www.nytimes.com/2022/07/12/world/interpreter -world-falling-apart.html.

7. Salim S. Virani et al., "Heart Disease and Stroke Statistics—2021 Update," American Heart Association, January 27, 2021, doi:10.1161/CIR.0000000000000950.

8. Fisher, "Is the World Really Falling Apart, or Does It Just Feel That Way?"

9. Adam Wong, "Every Major (and Minor) US Stock Market Crash Since 1950," The Fifth Person, March 2, 2020, https://fifthperson.com/every-us-stock-market-crash -since-the-1950s/.

CHAPTER 8

1. John C. Bogle, *Enough: True Measures of Money, Business, and Life* (New York: Wiley, 2009), 230.

2. Morgan Housel, "Wealth vs. Getting Wealthier," *Collab Fund* (blog), June 28, 2022, https://www.collaborativefund.com/blog/wealth-vs-getting-wealthier/.

3. Housel, *Psychology of Money*, 41.

4. Ibid.

5. Ibid., 42–43.

6. Housel, "Wealth vs. Getting Wealthier."

NOTES

CHAPTER 11

1. Andrew W. Lo and Stephen R. Foerster, *In Pursuit of the Perfect Portfolio* (Princeton, NJ: Princeton University Press, 2021), 21.
2. Ibid., 25.
3. Ibid., 27.
4. Ibid., 32.
5. Ibid., 77.
6. Ibid., 81.
7. Ibid.
8. Ibid., 77–78.
9. Ibid.
10. Ibid., 93 (emphasis added).
11. Ibid., 114.
12. Ibid., 123.
13. Ibid., 132.
14. Ibid., 134–39.
15. William J. Bernstein, *If You Can: How Millennials Can Get Rich Slowly* (Efficient Frontier Publications, 2014).

CHAPTER 12

1. "What Is Factor Investing?" BlackRock, accessed January 19, 2023, https://www.blackrock.com/us/individual/investment-ideas/what-is-factor-investing.
2. Ibid.
3. "Leverage: A Thoughtful Approach," J.P. Morgan, PDF file, accessed January 19, 2023, http://graphics8.nytimes.com/packages/pdf/business/Leverage_A_thoughtful_approach.pdf.
4. Paul Sullivan, "Some Dos and Don'ts About Leverage, Simply Put," *New York Times*, March 9, 2012, https://www.nytimes.com/2012/03/10/your-money/some-dos-and-donts-about-leverage.html.

CHAPTER 13

1. Adam Hayes, "Volatility: Meaning in Finance and How It Works with Stocks," Investopedia, August 23, 2022, https://www.investopedia.com/terms/v/volatility.asp.
2. Malkiel, *A Random Walk*, 26.
3. Ibid., 157–58.

CHAPTER 16

1. Will Kenton, "What Is Behavioral Economics? Theories, Goals, and Applications," Investopedia, January 16, 2023, https://www.investopedia.com/terms/b/behavioral economics.asp.
2. Richard H. Thaler, *Misbehaving: The Making of Behavioral Economics* (New York: Norton, 2015), 5.
3. Ibid.
4. Ibid., 7, 9.
5. "The Sveriges Riksbank Prize in Economic Sciences in Memory of Alfred Nobel 2017," The Nobel Prize, accessed January 19, 2023, https://www.nobelprize.org /prizes/economic-sciences/2017/summary/.
6. Thaler, *Misbehaving*, 215.
7. Ibid., 217.
8. Ibid.
9. Ibid., 240.
10. Ibid., 236.
11. Ibid., 251.

CHAPTER 17

1. James Surowiecki, *The Wisdom of Crowds* (New York: Anchor Books, 2005), xxi–xxiii.
2. Ibid., xii–xiv.
3. Ibid., xv.
4. Ibid., 7–8.
5. Ibid., 10.
6. Ibid., 230–31.
7. Ibid., 241–43.
8. Ibid., 243.
9. Ibid., 248.
10. Ibid., 249.
11. Ibid., 251.

CHAPTER 18

1. Terrance Odean, "Making Smart Financial Decisions," University of California Berkeley Haas School of Business, PDF file, accessed January 19, 2023, https:// faculty.haas.berkeley.edu/odean/Video%20Transcripts/Individual%20investors %20part%201%20heuristics.pdf.

2. Pinker, *Enlightenment Now*, 26.
3. Kahneman, *Thinking, Fast and Slow*, 202.
4. Heather Long, "Japan's Stock Market Peaked 25 Years Ago Today," CNN, December 29, 2014, https://money.cnn.com/2014/12/29/investing/japan-nikkei-stocks-1989-peak/.
5. "International Stocks: Why Bother?" BlackRock, PDF file, accessed January 19, 2023, https://www.blackrock.com/us/financial-professionals/literature/investor-education/why-bother-with-international-stocks.pdf.
6. Bernstein, *The Four Pillars of Investing*, 167.
7. Kahneman, *Thinking, Fast and Slow*, 119–20.
8. Ibid., 129–30.
9. Ibid., 137.
10. Malkiel, *A Random Walk*, 117.
11. Ibid., 157–58.

CHAPTER 19

1. "The Uncommon Average: Long-Term Context on Annual Returns," Atlas Wealth Advisers, May 9, 2019, https://www.atlaswealthadvisors.com/news/the-uncommon-average-long-term-context-on-annual-returns.

CHAPTER 20

1. "Advisors Add 2.88% in Value, Study Finds," *Advisor's Edge*, May 7, 2020, https://www.advisor.ca/my-practice/conversations/advisors-add-2-88-in-value-study-finds/.
2. Francis M. Kinniry Jr. et al., "Putting a Value on your Value: Quantifying Vanguard Advisor's Alpha," Vanguard, PDF file, accessed January 19, 2023, https://advisors.vanguard.com/iwe/pdf/IARCQAA.pdf.
3. Ibid.
4. Marc M. Kramer, "Financial Advice and Individual Investor Portfolio Performance," *Financial Management* 41, no. 2 (2012): 424, https://www.jstor.org/stable/41493871.
5. Ibid.

CHAPTER 21

1. Housel, *Psychology of Money*, 113.
2. Ibid., 103.

APPENDIX I

1. Jason Fernando, "What Is a Commodity and Understanding Its Role in the Stock Market," Investopedia, July 31, 2022, https://www.investopedia.com/terms/c/commodity.asp.

◄ APPENDIX I ►

Definitions and Concepts[*]

Assets. Assets are resources with value, which an owner, whether it be a corporation, individual, or government, expects to receive a future benefit. Defining an asset is sometimes tricky, since many investors believe that, to truly be an asset, it must generate positive cash flows. Therefore, stocks and bonds paying a dividend or interest would be an asset, while commodities, which produce no cash flow, would not be considered an asset. Indeed, while many people believe their primary residence is an asset, some would disagree, since it is not paying you a cash flow. Alternatively, a rental property that you lease out would be considered an asset, since it produces a cash flow. Assets can be divided between real assets and financial assets, which are both defined herein.

Benchmarks. A benchmark is a standard or measure that can be used to analyze the allocation, risk, and return of a given investment. Investors measure their investment performance by comparing their investments to a designated benchmark. For example, an investor investing in large, publicly traded U.S. corporations would use the S&P 500 index as his benchmark. If the investor purchases a portfolio of ten stocks and gets a 10 percent return, how did the investor perform? Well, we cannot answer that question without knowing what the benchmark did—here, the S&P 500 index. If the index returned 5 percent over the period, we could say that the

---

* Many of these definitions and concepts have been formulated with reference to Investopedia.com, which is a great, and free, resource for many different types of investment- and financial-related terms and concepts.

investor "outperformed the benchmark." If the index returned 15 percent, however, we could say that the investor "underperformed the benchmark." Importantly, we would not compare the investor's performance with the bond market's index. That's because bonds and stocks have different risk and return characteristics and are used for different reasons by investors. It would not be fair, and would not make sense, to say that an investor who got a 10 percent return on their ten-stock portfolio outperformed the bond index's 4 percent return. Bonds are lower-risk investments and, therefore, should have lower returns than stocks over the long term. In other words, their risk and return characteristics are not comparable. This goes for riskier investments too. For example, investing in venture capital (VC)—which are early-stage, private startup companies—is riskier than investing in the S&P 500. Therefore, if you invest in VC, your benchmark would not be the S&P, but instead the VC market average. So, it would be incorrect to say that your VC investment that returned 15 percent outperformed the S&P's return of 10 percent. To know how your VC investment did, you'd need to compare it to the VC benchmark.

Bonds. Bonds are debt instruments issued by governments, corporations, and other organizations. A bond is a type of legal contract whereby the investor lends money to an entity in exchange for a stated rate of return—called a "coupon," which just means interest—over a specified period. At the end of that period, called the bond's "maturity," the principal amount is returned to the bond investor. Thus, the return on a bond is simply all the coupon payments received, plus return of principal at maturity. For example, a company might issue a ten-year bond with a 4 percent coupon, paid annually. If the investor buys $1,000 worth of bonds and holds them for ten years, the investor will receive $40 a year for ten years, and then would receive the principal of $1,000 back at year 10. Importantly, a bond is a legal contract promising repayment. The only way the investor will not get paid back is if the bond issuer defaults, typically because of bankruptcy. In that case, the bondholders will be paid back first, and then the shareholders, if there's any money left over. Bonds are, therefore, less risky than stocks. In addition, bonds carry no upside potential. If you hold the bond to its maturity and the borrower doesn't default, you know the maximum amount of return you will get—the stated coupon payments, plus principal.

Bond Yields. Many bonds are publicly traded and have market values that change every trading day. That's because the value of the bond's coupon, or interest, payments will change based on the economic environment. A bond paying 4 percent may be valuable when inflation is low, say around 2 percent, and stocks are performing poorly, say during a recession; therefore, people may be willing to pay a premium for the bond if they want safe, steady cash flow. That same bond, however, might be less valuable if inflation is 9 percent, or if the stock market is performing well and returning 12 percent. In that case, a bond paying 4 percent doesn't seem so great. Moreover, newly issued bonds on the marketplace might be paying more than 4 percent due to rising interest rates, or other reasons. In that case, investors will only purchase the existing bond paying 4 percent if it's offered at a discount. So, the price of the bond might go down until it attracts buyers. When the bond goes up or down in price, this affects the "yield" the bond is paying. A bond's yield is simply the coupon amount divided by the bond's price. A bond's price and its yield are inversely related. Therefore, when a bond's price drops, its yield increases. So, if the ten-year bond with an initial $1,000 principal value is paying a 4 percent coupon, but its price drops on the market to $900, the bond's yield will now be 4.44 percent.

Bull and Bear Markets. A bull market is one that is rising or is expected to rise. "Bulls" refers to traders and investors who believe that the market will rise in the future—they are said to be "bullish." A bear market is one that is falling or expected to fall. "Bears" refers to traders and investors who believe that the market will fall in the future—they are said to be "bearish."

Capital Gains vs. Ordinary Income. Understanding the difference between capital gains and ordinary income is critical for investor performance. Capital gains refer to the price appreciation of an investment. For example, if you buy Apple stock for $100 and sell it five years later for $500, you have a capital gain of $400. Importantly, capital gains are taxed at a lower rate than ordinary income by the U.S. government. What's more, you can have short-term capital gains, when the investment is held for less than a year, and long-term capital gains, when the investment is held for more than a year. Short-term capital gains are taxed at a lower rate than long-term capital gains. Ordinary income refers to investment income that is taxed at the investor's normal income tax rate. Dividends earned from stocks and interest/coupon payments from bonds are considered ordinary income.

Commodities. A commodity is "a basic good used in commerce that.is interchangeable with other goods of the same type." Commodities are typically raw materials that are used as inputs for producing goods and services.[1] Commodities include energy products like oil and natural gas. They also include agricultural products like cotton, coffee, lumber, corn, and cattle. Metals, like gold, silver, platinum, and copper, are also commodities. Importantly, unlike most stocks and all bonds, commodities do not have cash flows. This means the value of a commodity is entirely dependent on supply and demand. As an investor, you can only make money from a commodity by selling it to another for more than you bought it for. Gold, silver, and a few other commodities, such as platinum, have historically had values above and beyond their industrial worth. For example, gold has some intrinsic value for use in electronics and jewelry, but gold's market value has traditionally been far greater than its intrinsic value. That's because humans have, for millennia, thought of gold as a store of value.

Compound Interest. Compound interest is "interest on interest," which compounds, or multiplies, the money invested. Compound interest accelerates the more compounding periods, or time, that there are, which is why compound interest really becomes impressive only after many decades of growth.

Diversification. Diversification refers to an investment strategy of holding a wide mix of investments within a portfolio. Diversification has been proven mathematically to reduce risk without sacrificing return in certain instances. It hinges on the notion that risk can be better managed by spreading it out—the adage of not "having all your eggs in one basket." Investors can diversify across securities (i.e., by owning numerous stocks instead of a few), across asset types (i.e., by owning stocks, bonds, commodities, and real estate), by sectors (i.e., having exposure to energy, industrials, technology, healthcare, etc.), and by countries and regions (i.e., having exposure to Europe, Latin America, Asia, Africa, etc.).

Exchange Traded Funds (ETF). ETFs are like a mutual fund in that they pool investor money together to then be managed by professional managers. Unlike mutual funds, however, ETFs can be purchased on exchanges the same way that an individual security like a stock is. That means that you can trade ETFs during the trading day, unlike a mutual fund. Like mutual funds, ETFs come in many different shapes and sizes, from passively managed index funds to actively managed funds.

Factors. Factors refer to characteristics of securities that have been, or are believed to be, drivers of return. Examples include things like value, size, momentum, quality, and volatility.

Financial Assets. Financial assets are those that get their value from a contractual right or ownership claim. In contrast to real assets, they do not physically exist. Examples include stocks, bonds, mutual funds, bank deposits, futures, and options.

Fundamental Security Analysis. This concept refers to determining an asset's intrinsic, true, or real value by examining a company's current and future financial prospects. Fundamental analysts believe they can determine a company's true, intrinsic value and then, based upon that company's current share price, decide whether it is a good buy or a good sell.

Hedge Funds. Hedge funds are private limited partnerships that pool investors' money and are managed by professional managers. Most hedge funds are actively managed and seek to beat their benchmarks. Hedge funds charge more money than passive funds because they are trying to beat the market. Hedge funds typically require high minimum investments, and many are not available to you unless you already have significant wealth. Many hedge funds are quite risky, buying and selling individual assets regularly.

Index Funds. An index fund is a type of mutual fund or exchange traded fund (ETF) that is constructed to match the components and performance of a financial market index, like the S&P 500. These funds seek to track their chosen index at a low cost. Index funds allow investors to passively invest in their chosen market to receive that market's return. Index funds typically outperform most actively managed funds (those trying to beat the market) over long time horizons.

Inflation. Inflation is the change, over a specified period, in the price of goods and services. Inflation is typically measured by government agencies, which look at the average price of a defined basket of goods and services over time. When goods and services inflate over time, that means the same amount of money will not buy the same amount of goods and services, on average. Not all goods and services inflate at the same rate; and some may deflate, or go down, over time. For example, the average price of things like televisions and computers has deflated over time, while the average price of things like healthcare, education, and housing has inflated over time. While inflation might sound like a negative, it is a crucial component of modern, capitalist economies. Indeed, the U.S. government, along with most others, mandates that their central banks try to create about 2 percent inflation every year. This is because the government wants people to do two things with their money: (1) spend it in the economy, since one person's spendings are another person's income, or (2) invest it with someone else who can put the funds to more productive use. Inflation running at 2 percent is seen as the sweet spot for giving people enough time to either spend the money or invest. Because inflation erodes the value of the currency, it means that people should not hoard cash, which is bad for the economy. High inflation is negative for an economy, however, because it can cause a runaway spiral that is hard to contain, where people's incomes are no longer sufficient to buy the goods and services they need. But deflation is likely even worse since nobody will want to spend or invest if their cash is worth *more* in the future.

Markets. A market is a place—whether physical or digital—where buyers and sellers come together to buy and sell goods, services, information, currency, and the like. In accordance with supply and demand, the number of buyers and sellers for a particular asset in a market will determine the price of that asset. So, if there are more buyers than sellers, the price of the asset will go up, which should attract more sellers. And if there are more sellers than buyers, the price of the asset will go down, which should attract more buyers. When most people hear the word "market" they typically think of the stock market, but there are markets for almost everything you can think of, including bonds, commodities, houses, and cryptocurrencies.

Mutual Funds. Mutual funds broadly refer to funds that take investors' money, pool them together, and invest them. They are managed by professional managers. Mutual funds have many different styles, strategies, and investment mandates. An index fund is a type of mutual fund, but so are actively managed funds that try to beat their index benchmark. You can invest in many different types of mutual funds, such as those focusing on replicating a particular market, sector, region, or country, or those that are actively managed—for example, a technology growth fund. Mutual funds do not have daily liquidity, like many publicly traded assets and ETFs, and can only be traded once a day after the market closes.

Opportunity Costs. Opportunity costs are all the benefits an investor misses out on when choosing one investment over another—the "road not taken." As investors, we only have a finite amount of money with which to invest. We must make choices and live with them. But blindly ignoring opportunity costs gets investors into trouble. Keeping in mind what you could have done with your money, or what you will give up when choosing one investment over all the others, is a crucial skill to develop as an investor. For example, many investors like purchasing rental properties, fixing them up, and renting them out. They relish the monthly cash flows and expect the property to appreciate nicely over time. But few take the time to compare whether the opportunity costs were worth it. Did your investment do well because of something unique to you or the property, or did the entire housing market appreciate? And what if the entire housing market appreciated more than your rental house? What if you could have taken less risk and earned more return by investing in the entire housing market through a low-cost, publicly traded single-family housing real estate fund? What if you could have done this without any work, like making repairs, paying taxes, and collecting rent? Were the opportunity costs you gave up worth it?

Passive vs. Active Investing. Passive investing means the investor looks to mimic the return of a certain market. This is usually accomplished by purchasing a low-cost index fund that replicates that market. For example, if an investor wants to match the return of the S&P 500, which is a well-known market index in the United States that tracks the stocks of the largest five hundred public companies in the country, the investor will buy an S&P 500 index fund. By investing in that fund, the investor is guaranteed to receive the return provided by the S&P 500, less any fees, costs, and taxes. On the other hand, an active investor looks to outperform the return of a certain market. Therefore, taking the S&P 500 example, an active investor will buy and sell one or more stocks, trying to pick stocks that do better than the S&P 500 index. Further, if an investor purchases an individual stock—say Amazon, for example— that investor is implicitly betting, whether they know it or not, that Amazon will do better than the S&P 500 index. Because, if they didn't believe that, why not just buy the index? Market timing strategies are also an attempt to outperform the index whereby investors try to be in the market for the good times and out for the bad. It's important to keep the difference between active and passive in mind when looking at funds, since a fund will either be active or passive in style. Active funds will charge investors more money, sometimes a lot more, for the chance to outperform. Passive investing is simple and low cost, while active investing is expensive, typically requiring many smart analysts and managers who are constantly trying to outperform.

Portfolio. An investment portfolio is simply a collection of different kinds of investments, which could include stocks, bonds, real estate, cash, and commodities. Many investors refer to all their investments as a singular portfolio, while others may split up their investments into different portfolios depending on their investment strategy and organization preferences.

Private Equity. Generally, this refers to investments made into privately held companies. Therefore, investing in a startup or into a friend's new company can technically be thought of as private equity. However, the term is usually used in reference to investing into a fund managed by a private equity firm. Private equity firms generally buy an equity stake in a portfolio of private companies, typically with debt, to effect positive change in the companies. These are called leveraged buyouts. Venture capital is technically a type of private equity but is usually thought of as a separate type of investment.

Real Assets. Real assets are tangible, physical assets that get their value from their physical properties. Examples include raw land, developed real estate, and commodities.

Real Estate Investment Trusts (REITs). A REIT is a corporation that owns, operates, or finances real estate. REITs are similar to mutual funds in that they pool investor money to be managed by professional managers. Most REITs are publicly traded like stocks, which makes them very liquid. You can buy REITs for many different types of real estate assets, like single family housing, multi-family housing, industrial, medical, and hotels.

Securities. Securities refer to fungible, negotiable financial instruments that can be freely bought and sold in private or public markets. Securities include stocks and bonds, as well as other instruments that derive their value from another asset, like futures and options.

Stocks. Stocks, also called "equities" or "shares," are pieces of ownership in a corporation. When you own a piece of stock, you are a part owner of that company. That means you get to participate in the company's growth or decline. Stocks will typically pay the stockholder a dividend from the company's profits. A dividend is a cash payment to the stockholder on a per-share basis. So, a company may pay a $1 per-share dividend per quarter. If you owned one hundred shares of that company's stock, you'd receive $100 in cash in your account every quarter. You can then choose to reinvest that dividend back into the company by purchasing more stock or to take the cash. Some companies, particularly companies that are growing quickly, will not pay a dividend, and will instead reinvest any profits back into the company to catalyze growth. In that case, the company's share price should hopefully increase if such growth is realized. To the stock investor, the only thing that matters is the "total return" with Total Return = Dividends + Share Price Appreciation. It does not matter, therefore, whether the company pays a dividend if the price of the stock appreciates equal to or greater than what the dividend would have been. Importantly, stocks offer no promise of return. The investor gets to participate in any upside, but if the company goes bankrupt, the stock could become worthless. That's because, in bankruptcy, the company's bondholders are paid out before any stockholders.

Systematic vs. Idiosyncratic Risk. Systematic risk refers to risks that affect most, if not all, assets and which largely cannot be diversified away. They include things like recessions, pandemics, war, and inflation. Idiosyncratic risks are those that affect individual assets and sectors, and which can be diversified away, in whole or in part, through sufficient diversification. They include things like a CEO making a bad decision, an employee defrauding the company, or a major lawsuit. It is key to understand that, pre-investment, investors should only expect to be compensated (i.e., to receive positive investment returns) for the systematic risks they take. That is because if you can diversify a risk away, you should not expect to be compensated for taking the risk. For example, if you invest in ExxonMobil and they perform poorly, other energy companies will take Exxon's business and market share. You could have received the energy sector's return by diversifying and owning the entire energy market, including ExxonMobil. You suffered idiosyncratic risk by choosing just Exxon. This does not mean, however, that you cannot get lucky and earn an outsized return by investing in a single company. In that case, the idiosyncratic risk that could have occurred did not, and the company you chose outperformed the market for that time period. The more diversified your portfolio, the less idiosyncratic risk it should have, leaving you only with systematic risk. Because you should not expect to be compensated for taking idiosyncratic risk, you should try to have maximum diversification to mostly eliminate it.

Tax-Deferred Accounts. Tax-deferred accounts are those that are given special tax treatment by the U.S. government. Some accounts, like many retirement accounts, are funded with "pre-tax" money, meaning that whatever money you put into such accounts will be subtracted from your income that year. For example, if you make $100,000 a year and put $20,000 into a tax-deferred 401(k) account, you will only be taxed by the U.S. government as if you were making $80,000 that year—a significant savings.

Technical Security Analysis. This concept refers to determining whether an asset will go up or down in price based on historical movements, like price, and historical market data, like trading volume. Those utilizing this technique call themselves "chartists." They look primarily at the past movements of stock prices to decide whether to buy or sell.

Venture Capital. Generally, this refers to investments made into privately held, early-stage companies, typically referred to as startup companies. Venture capital firms will invest in a basket of startups with the hopes that a few strike it big.

◄ APPENDIX II ►
Further Reading

The following are books we recommend if you want to learn more about investing, economics, risk, investor behavior, and more. They are listed here in no particular order.

A Random Walk Down Wall Street: The Time-Tested Strategy for Successful Investing, by Burton Malkiel

The Psychology of Money: Timeless Lessons on Wealth, Greed, and Happiness, by Morgan Housel

The Investment Answer: Learn to Manage Your Money & Protect Your Financial Future, by Daniel C. Goldie and Gordon S. Murray

The Little Book of Common Sense Investing: The Only Way to Guarantee Your Fair Share of Stock Market Returns, by John C. Bogle

The Wisdom of Crowds: Why the Many Are Smarter Than the Few and How Collective Wisdom Shapes Business, Economics, Societies and Nations, by James Surowiecki

Thinking, Fast and Slow, by Daniel Kahneman

The Four Pillars of Investing: Lessons for Building a Winning Portfolio, by William J. Bernstein

The Rational Optimist: How Prosperity Evolves, by Matt Ridley

Your Money & Your Brain: How the New Science of Neuroeconomics Can Help Make You Rich, by Jason Zweig

The Great Depression: A Diary, by Benjamin Roth

Success and Luck: Good Fortune and the Myth of Meritocracy, by Robert H. Frank

In Pursuit of the Perfect Portfolio: The Stories, Voices, and Key Insights of the Pioneers Who Shaped the Way We Invest, by Andrew W. Lo and Stephen R. Foerster

FURTHER READING

Winning the Loser's Game: Timeless Strategies for Successful Investing, by Charles D. Ellis

Simple Wealth, Inevitable Wealth: How You and Your Financial Advisor Can Grow Your Fortune in Stock Mutual Funds, by Nick Murray

Enlightenment Now: The Case for Reason, Science, Humanism, and Progress, by Steven Pinker

Devil Take the Hindmost: A History of Financial Speculation, by Edward Chancellor

Against the Gods: The Remarkable Story of Risk, by Peter L. Bernstein

Enough: True Measures of Money, Business, and Life, by John C. Bogle

Common Sense on Mutual Funds: New Imperatives for the Intelligent Investor, by John C. Bogle

Stay the Course: The Story of Vanguard and the Index Revolution, by John C. Bogle

The Delusions of Crowds: Why People Go Mad in Groups, by William J. Bernstein

The Power of Creative Destruction: Economic Upheaval and the Wealth of Nations, by Céline Antonin, Simon Bunel, and Philippe Aghion

Narrative Economics: How Stories Go Viral & Drive Major Economic Events, by Robert J. Shiller

Where Are the Customers' Yachts?: or a Good Hard Look at Wall Street, by Fred Schwed Jr.

The Black Swan: The Impact of the Highly Improbable, by Nassim Nicholas Taleb

Fooled by Randomness: The Hidden Role of Chance in Life and in the Markets, by Nassim Nicholas Taleb

Misbehaving: The Making of Behavioral Economics, by Richard H. Thaler

The Myth of the Rational Market: A History of Risk, Reward, and Delusion on Wall Street, by Justin Fox

◄ INDEX ►

ABOUT THE AUTHORS

Julio Cacho, PhD

Dr. Julio Cacho is the founder and chief investment officer of Quantor Capital, a Houston-based asset manager, and the co-chief investment officer of Inscription Capital, a registered investment-advisory firm managing over $1.4 billion. He provides highly personalized financial advice to family offices, financial advisors, bankers, asset managers, institutions, and wealthy individuals on their investment portfolios and financial products.

Julio was born in Puebla, Mexico, and after watching many peers and acquaintances fall victim to the common Mexican idiom "After the third generation, you lose all your money," he dedicated his life to teaching others about generational wealth and effective investment strategies. He has more than twenty years of combined professional and academic experience in financial statistical research, optimal investment selection, and investment-risk management.

Before founding Quantor Capital, Julio was a director of risk and performance at Ziff Brothers Investments, a private multibillion-dollar family office in New York City. At Ziff, Julio developed investment and hedging strategies as a quantitative researcher and implemented risk-management strategies.

He is currently a faculty member at Rice University and has taught at Princeton University, ITAM, and the Swiss Finance Institute. Julio has also been a seminar speaker at numerous top universities and financial institutions. In 2005, Julio won the 2005 Citi-Banamex research in economics prize and has published articles about optimal portfolio selection in peer-reviewed academic journals.

Julio holds a master of finance and doctor of philosophy in investment portfolios from Princeton University. He received a BSC in actuarial science and an MA in economics with highest honors from ITAM in Mexico City.

Cole Conkling, JD

Cole is a managing director at Inscription Capital, a registered investment advisor located in Houston, Texas, which has over $1.4 billion in assets under management. Cole also serves as a partner and managing director of Quantor Capital, an asset manager, in Houston. Cole was born and raised in Houston. He received his BA in biology from the University of Texas at Austin in 2005, and his JD from the University of Houston Law Center in 2010, where he graduated cum laude. Cole practiced commercial litigation for almost nine years before joining the investment industry in 2019. He is an avid writer of blogs and papers for his two investment firms and is also a co-host, with Juan Carlos Herrera, of the podcast *Now Know This*, which covers investing, economics, and investor behavior. Cole lives in Houston, Texas, with his wife and two daughters.

Juan Carlos Herrera

Juan Carlos is the chief of wealth management for Grupo Bursatil Mexicano (the largest independent broker dealer in Mexico), a managing director of Inscription Capital, and founding partner of Quantor Capital, LLC. After graduating from the University of Texas in Austin, Juan Carlos began his financial career in Madrid, Spain, working for a boutique consulting firm. In 2006, Juan Carlos came back to the United States and joined Citigroup where he held positions in wealth management and private banking for affluent families. In 2008, Juan Carlos left Citi to start a quantitative hedge fund, QL Capital Management. While at QL Capital Management, Juan Carlos helped design, develop, and trade unique short-term trading strategies that invested in over eighty markets. Juan Carlos has a BA from the University of Texas at Austin and currently holds Series 65 and Series 3 FINRA licenses.